Algorithms for Biomedical Image Analysis and Processing

Algorithms for Biomedical Image Analysis and Processing

Editors

Lucia Maddalena
Laura Antonelli

Basel • Beijing • Wuhan • Barcelona • Belgrade • Novi Sad • Cluj • Manchester

Editors
Lucia Maddalena
Consiglio Nazionale delle Ricerche
Naples, Italy

Laura Antonelli
Consiglio Nazionale delle Ricerche
Naples, Italy

Editorial Office
MDPI
St. Alban-Anlage 66
4052 Basel, Switzerland

This is a reprint of articles from the Special Issue published online in the open access journal *Algorithms* (ISSN 1999-4893) (available at: https://www.mdpi.com/journal/algorithms/special_issues/biomedical_image_analysis_processing).

For citation purposes, cite each article independently as indicated on the article page online and as indicated below:

Lastname, A.A.; Lastname, B.B. Article Title. *Journal Name* **Year**, *Volume Number*, Page Range.

ISBN 978-3-0365-9760-7 (Hbk)
ISBN 978-3-0365-9761-4 (PDF)
doi.org/10.3390/books978-3-0365-9761-4

Cover image courtesy of Laura Antonelli

© 2024 by the authors. Articles in this book are Open Access and distributed under the Creative Commons Attribution (CC BY) license. The book as a whole is distributed by MDPI under the terms and conditions of the Creative Commons Attribution-NonCommercial-NoDerivs (CC BY-NC-ND) license.

Contents

About the Editors vii

Laura Antonelli and Lucia Maddalena
Special Issue on "Algorithms for Biomedical Image Analysis and Processing"
Reprinted from: *Algorithms* 2023, 16, 544, doi:10.3390/a16120544 1

Lucia Maddalena, Laura Antonelli, Alexandra Albu, Aroj Hada and Mario R. Guarracino
Artificial Intelligence for Cell Segmentation, Event Detection, and Tracking for Label-Free Microscopy Imaging
Reprinted from: *Algorithms* 2022, 15, 313, doi:10.3390/a15090313 5

Mattia Conte, Andrea M. Chiariello, Alex Abraham, Simona Bianco, Andrea Esposito, Mario Nicodemi, et al.
Polymer Models of Chromatin Imaging Data in Single Cells
Reprinted from: *Algorithms* 2022, 15, 330, doi:10.3390/a15090330 27

Misgana Negassi, Diane Wagner and Alexander Reiterer
Smart(Sampling)Augment: Optimal and Efficient Data Augmentation for Semantic Segmentation
Reprinted from: *Algorithms* 2022, 15, 165, doi:10.3390/a15050165 35

Igor D. Rodrigues, Emerson A. de Carvalho, Caio P. Santana and Guilherme S. Bastos
Machine Learning and rs-fMRI to Identify Potential Brain Regions Associated with Autism Severity
Reprinted from: *Algorithms* 2022, 15, 195, doi:10.3390/a15060195 51

Bochong Li, Ryo Oka, Ping Xuan, Yuichiro Yoshimura and Toshiya Nakaguchi
Semi-Automatic Multiparametric MR Imaging Classification Using Novel Image Input Sequences and 3D Convolutional Neural Networks
Reprinted from: *Algorithms* 2022, 15, 248, doi:10.3390/a15070248 69

Mateus F. T. Carvalho, Sergio A. Silva, Jr., Carla Cristina O. Bernardo, Franklin César Flores, Juliana Vanessa C. M. Perles, Jacqueline Nelisis Zanoni and Yandre M. G. Costa
Cancer Identification in Walker 256 Tumor Model Exploring Texture Properties Taken from Microphotograph of Rats Liver
Reprinted from: *Algorithms* 2022, 15, 268, doi:10.3390/a15080268 83

Choirul Anam, Ariij Naufal, Heri Sutanto, Kusworo Adi and Geoff Dougherty
Impact of Iterative Bilateral Filtering on the Noise Power Spectrum of Computed Tomography Images
Reprinted from: *Algorithms* 2022, 15, 374, doi:10.3390/a15100374 99

Giorgia Franchini, Micaela Verucchi, Ambra Catozzi, Federica Porta and Marco Prato
Biomedical Image Classification via Dynamically Early Stopped Artificial Neural Network
Reprinted from: *Algorithms* 2022, 15, 386, doi:10.3390/a15100386 115

Zhongda Huang, Andy Ogilvy, Steve Collins, Warren Hare, Michelle Hilts and Andrew Jirasek
A Hybrid Direct Search and Model-Based Derivative-Free Optimization Method with Dynamic Decision Processing and Application in Solid-Tank Design
Reprinted from: *Algorithms* 2023, 16, 92, doi:10.3390/a16020092 129

Chadi Ghafari, Khalil Houissa, Jo Dens, Claudiu Ungureanu, Peter Kayaert, Cyril Constant and Stéphane Carlier
Clinical Validation of a New Enhanced Stent Imaging Method
Reprinted from: *Algorithms* **2023**, *16*, 276, doi:10.3390/a16060276 . . . . **153**

About the Editors

Lucia Maddalena

Lucia Maddalena received her Master's degree cum laude in Mathematics and her Ph.D. in Applied Mathematics and Computer Science from the University of Naples Federico II, Naples, Italy. She is currently is a Senior Researcher with the Consiglio Nazionale delle Ricerche, where she heads the Computational Data Science Group and the ICAR-CNR INdAM Research Unit. Her research has been primarily devoted to methods, algorithms, and software for image processing and multimedia systems in high-performance computational environments, with applications in digital film restoration, video surveillance, and biomedical imaging. She is also currently investigating the design of models, algorithms, and software tools to discover, understand, and model scientific phenomena through the analysis of experimental data and/or through the simulation of their generation processes.

Laura Antonelli

Laura Antonelli has a degree cum laude in Mathematics and a Ph.D. in Applied Mathematics and Computer Science. Currently, she is a researcher at Consiglio Nazionale delle Ricerche. Her research concerns numerical methods and computing solutions for biomedical imaging and analysis. Her primary research topics are imaging problems, such as image restoration, denoising, and segmentation, usually modeled as inverse problems. Her studies have mostly investigated the analytical and numerical solutions to imaging problems, including classical approaches such as regularization. Recently, her research interests have been in using machine learning methods to solve image segmentation and classification problems.

Editorial

Special Issue on "Algorithms for Biomedical Image Analysis and Processing"

Laura Antonelli *,† and Lucia Maddalena †

Institute for High-Performance Computing and Networking, Consiglio Nazionale delle Ricerche, Via P. Castellino 111, 80131 Naples, Italy; lucia.maddalena@cnr.it
* Correspondence: laura.antonelli@cnr.it
† These authors contributed equally to this work.

Citation: Antonelli, L.; Maddalena, L. Special Issue on "Algorithms for Biomedical Image Analysis and Processing". *Algorithms* **2023**, *16*, 544. https://doi.org/10.3390/a16120544

Received: 6 September 2023
Accepted: 22 November 2023
Published: 28 November 2023

Copyright: © 2023 by the authors. Licensee MDPI, Basel, Switzerland. This article is an open access article distributed under the terms and conditions of the Creative Commons Attribution (CC BY) license (https://creativecommons.org/licenses/by/4.0/).

Biomedical imaging is a broad field concerning image capture for diagnostic and therapeutic purposes. Biomedical imaging technologies utilize x-rays (CT scans) [1], magnetism (MRI) [2], sound (ultrasound) [3], radioactive pharmaceuticals (nuclear medicine: SPECT, PET) [4], or light (endoscopy, OCT, light microscopy) [5,6]. Algorithms for processing and analyzing biomedical images are commonly used to visualize anatomical structures or assess the functionality of human organs, point out pathological regions, analyze biological and metabolic processes, set therapy plans, and image-guided surgery [7]. At a different scale, microscopy images are generally produced using light microscopes, which provide structural and temporal information about biological specimens. In the most widely used light microscopy techniques, the light is transmitted from a source on the opposite side of the specimen to the objective lens. On the contrary, fluorescence microscopy uses the reflected light of the specimen [6]. Microscopy imaging requires methods for quantitative, unbiased, and reproducible extraction of meaningful measurements to quantify morphological properties and investigate intra- and inter-cellular dynamics [8]. New technologies have been developed to address this need, such as microscopy-based screening, sequencing, and imaging, with automated analysis (including high-throughput screening and high-content screening) [9], where basic image processing algorithms (e.g., denoising and segmentation) are fundamental tasks.

The large number of applications that rely on biomedical images increases the demand for efficient, accurate, and reliable algorithms for biomedical image processing and analysis, especially with the rising complexity of imaging technologies and the huge amount of images to be processed. This special issue aimed at bringing together both original research articles and topical reviews on the wide area algorithms for biomedical image processing and analysis techniques.

In response to the call for papers, a total of 14 manuscripts were submitted. Out of them, we selected ten submissions to appear in this Special Issue, coming from seven countries in three geographical regions: *America* (Brazil (2), Canada (1)), *Asia* (Indonesia (1), Japan (1)), and *Europe* (Belgium (1), Germany (1), Italy (3)). Two or three experts in the corresponding area have reviewed each submission. The List of Contributions for this Special Issue includes first two reviews and then the other eight published papers in chronological order of publication date, briefly described in the following.

In their review (Contribution 1), Maddalena et al. give an overview of methods, software, data, and metrics for various tasks related to label-free microscopy images, including cell segmentation, event detection and classification, and cell tracking and lineage, providing the reader with a unique source of information, with links for further details.

The review by Conte et al. (Contribution 2) discusses the application of models from polymer physics to understand the machinery underneath the chromosome architecture in the nucleus of the cells. Numerical simulations of the reviewed models are validated against imaging data from multiplexed super-resolution fluorescence in situ hybridization (FISH) imaging for chromatin conformation tracing, which allows unbiased determination of the structural features and their genomic coordinates with high resolution in single cells. This way, they show that this kind of novel data from microscopy can be complemented with quantitative models from physics to understand the mechanisms and function of the genome structure.

Negassi et al. (Contribution 3) afford the problem of automatic data augmentation for semantic image segmentation. They propose an optimal comprehensive method and a sub-optimal one that is computationally less demanding. The performance of these methods is evaluated against four existing annotated datasets for various applications, including crack detection in bridge images, autonomous driving, anomaly detection in cystoscopic medical images, and segmentation of brain electron microscopy images.

In Contribution 4, Rodrigues et al. aim to identify potential brain regions as biomarkers of Autism Spectrum Disorder (ASD) severity. Imaging data come from pre-processing the brain's resting-state functional magnetic resonance imaging (rs-fMRI). Classification of subjects affected by different autism grades is carried out using SVM to select the groups of atlas ROIs (Regions of Interest) that lead to the highest accuracy.

In Contribution 5, Li et al. consider the problem of classifying low and high risk of early prostate cancer. Imaging data consists of DWI and T2 sequences from multi-parametric magnetic resonance imaging (mp-fMRI) aligned and cropped to the prostate region, producing 3D sequences to be fed to a 3D-CNN. The experiments are carried out using various combinations of the input data and different 3D-CNN models and analyse the cancer response maps produced from the last convolution layer of the network.

Contribution 6 by Carvalho et al. affords the problem of classifying healthy and tumor cases in microphotograph images of rats' liver tissue. They consider different texture features and their fusion, combined with three traditional machine learning classifiers.

In Contribution 7, Anam et al. analyze the effect of the iterative application of bilateral filtering to Computed Tomography images. The experiments are carried out on homogeneous phantom images scanned with different tube currents to investigate the impact on noise texture and spatial resolution and on anthropomorphic phantom images of the head to simulate clinical scenarios.

Franchini et al. (Contribution 8) propose an adaptive early stopping technique for optimising the training phase of neural networks for image classification, reducing the required epochs. Numerical experiments are carried out using different CNN models on the standard CIFAR-100 database and two biomedical databases obtained by computed tomography, involving various numbers of classes.

In Contribution 9, Huang et al. present in their work, a derivative-free optimization (DFO) framework that allows direct and model-based search methods in a single algorithm, analyzing their optimal combinations. They propose a smart version of the method that dynamically and adaptively chooses the search strategies. These methods are applied for the design of a solid-tank fan-beam optical CT scanner.

Contribution 10 by Ghafari et al. proposes a clinical validation of recent stent imaging methods. The imaging data consists of coronary angiographies post-processed by two enhanced stent imaging methods, one vendor-specific and the other independent from the angiographic system. The experiments are devoted to comparing the visualization obtained by the two methods in terms of image quality as perceived by expert cardiologists and to quantitatively analyze the stent expansion measurements achieved with the independent method.

As the editors, it is our pleasure to thank the editorial staff of the journal Algorithms for their helpful cooperation during the preparation of the Special Issue and of this volume. We would also like to thank all reviewers for their thorough and timely reports on the reviewed papers and all the authors for submitting many interesting works from a broad spectrum in the field of interest of this volume.

Acknowledgments: This work has been carried out also under the PRIN 2022 project P2022PMEN2 and within the activities of the authors as members of the INdAM Research group GNCS and the ICAR-CNR INdAM Research Unit.

Conflicts of Interest: The authors declare no conflict of interest.

List of Contributions

1. Maddalena, L.; Antonelli, L.; Albu, A.; Hada, A.; Guarracino, M.R. Artificial Intelligence for Cell Segmentation, Event Detection, and Tracking for Label-free Microscopy Imaging. *Algorithms* **2022**, *15*, 313. https://doi.org/10.3390/a15090313.
2. Conte, M.; Chiariello, A.M.; Abraham, A.; Bianco, S.; Esposito, A.; Nicodemi, M.; Matteuzzi, T.; Vercellone, F. Polymer Models of Chromatin Imaging Data in Single Cells. *Algorithms* **2022**, *15*, 330. https://doi.org/10.3390/a15090330.
3. Negassi, M.; Wagner, D.; Reiterer, A. Smart(Sampling)Augment: Optimal and Efficient Data Augmentation for Semantic Segmentation. *Algorithms* **2022**, *15*, 165. https://doi.org/10.3390/a15050165.
4. Rodrigues, I.D.; de Carvalho, E.A.; Santana, C.P.; Bastos, G.S. Machine Learning and rs-fMRI to Identify Potential Brain Regions Associated with Autism Severity. *Algorithms* **2022**, *15*, 195. https://doi.org/10.3390/a15060195.
5. Li, B.; Oka, R.; Xuan, P.; Yoshimura, Y.; Nakaguchi, T. Semi-Automatic Multiparametric MR Imaging Classification Using Novel Image Input Sequences and 3D Convolutional Neural Networks. *Algorithms* **2022**, *15*, 248. https://doi.org/10.3390/a15070248.
6. Carvalho, M.F.T.; Silva, S.A.; Bernardo, C.C.O.; Flores, F.C.; Perles, J.V.C.M.; Zanoni, J.N.; Costa, Y.M.G. Cancer Identification in Walker 256 Tumor Model Exploring Texture Properties Taken from Microphotograph of Rats Liver. *Algorithms* **2022**, *15*, 268. https://doi.org/10.3390/a15080268.
7. Anam, C.; Naufal, A.; Sutanto, H.; Adi, K.; Dougherty, G. Impact of Iterative Bilateral Filtering on the Noise Power Spectrum of Computed Tomography Images. *Algorithms* **2022**, *15*, 374. https://doi.org/10.3390/a15100374.
8. Franchini, G.; Verucchi, M.; Catozzi, A.; Porta, F.; Prato, M. Biomedical Image Classification via Dynamically Early Stopped Artificial Neural Network. *Algorithms* **2022**, *15*, 386. https://doi.org/10.3390/a15100386.
9. Huang, Z.; Ogilvy, A.; Collins, S.; Hare, W.; Hilts, M.; Jirasek, A. A Hybrid Direct Search and Model-Based Derivative-Free Optimization Method with Dynamic Decision Processing and Application in Solid-Tank Design. *Algorithms* **2023**, *16*, 92. https://doi.org/10.3390/a16020092.
10. Ghafari, C.; Houissa, K.; Dens, J.; Ungureanu, C.; Kayaert, P.; Constant, C.; Carlier, S. Clinical Validation of a New Enhanced Stent Imaging Method. *Algorithms* **2023**, *16*, 276. https://doi.org/10.3390/a16060276.

References

1. Withers, P.J.; Bouman, C.; Carmignato, S.; Cnudde, V.; Grimaldi, D.; Hagen, C.; Maire, E.; Manley, M.; Du Plessis, A.; Stock, S. X-ray computed tomography. *Nat. Rev. Methods Prim.* **2021**, *1*, 18. [CrossRef]
2. Mukhatov, A.; Le, T.A.; Pham, T.T.; Do, T.D. A comprehensive review on magnetic imaging techniques for biomedical applications. *Nano Sel.* **2023**, *4*, 213–230. [CrossRef]
3. Moran, C.M.; Thomson, A. Preclinical Ultrasound Imaging—A Review of Techniques and Imaging Applications. *Front. Phys.* **2020**, *8*, 124. [CrossRef]
4. Wadsak, W.; Mitterhauser, M.; Mitterhauser, M. Basics and principles of radiopharmaceuticals for PET/CT. *Eur. J. Radiol.* **2010**, *73*, 461–469. [CrossRef] [PubMed]
5. Easti, J.E.; Vleugels, J.L.; Roelandt, P.; Bhandari, P.; Bisschops, R.; Dekker, E.; Hassan, C.; Horgan, G.; Kiesslich, R.; Longcroft-Wheaton, G.; et al. Advanced endoscopic imaging: European Society of Gastrointestinal Endoscopy (ESGE) Technology Review. *Endoscopy* **2016**, *48*, 1029–1045. [CrossRef] [PubMed]
6. Thorn, K. A quick guide to light microscopy in cell biology. *Mol. Biol. Cell* **2016**, *27*, 219–222. [CrossRef]
7. Raghavendra, P.; Pullaiah, T. Chapter 4—Biomedical Imaging Role in Cellular and Molecular Diagnostics. In *Advances in Cell and Molecular Diagnostics*; Raghavendra, P., Pullaiah, T., Eds.; Academic Press: Cambridge, MA, USA, 2018; pp. 85–111. [CrossRef]

8. Bullen, A. Microscopic imaging techniques for drug discovery. *Nat. Rev. Drug Discov.* **2008**, *7*, 54–67. [CrossRef]
9. Blay, V.; Tolani, B.; Ho, S.; Arkin, M. High-Throughput Screening: Today's biochemical and cell-based approaches. *Drug Discov. Today* **2020**, *25*, 1807–1821. [CrossRef] [PubMed]

Disclaimer/Publisher's Note: The statements, opinions and data contained in all publications are solely those of the individual author(s) and contributor(s) and not of MDPI and/or the editor(s). MDPI and/or the editor(s) disclaim responsibility for any injury to people or property resulting from any ideas, methods, instructions or products referred to in the content.

Review

Artificial Intelligence for Cell Segmentation, Event Detection, and Tracking for Label-Free Microscopy Imaging

Lucia Maddalena [1,†], Laura Antonelli [1,*,†], Alexandra Albu [2], Aroj Hada [2] and Mario Rosario Guarracino [1,2]

[1] Institute for High-Performance Computing and Networking, National Research Council, 80131 Naples, Italy
[2] Department of Economics and Law, University of Cassino and Southern Lazio, 03043 Cassino, Italy
* Correspondence: laura.antonelli@cnr.it
† These authors contributed equally to this work.

Abstract: Background: Time-lapse microscopy imaging is a key approach for an increasing number of biological and biomedical studies to observe the dynamic behavior of cells over time which helps quantify important data, such as the number of cells and their sizes, shapes, and dynamic interactions across time. Label-free imaging is an essential strategy for such studies as it ensures that native cell behavior remains uninfluenced by the recording process. Computer vision and machine/deep learning approaches have made significant progress in this area. Methods: In this review, we present an overview of methods, software, data, and evaluation metrics for the automatic analysis of label-free microscopy imaging. We aim to provide the interested reader with a unique source of information, with links for further detailed information. Results: We review the most recent methods for cell segmentation, event detection, and tracking. Moreover, we provide lists of publicly available software and datasets. Finally, we summarize the metrics most frequently adopted for evaluating the methods under exam. Conclusions: We provide hints on open challenges and future research directions.

Keywords: label-free microscopy; cell segmentation; cell classification; cell event detection; cell tracking; artificial intelligence; machine learning; deep learning

1. Introduction

Microscopy is a fundamental research pillar enabling scientists to discover the structures and dynamics of cells and subcellular components. Most of these components are *phase objects*, which means they are transparent and colorless and cannot be visualized under a light microscope. To overcome this limit, a solution consists in staining the components with dyes, also known as *fluorophores* or *fluorochromes*. Such molecules absorb short-wavelength light, generally UV, and emit fluorescence light at a longer wavelength. This mechanism represents the basic premise of *fluorescence microscopy techniques*, and the fluorescence images show the specimen bright on a dark background. The staining techniques use different dyes to point out a specific cellular component. Then, the same specimen can appear with a red, blue, or green color and appearance, as depicted in Figure 1a,b.

As the molecular genetic methodologies and tools advance, the fluorescence techniques become more specific and can be applied to a larger set of different model organisms [1,2]. However, to ensure high-quality images, they require laborious and expensive sample preparation. Furthermore, the dyes reduce their luminance over time due to a light-induced degradation process called *photobleaching* [3]. Finally, fluorescent techniques are invasive and interfere with the biological processes causing phototoxicity.

On the contrary, *Label-free Imaging (LI)* techniques can visualize many cellular structures simultaneously with minimal sample preparation, phototoxicity, and no photobleaching, making them particularly suitable for live-cell imaging. Thus, LI provides measurements complementary to fluorescence imaging for several biological studies. Based on optical principles, these techniques measure the light phase change (i.e., the refractive index) passing through the specimen and converting it into intensity modulations producing *qualitative* phase contrast images, as exemplified in Figure 1c (the phase change information contained in LI images is non-linearly coupled with its luminance intensity and cannot be retrieved quantitatively. An image produced by LI techniques is a map of path-length shifts associated with the specimen, containing information about both the thickness and refractive index of its structure; for further details and explanations, see [4]). Among the traditional techniques to phase change imaging, there are *Phase Contrast* (PhC) [5] and *Differential Image Contrast* (DIC) [6] based on the phase gradient method and differential interference contrast, respectively, to measure the refractive index. Another LI technique very similar to DIC is the *Hoffman Modulation Contrast* (HMC) [7]. Due to intrinsic limitations of the numerical conversion methods, phase contrast images contain artifacts [8] (i.e., bright halo surrounding cell contours) and the "shade-off effect", which produces low contrast inside the cells with an intensity very similar to the background. Although several methods have been developed to overcome these artifacts, automatic image processing of label-free images is still challenging, especially the segmentation task for separating cells from the background.

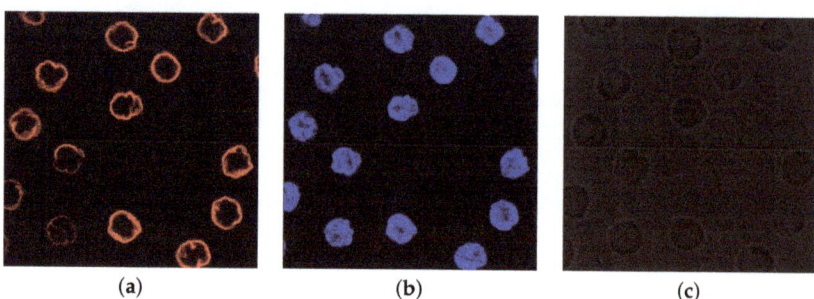

Figure 1. Example of differences in appearance of fluorescence and phase contrast microscopy images (culture of human lymphocyte cells [9]): (**a**) fluorescence image of nuclear envelope; (**b**) fluorescence image of interior nuclei (DNA); (**c**) phase contrast image of whole cells.

Unlike the previous techniques, quantitative LI provides higher contrast and reduces artifacts. Among them, *Quantitative Phase Imaging* (QPI) techniques refer to the microscopes showing phase quantitative information. Details concerning QPI techniques can be found in [10].

A further alternative to noninvasive techniques is Bright-Field (BF) microscopy. It represents the most straightforward configuration for the light microscope, which is not only cheaper but also does not require sample preparation [11]. BF images provide information about the cellular organization, and they are preferred to visualize specimens with low contrast from the background (unlike in fluorescence) or with low resolution and magnification visualization of thin cellular components (unlike in phase contrast). Several studies describe the use of the BF channel in cell detection and automated image analysis of cell populations [12,13].

With the aim of observing the dynamic behavior of living cells over time, LI microscopes are also equipped with a real-time imaging tool named *time-lapse*. Broadly speaking, time-lapse is a speed-up technique to observe events changing over time. This is usually realized by taking images at regular time intervals and merging them into a video. One of the most significant applications of time-lapse microscopy is cell population monitoring to study single-cell behavior in response to physiological or external stimuli and understand the underlying mechanisms. For example, in drug discovery and cancer research [14], time-lapse microscopy is used to look at cell response to anti-mitotic drugs in terms of cell division and cell death. To achieve this goal, quantitative information on cell behavior needs to be obtained and analyzed [15]. Cell proliferation, lineage, and fate are of primary importance among various cellular events. Image analysis of these biological processes is usually performed manually with suitable protocols [16]. As manual analysis of a large volume of light microscopy images is slow, tedious, time-consuming, and subject to observer subjectivity, biological studies see an increased demand for reliable automatic imaging tools. As in many scientific disciplines, Artificial Intelligence (AI) has been changing how imaging data are processed and analyzed and how experiments are carried out. AI refers to artificial systems aiming to adapt previous knowledge to new situations and recognize meaning in data patterns. Machine Learning (ML) [17] is a subset of AI methods that extracts valuable features from large data sets to make predictions or decisions on unseen data. An ML algorithm is not designed to solve a specific problem but rather to train a computer to solve problems. The training is data-driven. Deep Learning (DL) is a set of ML algorithms using a multi-layer "neural networks" to progressively extract higher-level features from data (the number of layers is the depth of the model, hence the terminology "deep learning"; for a quick overview on DL key concepts for microscopy image data, the reader can refer to [18]).

This review mainly focuses on AI methods for the most used traditional LI microscopy techniques, i.e., PhC, DIC, and BF, to investigate fundamental biological events. A comprehensive description of the state-of-the-art methods using QPI data and AI approaches, which are out of our focus, can be found in [19] and references therein. Few recent surveys are available in the literature covering methods for these types of microscopy images and videos. The study presented by Vicar et al. [20] performs a comprehensive comparison of cell image segmentation methods for the most common label-free microscopy techniques, including PhC, DIC, HMC, and QPI. The review covers traditional methods, providing only hints on DL-based segmentation methods. The authors identify an effective image segmentation pipeline composed of four main steps: *image reconstruction, foreground-background segmentation, seed-point extraction*, and *cell segmentation*. They discuss and assess the most effective combination of the above steps for the specific microscopy techniques based on software and tools available in the state-of-the-art literature. Furthermore, they compare the accuracy and efficiency of tools containing all the above four steps (named "all-in-one" tools) as well as software implementing only one of them. Software and data were made publicly available (see Sections 3 and 4). In [21], Emami et al. present a review of methods and tools for cell tracking. Following the traditional object tracking literature, the methods are subdivided into three groups, according to whether tracking is achieved by detection, model evaluation, or filtering, with limited space given to DL approaches. Well-known commercial and open-source cell tracking tools are summarized, and typical challenges are highlighted. Ulman et al. [22] present a comparison of 21 cell-tracking algorithms participating in three editions of the Cell Tracking Challenge (CTC), an initiative promoting the development and objective evaluation of cell segmentation and tracking algorithms. The compared methods are summarized based on common principles, features, and methodologies, as well as pre- and post-processing strategies. They are evaluated for both the segmentation and tracking tasks (see Section 5), and their overall average performance is used to compile the final ranking. Started in 2013, this challenge is still ongoing, and since 2019, it has been articulated into two different challenges, the Cell Tracking Benchmark (CTB) and the Cell Segmentation Benchmark (CSB), sharing the same dataset (see Section 4).

Although the described surveys provide extremely useful insights on specific tasks or specific datasets, the landscape of the scientific research on the subject still appears fragmented. The aim of our review is to provide a broad and up-to-date view of AI methods for the analysis of label-free images and videos acquired by traditional LI microscopy techniques and all the ingredients needed to afford it. Thus, it covers the most recent methods, especially for cellular segmentation, event detection, and tracking over time-lapse videos, available datasets, software, and evaluation metrics.

The review is organized as follows. In Section 2, we introduce the considered microscopy analysis tasks and provide brief descriptions of the reviewed literature methods for each of them. Sections 3 and 4 provide brief descriptions and links to the publicly available software and data. Section 5 introduces the most frequently used metrics to evaluate the AI algorithms for the considered tasks. Section 6 summarizes the open problems, providing hints on possible future research directions.

2. Literature
2.1. Cell Segmentation

Image segmentation is the main task for producing numerical data from live-cell imaging experiments, thus providing direct insight into the living system from the quantitative cell information [23,24]. Cell segmentation is the process of splitting a microscopy image into "segments", i.e., Regions Of Interest (ROIs), and produces an image where cells are separated from the image background by cell contours or cell labels. Accurate cell segmentations are crucial for many challenges involved in cellular analysis, including but not limited to cell tracking [25], cellular features quantification, proliferation, morphology, migration, interactions, and counting [26–29].

Several steps are considered in the literature for achieving cell segmentation. Some authors [8,20,30] consider crucial to initially perform an image reconstruction step, which produces images with higher contrast between foreground and background, increasing the success of the subsequent image processing tasks. The image formation model in phase contrast microscopy can be studied to reduce artefacts and solve the inverse problem through a regularization approach [8]. Some ML-based methods are reviewed by Vicar et al. [20] for PhC and DIC images, while De Haan et al. [30] present an overview of how DL-based frameworks solve these inverse problems in optical microscopy.

Cell detection (or identification) is also frequently adopted previous to segmentation [20,22], with the aim of locating the cells in the image (e.g., via bounding boxes, as exemplified in Figure 2a).

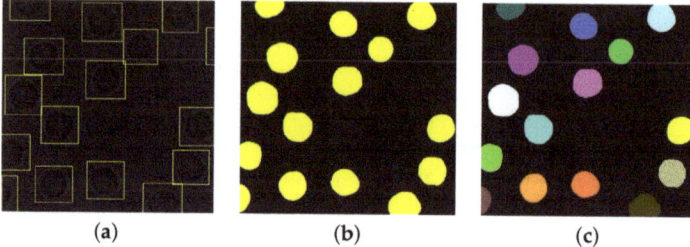

Figure 2. Results of different image processing tasks: (**a**) cell detection; (**b**) cell semantic segmentation; (**c**) cell instance segmentation.

Some specific types of segmentation are frequently considered for cellular images [20,31–33]. Semantic segmentation identifies the object (i.e., the cell) category of each pixel for every known object within an image, as exemplified in Figure 2b. Instance segmentation, instead, identifies the object instance (i.e., the cell with specific features) of each pixel for every known object within an image [34]; an example is given in Figure 2c. It should be observed that the problem of cell instance segmentation is sometimes intended as joint cell detection and segmentation (e.g., see [32]), while other times (e.g., see [20]) instant segmentation is used as a synonym for single cell segmentation.

Some of the most recent segmentation algorithms are described in the following. In [23], Van Valen et al. in the software named **DeepCell** adopt deep convolutional neural networks for cell segmentation for various types of microscopy images (PhC, Fluo, and PhC coupled with images of a fluorescent nuclear marker), also providing hints on design rules in training CNNs for this task (image normalization, data augmentation, hyper-parameter tuning, and segmentation refinement). They also extend the deep convolutional neural networks to perform semantic segmentation (i.e., not only image segmentation but also cell type prediction). The software and the adopted data are publicly available (see Sections 3 and 4).

Hilsenbeck et al. [25] present **fastER**, a fast and trainable tool for cell segmentation that extracts texture and shape features from candidate regions, estimates their likelihood to be a cell with a support vector machine (SVM) algorithm, and calculates an optimal set of non-overlapping candidate regions using a divide and conquer approach. Candidate regions are chosen as the so-called extremal regions (regions with maximal size containing only pixels whose intensities are no greater than a specific threshold), similarly to CellDetect [35]. For each candidate region, a feature vector is extracted to train the SVM model, including typical shape and intensity information (size, major/minor axis lengths, eccentricity, average intensity inside and in its neighborhood, average and standard deviation gradient, and average heterogeneity) [36]. Pre-processing of the images consists of denoising with bilateral filtering, while post-processing of the resulting masks includes hole-filling and size filtering. The software made publicly available (see Section 3) is shown to be robust against common cell segmentation challenges but still suffers high cell densities and blurring. Compared with other state-of-the-art methods (e.g., U-Net [37], ilastik [38], CellProfiler [39], and CellDetect), it is shown to be more efficient on various types of data made publicly available (see Section 4) still achieving similarly accurate results.

Yi et al. [32] propose the software **ANCIS** an Attentive Neural Cell Instance Segmentation method to predict each cell's bounding box and its segmentation mask simultaneously. The method builds on a joint network that combines the single shot multi-box detector (SSD) one-stage object detector [40] and U-net [37] for cell segmentation. Attention mechanisms are adopted in detection and segmentation modules to focus the model on useful features while suppressing irrelevant information. The software, tested on DIC images of neural cells, is publicly available (see Section 3).

In [24], Lux and Matula use a watershed [41] marker-based approach with two convolutional neural networks (CNN) of hour-glass architecture shape to segment clustered cells in images consisting of five datasets, three of which originate from the Cell Tracking Challenge [22] (DIC-C2DH-HeLa, Fluo-N2DH-SIM+, and PhC-C2DL-PSC). They used normalization by histogram equalization and median scaling as a pre-processing step. Afterwards, they augment the data by randomized rigid geometric transformations and scaling. Then, Lux et al. use one CNN to predict cell marker pixels and the other CNN for image foreground predictions. They utilize these outputs to compute the marker function to obtain the segmentation seeds and the segmentation function to define cell regions that are further used in the marker-controlled watershed segmentation.

Scherr et al. [42] present a method for segmenting touching cells in BF images from the Cell Tracking Challenge [22] by using a novel representation of cell borders, inspired by distance maps. The proposed method uses an adapted U-Net with two decoder paths, one for prediction of cell distance and another for prediction of neighbor distance. These distances are then used for the watershed-based post-processing to obtain segmentations. Results are evaluated using the SEG, DET, and CSB metrics (see Section 5) and show accurate performances, with average SEG and DET scores of 0.726 and 0.975, respectively.

Nishimura et al. [43] propose a weakly supervised cell instance segmentation method that recognizes each cell region by only using weak labels, i.e., point-level (cell centroid positions) rather than pixel-level annotations, as training data. This approach strongly reduces the annotation cost compared with the standard annotation method required for supervised segmentation. They train a cell detection CNN (U-net) and then use it to estimate rough cell positions. The rough cell shapes are extracted from the detection network by backpropagating the activation from output to input, obtaining a relevance map that shows how each pixel in the input image is relevant to the output. The final cell shapes are estimated by graph-cut [44] using the estimated relevance map as a seed. Results on different datasets show that the method works well with different types of microscopy and different contrasts.

Stringer and Pachitariu introduce **Cellpose** [45] a software library for the instance segmentation of cell images. It implements a CNN using the U-net architecture style. Cellpose provides the probability of a pixel being inside a cell and the flows of pixels in xy coordinates towards the cell center. The flows are then used to construct the cell ROIs. Several results confirm its reliability on a wide range of label-free images without model retraining or parameter adjustment. The authors also propose a 3D extension of the library that does not use 3D-labeled data but works on the 2D model. The recent furthest extension of Cellpose [46] can adapt CNN segmentation models to new microscopy images with very little training data. Code and data are publicly available (see Sections 3 and 4).

2.2. Event Detection and Classification

Even though segmentation remains the core of the subsequent imaging tasks, automated analysis of microscopy image sequences often bypasses the segmentation task. Usually, the detection of cell events under investigation is performed directly from heuristically generated ROIs. Detecting changes in cellular behavior plays a central role in different studies, where the focus is on identifying the changes in cellular growth, mitosis, and death. Such changes may be related to cell shape, division, and movement. They cannot be detected in a single image but require the analysis of video or time-lapse sequences. The difficulty primarily relies on the wide spatial-temporal variability of such phenomena, which requires suitable methods to handle time-varying phenomena. Nevertheless, the infinite spectrum of possible events faces an inherent shortage of labeled data.

Automatic and robust approaches to detecting the time and location of cell events from image sequences often make use of the classification task. In microscopy, classification refers to identifying and distinguishing different cell types or states. Classification between other cells, types of tumors (benign or malignant), types of cell states (mitosis detection, alive-dead classification), and types of CIC (Cell-In-Cell) structures [47] are some typical applications.

Some recent AI approaches for event cell detection are here presented. Su et al. [48] and Mao and Yin [49] propose a convolutional long short-term memory (CNN-LSTM) network and a Two stream Bidirectional CNN-LSTM network, respectively, on sequences of single-cell image patches and utilize both spatial and temporal information to detect mitosis events. They report an average precision of 0.96 and 0.98, respectively. However, these models need a large amount of manually annotated data to train on, and both papers also report a sharp decrease in accuracy when testing the model on other cell datasets.

A CNN-LSTM model that learns spatial and temporal locations of the cells from a detection map in a semi-supervised manner is proposed by Phan et al. [50] for the detection of mitosis in PhC videos. The method needs only 1050 annotated frames to achieve an F1 score of 0.544–0.822, depending on the video. However, it also shows a decrease in performance with the increase in the input sequence length, which is not ideal for practical situations where time-lapse experiment's video sequences may contain thousands of frames. The method also will only be able to detect a single event at a time, such as mitosis, whereas these events can randomly occur in multiple places in a single frame.

Nishimura and Bise [51] propose a method for multiple mitosis event detection and localization by estimating a spatial-temporal likelihood map using the 3D CNN architecture V-Net [52]. In the likelihood map, a mitosis position is represented as an intensity peak with a Gaussian distribution, in which multiple mitoses are represented as multiple peaks. The method has an average precision of 0.862 on a private dataset. While the method does take into account the spatial and temporal information, it is only limited to detecting mitosis events and not any other events that may be associated with mitosis. In order to identify other events as well, multiple models based on this method would be needed. Furthermore, the use of this method for other datasets or cell lines requires the generation of laborious manual annotations in the form of Gaussian distributed likelihood maps.

Su et al. [53] present a deep reinforcement learning-based progressive sequence saliency discovery network (PSSD) for mitosis detection in time-lapse PhC images. The discovery of these salient frames is formulated as a Markov Decision Process that progressively adjusts the selection positions of salient frames in the sequence. Then, the pipeline leverages deep reinforcement learning to learn the policy in the salient frame discovery process. The method consists of two parts: (1) the saliency discovery module, which selects the salient frames from the input cell image sequence by progressively adjusting the selection positions of salient frames; (2) the mitosis identification module, which takes a sequence of salient frames and performs temporal information fusion for mitotic sequence classification. The method is evaluated on the C2C12-16 mitosis detection dataset [54] (see Section 4), and is found to outperform the previous state-of-the-art methods, including CNN-LSTM and 3D-CNN among the others.

Theagarajan and Bhanu [55] present **DeephESC 2.0**, an ML method to detect and classify human embryonic stem cells (hESC) in PhC images. Firstly, they use a mixture of Gaussians to detect the cells [56], where two Gaussian distributions model the intensity distributions of the foreground (cells) and the background (substrate). Then, Generative Multi Adversarial Networks (GMANs) [57] augment data with new synthetic images and improve the performance of the classification step. To classify the images into six different classes, they implement a hierarchical classifier consisting of a CNN and two Triplet CNNs. The software and dataset are publicly available (see Sections 3 and 4).

La Greca et al. [58] use in the **celldeath** software some classical DL approaches such as ResNet [59], where they classify cells as dead or alive by using complete frames as input images. On images containing both alive and dead cells, the model can predict the dead ones, which are localized by heat map-like visualizations merging the information provided by the last convolutional layer and the model predictions. These predictions are compared with human performance and are found to largely outperform human ability. The software is publicly available (see Sections 3 and 4).

2.3. Cell Tracking

Object tracking consists in locating and monitoring one or more objects of interest and their behavior over time [21]. The image sequence containing cells can be acquired at specific time intervals using the time-lapse technique. When discussing cell tracking, it is generally assumed that segmentation or detection and classification have been performed.

Some recent tracking methods are here reviewed. Magnusson et al. [60] propose a global track linking algorithm, which links into tracks cell outlines generated by a segmentation algorithm. It is a batch algorithm that uses the entire image sequence to decide the links. Starting with the hypothesis that there are no cells in the image sequence, it adds one cell track at a time, in a greedy way, choosing the one maximizing a suitable scoring function, using the Viterbi algorithm. The algorithm can handle cell mitosis, apoptosis, and migration in and out of the imaged area and can also deal with false positives, missed detections, and clusters of jointly segmented cells. It has been tested on BF sequences, but in principle, it can be applied to any type of sequences, given a suitable segmentation algorithm to outline the cells. The algorithm has been implemented in several cell trackers, see for example the Baxter Algorithms package (see Section 3).

Grah et al. [61] propose **MitosisAnalyser**, a framework for detecting, classifying, and tracking mitotic cells in live-cell phase contrast imaging based on mathematical imaging methods. As pre-processing, denoising by Gaussian filter smoothing is applied, followed by rescaling. In the workflow, each mitosis is detected by using the circular Hough transform. The obtained circular contours are used for initializing the tracking algorithm, which is based on variational methods. Backward tracking is used to establish the beginning of mitosis by detecting a change in the cell morphology. This step is followed by forward tracking until the end of mitosis. The output provides the duration of mitosis and information on cell fates (e.g., number of daughter cells, cell death). The Matlab code is publicly available (see Section 3).

In [62], Rea et al. propose a Graphics Processing Unit (GPU)-based algorithm for tracking yeast cells in PhC microscopy images in real-time. The tracking by detection approach determines a minimum cost configuration for each couple of frames, given by the solution of a linear programming (LP) problem. The GPU-parallel software based on the simplex method, a common tool for solving LP problems, is obtained by exploiting parallelization strategies to maximize the overall throughput and minimize memory transfers between host and device, thus exploiting data locality. The software is publicly available (see Section 3).

Tsai et al. [63] introduce **Usiigaci**, a semi-automated pipeline to segment, track, and visualize cells in PhC sequences. Segmentation is based on a mask regional convolutional neural network (Mask R-CNN) [64], while the tracking module relies on the Trackpy library [65]. A graphical user interface allows the user to verify the results. The software and annotated data are publicly available (see Sections 3 and 4).

Scherr et al. [42], in the same paper as for segmentation, also propose a graph-based cell tracking algorithm for touching cells in BF microscopy images (BF-C2DL-HSC and BF-C2DL-MuSC datasets) from the Cell Tracking Challenge [22]. The adapted tracking algorithm includes a movement estimation in the cost function to re-link tracks with missing segmentation masks over a short sequence of frames. Their algorithm can track all segmented cells in an image sequence and only a subset, e.g., a selection of manually marked cells. Results for cell tracking are evaluated using the TRA and CTB metrics (see Section 5) and are shown to perform very well, with TRA scores of 0.929 and 0.967 for the BF-C2DL-HSC and BF-C2DL-MuSC images, respectively.

3. Software

As also already discovered in Section 2, it is every day more common for newly proposed methods to make their implementations publicly available, in the light of the recent trend toward open science. In Table 1, we provide links to existing publicly available software, subdivided by task. Moreover, we provide links to software platforms, providing more diverse functionalities for analyzing microscopy images and videos. Besides the software already described in Section 2, here we briefly summarize the remaining ones.

TWS (Trainable Weka Segmentation) is a Fiji plugin that combines ML algorithms with a set of selected image features to produce pixel-based segmentations. Weka (Waikato Environment for Knowledge Analysis) [66] can itself be called from the plugin.

Baxter Algorithms is a software package for tracking and analyzing cells in microscope images, providing an implementation of the global track-linking algorithm in [60]. The software can handle images produced using both 2D transmission microscopy and 2D or 3D fluorescence microscopy.

CellProfiler is a commonly used program designed for biologists with minimal programming knowledge to measure biological phenotypes quantitatively [39]. Algorithms for image analysis are available as individual modules that can be placed in sequential order to create a pipeline. Several commonly used pipelines are available for download and can be used to detect and measure various properties of biological objects.

ilastik [38] is an interactive machine learning tool based on a random forest classifier [67] for image analysis and is widely used by biologists since it no require specific ML knowledge. It provides pipelines for segmentation, classification, tracking, and lineage, performing on multidimensional data (including 3D space, time, and channels). A friendly user interface enables users to interactively implement their image analysis through a supervised machine learning workflow. ilastik classifies pixels and objects by learning from annotations to predict the class of each unannotated pixel and object. It provides an automatic selection of image features based on a first optimization step. Users can introduce sparse annotations or use labeled data or even provide training examples, then correct the classifier precisely at the position where it is wrong. Once a classifier has been trained, new data can be processed in batch mode.

Table 1. Software: name (Name); reference ([Ref]); year of publication (Year); url (Link); programming language or environment (Language). All links were accessed on 28 August 2022.

Name	[Ref]	Year	Link	Language
Cell segmentation				
DeepCell	[23]	2016	https://simtk.org/projects/deepcell	Python, C, Ruby
fastER	[25]	2017	https://bsse.ethz.ch/csd/software/faster.html	C++
TWS	[68]	2017	https://imagej.net/plugins/tws/	Java
ANCIS	[32]	2019	https://github.com/yijingru/ANCIS-Pytorch	Python
Vicar et al.	[20]	2019	https://github.com/tomasvicar/Cell-segmentation-methods-comparison	Matlab
Cellpose	[45,46]	2022	https://github.com/MouseLand/cellpose	Python
Cell classification				
DeephESC 2.0	[55]	2019	https://www.vislab.ucr.edu/SOFTWARE/software.php	Python
celldeath	[58]	2021	https://github.com/miriukaLab/celldeath	Python
Cell tracking				
Baxter Algorithms	[60]	2015	https://github.com/klasma/BaxterAlgorithms	Matlab/C
Rea et al.	[62]	2019	https://dibernardo.tigem.it/software-data	Matlab/C
Software platforms				
CellProfiler	[39]	2006	http://cellprofiler.org	Python
MitosisAnalyser	[61]	2017	https://github.com/JoanaGrah/MitosisAnalyser	Matlab
ilastik	[38]	2019	https://www.ilastik.org/index.html	Python
Usiigaci	[63]	2019	https://github.com/ElsevierSoftwareX/SOFTX_2018_158	Python
ZeroCostDL4Mic	[69]	2020	https://github.com/HenriquesLab/ZeroCostDL4Mic	Python
DeepImageJ	[70]	2021	https://deepimagej.github.io/deepimagej	Python
BioImage Model Zoo	[71]	2022	https://bioimage.io	Python
LIM Tracker	[72]	2022	https://github.com/LIMT34/LIM-Tracker	Python/Java
TrackMate 7	[73]	2022	https://imagej.net/plugins/trackmate/trackmate-v7-detectors	Java

ZeroCostDL4Mic is a cloud-based platform proposed by von Chamier et al. [69] aiming to simplify the use of DL architectures for various microscopy tasks. It is a collection of Jupyter Notebooks that can efficiently and interactively run Python code, leveraging the free, cloud-based computational resources of Google Colab. Concerning our focus, the tasks covered by ZeroCostDL4Mic include object detection, for which it implements YOLOv2, and cell segmentation, where it implements both the U-net and StarDist [74,75] networks. The outputs generated by StarDist are directly compatible with the TrackMate tracking software, enabling also automated cell tracking.

DeepImageJ [70] is a plugin for ImageJ and Fiji to facilitate the usage of DL models. It aims to offer user-friendly access to pre-trained models designed for various image modalities, including PhC and DIC. Currently, for the two previously mentioned modalities, the DL models are designed for segmentation.

BioImage Model Zoo [71] is an online repository for AI models to facilitate the usage of these pre-trained models by the bioimaging community. They provide a standard and tutorials to upload new models. The users can either download the projects in community partners' format or in user-friendly Python notebooks that can be used by anyone with the user's own dataset to perform bioimage analysis tasks. The current community partners are ilastik, ImJoy [76], Fiji [77], deepImageJ, ZeroCostDL4Mic, and HPA [78].

LIM Tracker is a Fiji plugin for cell tracking and analysis expressly aimed at advanced interactivity, usability, and versatility. Three tracking methods are implemented, suitable for fluorescence or PhC microscopy sequences. In the link-type tracking (tracking by detection), cells are first detected based on a Laplacian of Gaussian filter and watershed segmentation. Their ROIs are then linked by the Linear Assignment Problem algorithm [79]. In the sequential search-type tracking method, based on the particle filter framework, a user-specified ROI is tracked by sequentially searching for its corresponding ROI in subsequent frames by pattern matching. The third type of tracking is manual tracking, which allows users to specify the position of ROIs while moving along sequence frames.

Several additional functions allow interactive visualization and error correction. A plugin mechanism is provided for using different segmentation modules, including user-defined algorithms or DL algorithms (e.g., StarDist, Cellpose [45,46], YOLACT++ [80], Matterport MaskR-CNN [81], and Detectron2 MaskR-CNN [82]).

TrackMate 7 [73] is an extension of the TrackMate tracking software [83] distributed as a Fiji plugin. It integrates into tracking pipelines (based on five possible particle-linking algorithms) ten segmentation algorithms (including ilastik, Weka, StarDist, and Cellpose), besides any mask or label images computed with any other segmentation algorithm. It can handle fluorescence or label-free microscopy images, both 2D and 3D. The additional TrackMate helper facilitates choosing an optimal combination of segmentation and tracking modules, also allowing a systematic optimization of the tracking parameters for a whole dataset.

For an extended list of commercial and open source tools for tracking, the interested reader can also refer to [21]. A list of publicly available executable versions of 19 algorithms participating in the 2013–2015 CTC challenges is provided in Table 3 of the Supplementary Material of [22]; further links can also be found through the CTC web pages. Open-source DL software for bioimage segmentation is nicely surveyed in [84], where tools in different forms, such as web applications, plug-ins for existing imaging analysis software, and preconfigured interactive notebooks and pipelines are reviewed. Finally, further suggestions can come from the review by Smith et al. [85]. Indeed, even though their survey focuses on phenotypic image analysis, some of the referred software includes cell segmentation and time-lapse analysis tools.

4. Data

Datasets publicly available can be broadly subdivided into those devoted solely to segmentation (see Table 2), event detection and classification (and eventually also tracking, see Table 3), or tracking (and eventually also segmentation, see Table 4). Observe that the numbers reported in these tables refer solely to traditional label-free images/image sequences, which is the focus of this review; nonetheless, many of the reported datasets also have data from other microscopy types. The reported numbers specify only images for which annotations exist (there could be other images but without annotations).

Table 2. Details of available annotated data for cell segmentation in traditional label-free images: dataset name (Name); reference ([Ref]); type of microscopy data (Content); url (Link); number of annotated images (# imgs), annotated cells (# cells), and cell lines (#cell lines). All links were accessed on 28 August 2022.

Name	[Ref]	Content	Link	# Imgs	# Cells	# Cell Lines
Allen Cell Explorer	[86]	3D Label-Free	https://www.allencell.org/data-downloading.html/#sectionLabelFreeTrainingData	~18,000	~39,000	1
BU-BIL	[87]	PhC	https://www.cs.bu.edu/fac/betke/BiomedicalImageSegmentation/	151	151	3
CTC	[22]	PhC, DIC, BF	http://www.celltrackingchallenge.net	213	1980	5
DeepCell	[23]	PhC	https://doi.org/10.1371/journal.pcbi.1005177.s021, https://doi.org/10.1371/journal.pcbi.1005177.s022, https://doi.org/10.1371/journal.pcbi.1005177.s023	45	~4300	1
EVICAN	[88]	PhC, BF	https://edmond.mpdl.mpg.de/dataset.xhtml?persistentId=doi:10.17617/3.AJBV1S	4640	26,428	30
fastER	[25]	PhC, BF	https://bsse.ethz.ch/csd/software/faster.html	39	1653 (+953) [1]	2
LIVEcell	[26]	PhC	https://sartorius-research.github.io/LIVECell/	5239	1,686,352	8
Usiigaci	[63]	PhC	https://github.com/ElsevierSoftwareX/SOFTX_2018_158	37	2641	1
Vicar et al.	[20]	PhC, DIC, HMC	https://zenodo.org/record/1250729	32	4546	1

[1] For other 953 cells, only centroids are provided.

Allen Cell Explorer [86] includes a massive collection of light microscopy cell images with manually curated segmentation masks for 12 cellular components, as reported in [88].

BU-BIL (Boston University-Biomedical Image Library) [87] includes six datasets, three of which consisting of PhC images from different cell lines. The main aim of [87] is to evaluate and compare the performance of biomedical image segmentation made by trained experts, non-experts, and automated segmentation algorithms. Therefore, for each image, only one cell is annotated and provided as binary masks obtained in those three different ways. The gold standard annotation is obtained by majority voting of annotations created by the ten trained experts.

CTC (Cell Tracking Challenge) is a time-lapse cell segmentation and tracking benchmark on publicly available data, launched in 2012 to objectively compare and evaluate state-of-the-art whole-cell and nucleus segmentation and tracking methods [22,89]. The datasets consist of 2D and 3D time-lapse video sequences of fluorescent counterstained nuclei or cells moving on top or immersed in a substrate, along with 2D PhC and DIC microscopy videos of cells moving on a flat substrate. The videos cover a wide range of cell types and quality (spatial and temporal resolution, noise levels, etc.). The ground truth consists of manually annotated cell masks (for segmentation) and cell markers interlinked between frames to form cell lineage trees (for tracking).

DeepCell comes from the supporting material of [23]. It consists of a PhC image sequence of HeLa-S3 cells. Annotations for each image are given in terms of cell and nuclei segmentation masks.

EVICAN (Expert VIsual Cell ANnotation) [88] includes partially annotated grayscale images of 30 different cell lines from multiple microscopes, contrast mechanisms, and magnifications. For each image, a subset of cells and nuclei is annotated and provided both as json annotation files and as binary masks. An example is shown in Figure 3a,b. To reduce the influence of unannotated cells on the background class, in their experiments, the authors pre-processed the dataset by blurring (with a Gaussian filter) the images but leaving unchanged the annotated instances. The pre-processed images are also provided with the dataset (see Figure 3c).

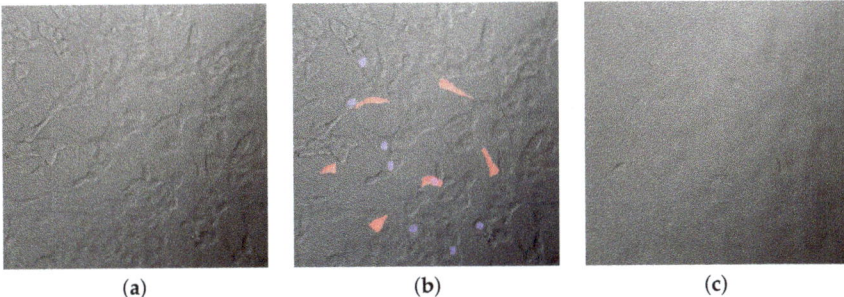

Figure 3. Example data from the EVICAN dataset [88]: (**a**) original image (ID 92_ACHN); (**b**) image with annotated cells (red) and nuclei (blue); (**c**) image where non-annotated areas have been blurred.

fastER [25] includes PhC, BC, and synthetic Fluo images of three different cell lines. For each image, the annotations consist of binary masks that enclose the segmentation of most of the cells and just the centroid for the remaining cells.

LIVEcell [26] is a recently proposed large-scale, manually annotated, and expert-validated dataset of PhC images for benchmarking cell segmentation. It consists of over 5 thousand images, including over 1.6 million cells of seven cell types (human and mouse) having different cell morphologies and culture densities. Annotations are provided as json files.

Usiigaci [63] includes 37 PhC images of T98G cells. Annotations consist of indexed masks, with an index for each cell, followed in time (see Figure 4). Thus, these can be used for both segmentation and tracking. A spreadsheet file is also enclosed, providing information from tracking and various features for each tracked cell.

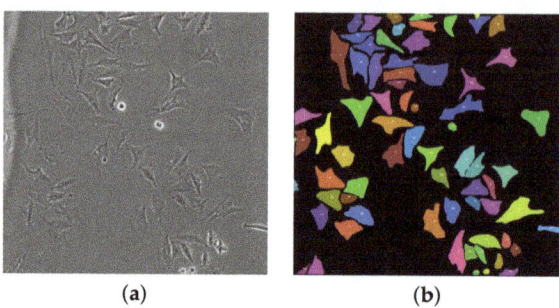

(a)   (b)

Figure 4. Example data from the Usiigaci dataset [63]: (**a**) original image (20180101ef002xy01t01.tif); (**b**) corresponding indexed mask, where each color indicates a different cell in all sequence images.

Table 3. Details of annotated data for cellular event detection and classification in traditional label-free sequences: dataset name (Name); reference ([Ref]); application of the data (Task); type of microscopy data (Content); url (Link); number of annotated images (# imgs), and number of annotated events (# events). All links were accessed on 28 August 2022.

Name	[Ref]	Task	Content	Link	# Imgs	# Events
C2C12-16	[54]	Mitosis Detection	DIC	https://www.iti-tju.org/mitosisdetection/download/ [1]	16,208	7159
CTMC	[90]	Mitosis Detection	DIC	https://ivc.ischool.utexas.edu/ctmc/ [1]	80,389	1616
DeephESC	[55]	Classification	PhC	https://www.vislab.ucr.edu/SOFTWARE/software.php [2]	785	NA

[1] Unavailable at the time of writing. [2] Accessed on 30 August 2022.

C2C12-16 [54] was released as a large-scale time-lapse phase-contrast microscopy image dataset for the mitosis detection task at the first international contest on mitosis detection in phase-contrast microscopy image sequences, held with the workshop on computer vision for microscopy image analysis (CVMI) at CVPR 2019. It is an extension of the Ker et al. dataset [91] with manual annotations of mitosis. The complete dataset contains 16 sequences with 1013 frames per sequence and a total of 7159 mitosis events within the images.

Cell Tracking with Mitosis Detection Challenge (CTMC) is a benchmarked challenge that provides DIC images for 14 cell lines [90]. The data adds up to 86 live-cell imaging videos consisting of 152,584 frames in total. In addition to the images, the challenge grants bounding box-based detection and tracking ground truths for each cell line, in the form of csv files for each video, including, for each frame and each cell, the cell ID and its bounding box coordinates. Recently, the dataset has also been adopted for the CTMC-v1 Challenge at CVPR 2022 (https://motchallenge.net/data/CTMC-v1/, accessed on 30 August 2022).

DeephESC [55] consists of 785 PhC hESC images subdivided according to six classes (cell clusters, debris, unattached cells, attached cells, dynamically blebbing cells, and apoptically blebbing cells).

Table 4. Details of available annotated data for cell tracking in traditional label-free sequences: dataset name (Name); reference ([Ref]); type of microscopy data (Content); url (Link); number of annotated images (# imgs), annotated cells/tracks (# cells/tracks), and cell lines (#cell lines). All links were accessed on 28 August 2022.

Name	[Ref]	Content	Link	# Imgs	# Cells/Tracks	# Cell Lines
CTC	[22]	PhC, DIC, BF	http://www.celltrackingchallenge.net [1]	213	1980/2944	5
CTMC	[90]	DIC	https://ivc.ischool.utexas.edu/ctmc/ [2]	80,389	1,097,223 [3] /1616	14
Ker et al.	[91]	PhC	https://osf.io/ysaq2/ [1]	19134	NA [4] /2011	1
Usiigaci	[63]	PhC	https://github.com/ElsevierSoftwareX/SOFTX_2018_158 [1]	37	2641/105	1

[1] Accessed on 30 August 2022. [2] Unavailable at the time of writing. [3] Only bounding boxes are provided. [4] Only centroids are provided.

The dataset by **Ker et al.** [91] includes 48 PhC image sequences of mouse C2C12 cells under various treatments. Annotations consist of manually tagged centroids and state (e.g., newborn, divided, or mitotic) for 10% of the cells for all the sequences; only for one of the sequences, all the cells are manually annotated. The dataset is also provided with annotations automatically generated for all the cells using in-house software based on segmentation, mitosis detection, and association.

Other annotated microscopy image sets can be downloaded from the Broad Bioimage Benchmark Collection (BBBC) [92]. It is a publicly available collection of microscopy images intended as a resource for testing and validating automated image-analysis algorithms. Being contributed by many different research groups and for various applications, annotations are provided in varying forms (e.g., cell counts, masks, outlines, or bounding boxes).

5. Metrics

Below, we present some metrics commonly adopted to evaluate the results quantitatively. Some of these metrics are directly used from the computer vision and ML/DL domains, while others are more specific to cellular image analysis.

5.1. Metrics for Pixel-Wise Cell Segmentation

Many different metrics are adopted in the literature to evaluate the performance of (cell) segmentation algorithms. The most frequently used is the one adopted for the CTC [22], generally denoted as **SEG**. Given the ground truth cell segmentation GT and the corresponding segmentation S computed with any segmentation algorithm, the Jaccard similarity index, also known as Intersection over Union (IoU), evaluates the degree of overlap between the true and the computed results and is defined as

$$\text{IoU}(GT, S) = \frac{|GT \cap S|}{|GT \cup S|}, \tag{1}$$

where $|\cdot|$ indicates the cardinality of a set (i.e., the number of pixels) and $\cap$ and $\cup$ indicate the set intersection and union, respectively. This metric [63] is sometimes equivalently expressed in terms of the number of true positive pixels TP ($TP = |GT \cap S|$), false negative pixels FN ($FN = GT - S$), and false positive pixels FP ($FP = S - GT$) as

$$\text{IoU}(GT, S) = \frac{TP}{FN + TP + FP}.$$

The SEG metric adopted in the CTC for a particular video is then computed as the mean IuO over all the GT cells of the video. It should be observed that, although many authors refer to this metric as SEG [72,93], others just refer to it as AP [45,46,74,75,88]. Further metrics frequently adopted [23,25,63] include

- the **Recall**, also known as Sensitivity or True Positive Rate,

$$\text{Recall} = \frac{TP}{TP + FN}, \tag{2}$$

that gives the percentage of detected true positive pixels as compared to the total number of true positive pixels in the ground truth;
- the **Precision**, also known as Positive Prediction,

$$\text{Precision} = \frac{TP}{TP + FP}, \qquad (3)$$

that gives the percentage of detected true positive pixels as compared to the total number of pixels detected by the algorithm, providing an indication on the degree of exactness of the algorithm in identifying only relevant pixels;
- the **F-score**, also known as F-measure or Figure of Merit,

$$F_1 = \frac{2 \cdot \text{Recall} \cdot \text{Precision}}{\text{Recall} + \text{Precision}} = \frac{2 \cdot TP}{2 \cdot TP + FP + FN}, \qquad (4)$$

that is the weighted harmonic mean of Precision and Recall.

All the above metrics assume values in [0,1] and higher values indicate better results.

5.2. Metrics for Object-Wise Cell Detection

Generally, in the case of cell detection, the ground truth is given in terms of bounding boxes of the cells contained in the images. Here, the IoU metric of Equation (1) can be adapted to evaluate the degree of overlap between the ground truth bounding boxes (GT) and the predicted bounding boxes (S). IoU tresholding can then be used to decide if a detection is correct or not. For a given IoU threshold α, a true positive (TP), i.e., a correct positive prediction, is a detection for which $\text{IoU}(GT, S) \geq \alpha$ and a false positive (FP), i.e., a wrong positive detection, is a detection for which $\text{IoU}(GT, S) < \alpha$. A false negative (FN) is an actual instance that is not detected.

Given these adapted concepts, the Recall, Precision, and F-score metrics defined in Equations (2)–(4) can be used to evaluate cell detection algorithms. These are also used to compute the **Average Precision at a given IoU threshold** α, denoted as AP@α, defined as the Area Under the Precision-Recall Curve (AUC-PR) evaluated at the IoU threshold α, given as

$$\text{AP@}\alpha = \int_0^1 p(r)\, dr.$$

According to the Common Objects in Context (COCO) [94] evaluation protocol (https://cocodataset.org/#detection-eval, accessed on 28 August 2022), single values for α can be chosen for thresholding IoU (generally equal to 0.5 or 0.75). Moreover, a set of thresholds can be chosen and the **mean Average Precision** mAP over these IoU thresholds considered for cell detection evaluation. With the usual choice [26,74,75] of values for α from 0.5 to 0.95 with a step size of 0.05, mAP is thus given by

$$\text{mAP} = \frac{AP@0.5 + AP@0.55 + \ldots + AP@0.95}{10}.$$

In the CTC [22], the detection accuracy of the methods, denoted as **DET**, is adopted to estimate how accurately each given object has been identified (http://celltrackingchallenge.net/evaluation-methodology/, accessed on 28 August 2022). It is based on the comparison of the nodes of the acyclic oriented graphs representing the objects in both the ground truth and the computed object detection result. Exploiting the Acyclic Oriented Graph Matching measure for detection (AOGM-D) [95], that gives the cost of transforming the set of nodes of the computed objects into the set of ground truth nodes, DET is defined as

$$\text{DET} = 1 - \frac{\min(\text{AOGM-D}, \text{AOGM-D}_0)}{\text{AOGM-D}_0},$$

where AOGM-D$_0$ is the cost of creating the set of ground truth nodes from scratch. DET always falls in the [0,1] interval, with higher values corresponding to better detection performance. The DET metric is averaged with the SEG metric described in Section 5.1 to provide the overall performance for the CSB

$$\text{OP}_{CSB} = \frac{1}{2}(\text{DET} + \text{SEG}).$$

5.3. Metrics for Cell Event Detection

For mitosis detection, Ref. [54] represents each detected mitosis as a triple (x, y, t) of spatial and temporal position of the event. The detection is considered a true positive (TP) if its distance from the corresponding ground truth triple is below preset spatial and temporal thresholds. Otherwise, it is considered a false positive (FP). Undetected ground truth mitotic events are considered as false negative (FN). Having so defined TP, FP, and FN, Ref. [54] adopts Precision, Recall, and F-score metrics defined in Equations (2)–(4), respectively, to evaluate the performance of mitosis detection algorithms. The same metrics are also adopted in [60], where they are extended also to apoptic events.

In [23], **DeepCell** is also used to perform semantic segmentation, i.e., to both segment individual cells and predict their cell type. For evaluating the obtained results, the authors consider the **Cellular Classification Score** (CCS_c) for each class c, defined as

$$CCS_c = \frac{\sum_{i \in Cells} s_{i,c}}{\sum_{j \in Classes} \sum_{i \in Cells} s_{i,j}},$$

where $s_{i,j}$ indicates the classification score of pixel i for class j. The authors showed that the closer the CCS_c is to 1, the more likely the prediction is correct.

5.4. Metrics for Cell Tracking

The metrics most frequently adopted for evaluating cell tracking are those introduced by the Multiple Object Tracking (MOT) [96]. The Multiple Object Tracking Accuracy (**MOTA**) [97] is a MOT tracking metric that represents the object coverage [90], also used for example in [63]. It can be defined as

$$\text{MOTA} = 1 - \frac{FN + FP + IDSW}{T},$$

where FN is the sum over the entire video of all missed cells (number of ground truth bounding boxes not covered by any computed bounding box), FP is the sum over the entire video of all false positives (number of bounding boxes not covering any ground truth bounding box), $IDSW$ is the number of object identities switched from one frame to the next (number of bounding boxes covering a ground truth bounding box from a track different than in the previous frame), and T is the total number of detections in the ground truth.

Multiple Object Tracking Precision (**MOTP**) [98] is the average dissimilarity between all correctly assigned detections (true positives) and their ground-truths, defined as

$$\text{MOTP} = \frac{\sum_{t,i} d_{t,i}}{\sum_t c_t},$$

where c_t indicates the number of matches in frame t and $d_{t,i}$ is the bonding bob overlap of the detection i with its ground truth. This MOT tracking metric shows the ability of the tracker to estimate precise object positions, independent of its skill at recognizing object configurations, keeping consistent trajectories, and so forth [97].

More recently, the MOT challenge introduced another tracking metric, named **IDF1**, that quantifies the object's identity across the frames of a sequence [90] and represents the ratio of the detections that were properly identified over the average number of ground-truth and computed detections [99]. It is an F-score as in Equation (4).

$$\text{IDF1} = \frac{2 * IDTP}{2 * IDTP + IDFP + IDFN},$$

where $IDTP, IDFP,$ and $IDFN$ indicate the number of true positive, false positive, and false negative IDs, respectively.

Many other metrics introduced for evaluating MOT challenges could also be applied to the case of cell tracking, such as the Higher Order Tracking Accuracy (HOTA) [100].

Focusing more specifically on cellular microscopy, the metric adopted in CTC [22] for evaluating cell tracking results is the Tracking Accuracy, denoted as **TRA**, used for example in [72,90,93]. It is a normalized weighted distance between the tracking ground truth and the result of the algorithm, with weights chosen to reflect the effort it takes a human curator to manually carry out the edits needed for matching the two. Tracking results are first represented as acyclic oriented graphs providing the cells lineage. Then the difficulty in transforming a computed tracking graph into the corresponding ground truth graph is estimated as

$$\text{TRA} = 1 - \frac{\min(\text{AOGM}, \text{AOGM}_0)}{\text{AOGM}_0},$$

where AOGM is the Acyclic Oriented Graph Matching (AOGM) measure [95] and AOGM_0 is the AOGM value required for creating the ground truth graph from scratch. TRA assumes values in [0, 1], with higher values corresponding to better tracking performance. The overall performance for the CTB is calculated as the average of the SEG (see Section 5.1) and TRA metrics:

$$\text{OP}_{CTB} = \frac{1}{2}(\text{SEG} + \text{TRA}).$$

6. Open Problems and Future Research Directions

Common challenges in microscopy image processing include increasingly high image sizes, image artifacts, and batch effects, especially in the presence of object crowding and overlapping. Nevertheless, insufficient, imbalanced, and inconsistent data annotations [101] prevent the effective usage of data analysis methods. The image size affects computational and storage time, which might prevent the use of modern image processing techniques on standard hardware. Nevertheless, the batch acquisition of images poses problems, as small variations might be present in successive applications of the same technical procedure. That implies that the hypothesis that all images are independently identically distributed statistical units sampled from the same population, which means they all describe the same process independently of its natural variability, might not be true anymore. As a consequence, the training of AI/ML/DL/methods can be biased and produce results that are not reflecting the probability distribution of the original phenomena. Despite the results reviewed here, these problems require further investigation, as the number of images required for training the parameters of a multi-layer architecture is in the order of tens of thousands. The performance of AI systems and their generalization capabilities strongly depend on the quality of annotations from the available datasets. Although many unsupervised algorithms may not require annotated data, these are crucial for understanding and interpreting such systems. As evident from Tables 2 and 4, which represent available data collections at the publication time, there is a lack of large-scale curated and annotated datasets of light microscopy images. In particular, this is true for adherent cells or suspension-cultured counterparts, where the lack of annotated datasets makes the segmentation difficult for different LI techniques [20]. This difficulty is exacerbated by the natural variability of the observed phenomena, which often show high cell densities, cell-to-cell variability, complex cellular shapes and texture, cell shape varying over time (e.g., due to drug treatments [26,93]), varying image illumination, and low signal-to-noise ratios

(SNRs) [24,25]. These problems are also common in cell detection and tracking, making them even more challenging, especially when using AI approaches. An extreme example is neural cell instance segmentation in neuroscience applications [32], which aims at detecting and segmenting every neural cell in a microscopy image. In these experiments, further limiting factors include cell distortion, unclear cell contours, low-contrast cell protrusion structures, and background impurities. However, accurate detection of objects is crucial for the tracking process, as aberrant object detection leads to missing links and the generation of tracks that end prematurely, with multiple short tracks representing the same individual object over time as different entities. Most detection algorithms treat tightly packed objects (e.g., touching and overlapping cells) as a single entity, resulting in breaks in tracks or single tracks linking groups of objects. In addition, cell tracking can produce terabyte-scale movies as experiments often require multi-day monitoring [93]. In such experiments, rapid cell migrations, high cell density, and multiple rounds of mitoses result in multiple neighboring cells being mis-tracked. Extensive 3D data present additional challenges due not only to the size of the image data itself but also to the very high cell densities they show toward the end of the videos [22].

Other key factors that affect the tracking results [21] include noise, occlusions, difficult object motion, complex objects structures, and background subtraction. Further work is also needed for handling scenarios with low SNR or contrast ratio [22]. These challenges can explain why few cell tracking platforms have been developed for label-free microscopy images. The benchmarked ranking of the Cell Tracking Challenge [22] confirms the difficulties in processing these images and highlights further related research, particularly for DIC images [90]. All these current factors limit the possibility of assessing and comparing the capabilities of different methods used to analyze data. Perspectives and future work in LI also include handling big data of continuously growing size, improving the quality and completeness of annotated datasets, continuous modeling of biological processes using regression rather than classification, and interpretability of ML and DL algorithms.

Finally, investigations should be devoted to the integration of multiple microscopy techniques on the same sample to overcome the proper limits of each technique and the lack of training data. We believe that a holistic view of biological processes and functions might be attained by *omics imaging* [36], which consists in the integration and analysis of next-generation sequencing data with images, in order to provide more insight into available data.

Author Contributions: Conceptualization, L.M., L.A. and M.R.G.; methodology, all; software, A.A. and A.H.; validation, A.A. and A.H.; formal analysis, L.M., L.A. and M.R.G.; investigation, all; resources, all; data curation, L.M., A.A. and A.H.; writing—original draft preparation, L.M. and L.A.; writing—review and editing, all; visualization, all; supervision, M.R.G.; project administration, M.R.G.; All authors have read and agreed to the published version of the manuscript.

Funding: This research received no external funding.

Institutional Review Board Statement: Not applicable.

Informed Consent Statement: Not applicable.

Data Availability Statement: Not applicable.

Acknowledgments: This work has been partially funded by the BiBiNet project (H35F21000430002) within POR-Lazio FESR 2014–2020. It was carried out also within the activities of L.M., L.A. and M.R.G. as members of the ICAR-CNR INdAM Research Unit and partially supported by the INdAM research project "Computational Intelligence methods for Digital Health". The work of M.R.G. was conducted within the framework of the Basic Research Program at the National Research University Higher School of Economics (HSE).

Conflicts of Interest: The authors declare no conflict of interest.

Abbreviations

The following abbreviations are used in this manuscript:

AI	Artificial Intelligence
ANCIS	Attentive Neural Cell Instance Segmentation
AOGM-D	Acyclic Oriented Graph Matching measure for Detection
BBBC	Broad Bioimage Benchmark Collection
BF	Bright-Field
BU-BIL	Boston University - Biomedical Image Library
CCS	Cellular Classification Score
CIC	Cell-In-Cell
CNN	Convolutional Neural Network
COCO	Common Objects in Context
CSB	Cell Segmentation Benchmark
CTB	Cell Tracking Benchmark
CTC	Cell Tracking Challenge
CTMC	Cell Tracking with Mitosis Detection Challenge
CVMI	Computer Vision for Microscopy Image Analysis
DIC	Differential Interphase Contrast
DL	Deep Learning
DNA	Deoxyribonucleic Acid
EVICAN	Expert VIsual Cell ANnotation
FN	False Negative
FNA	False Negative Association
FP	False Positive
GMAN	Generative Multi Adversarial Networks
GPU	Graphics Processing Unit
GT	Ground Truth
HMC	Hoffman Modulation Contrast
HOTA	Higher Order Tracking Accuracy
IoU	Intersection over Union
LI	Label-free Imaging
LP	Linear Programming
LSTM	Long Short-Term Memory
ML	Machine Learning
MOT	Multiple Object Tracking
MOTA	Multiple Object Tracking Accuracy
MOTP	Multiple Object Tracking Precision
PhC	Phase Contrast
PSSD	Progressive Sequence Saliency Discovery Network
QLI	Quantitative Label-free Imaging
QPI	Quantitative Phase Imaging
ROI	Regions of Interest
SSD	Single Shot multi-box Detector
SNR	Signal-to-Noise Ratio
SVM	Support Vector Machine
TP	True Positive
TWS	Trainable Weka Segmentation
UV	Ultraviolet
Weka	Waikato Environment for Knowledge Analysis

References

1. Sebestyén, E.; Marullo, F.; Lucini, F.; Petrini, C.; Bianchi, A.; Valsoni, S.; Olivieri, I.; Antonelli, L.; Gregoretti, F.; Oliva, G.; et al. SAMMY-seq reveals early alteration of heterochromatin and deregulation of bivalent genes in Hutchinson-Gilford Progeria Syndrome. *Nat. Commun.* **2020**, *11*, 1–16. [CrossRef] [PubMed]
2. Marullo, F.; Cesarini, E.; Antonelli, L.; Gregoretti, F.; Oliva, G.; Lanzuolo, C. Nucleoplasmic Lamin A/C and Polycomb group of proteins: An evolutionarily conserved interplay. *Nucleus* **2016**, *7*, 103–111. [CrossRef] [PubMed]

3. Song, L.; Hennink, E.; Young, I.; Tanke, H. Photobleaching kinetics of fluoresce in quantitative fluorescence microscopy. *Biophys J.* **1995**, *68*, 2588–2600. [CrossRef]
4. Mir, M.; Bhaduri, B.; Wang, R.; Zhu, R.; Popescu, G. Quantitative Phase Imaging. *Prog. Opt.* **2012**, *57*, 133–217. [CrossRef]
5. Zernike, F. How I Discovered Phase Contrast. *Science* **1955**, *121*, 345–349. [CrossRef] [PubMed]
6. Nomarski, G. Differential microinterferometer with polarized waves. *J. Phys. Radium Paris* **1955**, *16*, 9S.
7. Hoffman, R.; Gross, L. Modulation Contrast Microscope. *Appl. Opt.* **1975**, *14*, 1169–1176. [CrossRef]
8. Yin, Z.; Kanade, T.; Chen, M. Understanding the phase contrast optics to restore artifact-free microscopy images for segmentation. *Med. Image Anal.* **2012**, *16*, 1047–1062. [CrossRef]
9. Gregoretti, F.; Lucini, F.; Cesarini, E.; Oliva, G.; Lanzuolo, C.; Antonelli, L. Segmentation, 3D reconstruction and analysis of PcG proteins in fluorescence microscopy images in different cell culture conditions. In *Methods in Molecular Biology*; Springer: New York, NY, USA, 2022.
10. Popescu, G. *Quantitative Phase Imaging of Cells and Tissues*; Mc-Graw-Hill: New York, NY, USA, 2011.
11. Helgadottir, S.; Midtvedt, B.; Pineda, J.; Sabirsh, A.; Adiels, C.B.; Romeo, S.; Midtvedt, D.; Volpe, G. Extracting quantitative biological information from bright-field cell images using deep learning. *Biophys. Rev.* **2021**, *2*, 031401. [CrossRef]
12. Buggenthin, F.; Marr, C.; Schwarzfischer, M.; Hoppe, P.S.; Hilsenbeck, O.; Schroeder, T.; Theis, F.J. An automatic method for robust and fast cell detection in bright field images from high-throughput microscopy. *BMC Bioinform.* **2013**, *14*, 297. [CrossRef]
13. Selinummi, J.; Ruusuvuori, P.; Podolsky, I.; Ozinsky, A.; Gold, E.; Yli-Harja, O.; Aderem, A.; Shmulevich, I. Bright Field Microscopy as an Alternative to Whole Cell Fluorescence in Automated Analysis of Macrophage Images. *PLoS ONE* **2009**, *4*, 1–9. [CrossRef] [PubMed]
14. Naso, F.D.; Sterbini, V.; Crecca, E.; Asteriti, I.A.; Russo, A.D.; Giubettini, M.; Cundari, E.; Lindon, C.; Rosa, A.; Guarguaglini, G. Excess TPX2 interferes with microtubule disassembly and nuclei reformation at mitotic exit. *Cells* **2020**, *9*, 374. [CrossRef] [PubMed]
15. Jiang, Q.; Sudalagunta, P.; Meads, M.B.; Ahmed, K.T.; Rutkowski, T.; Shain, K.; Silva, A.S.; Zhang, W. An Advanced Framework for Time-lapse Microscopy Image Analysis. *bioRxiv* **2020**. [CrossRef]
16. Caldon, C.E.; Burgess, A. Label free, quantitative single-cell fate tracking of time-lapse movies. *MethodsX* **2019**, *6*, 2468–2475. [CrossRef]
17. Janiesch, C.; Zschech, P.; Heinrich, K. Machine learning and deep learning. *Electron. Mark.* **2021**, *31*, 685–695. [CrossRef]
18. Gupta, A.; Harrison, P.J.; Wieslander, H.; Pielawski, N.; Kartasalo, K.; Partel, G.; Solorzano, L.; Suveer, A.; Klemm, A.H.; Spjuth, O.; et al. Deep Learning in Image Cytometry: A Review. *Cytometry Part A* **2019**, *95*, 366–380. [CrossRef] [PubMed]
19. Jo, Y.; Cho, H.; Lee, S.Y.; Choi, G.; Kim, G.; Min, H.s.; Park, Y. Quantitative Phase Imaging and Artificial Intelligence: A Review. *IEEE J. Sel. Top. Quantum Electron.* **2019**, *25*, 1–14. [CrossRef]
20. Vicar, T.; Balvan, J.; Jaros, J.; Jug, F.; Kolar, R.; Masarik, M.; Gumulec, J. Cell segmentation methods for label-free contrast microscopy: Review and comprehensive comparison. *BMC Bioinform.* **2019**, *20*, 1–25. [CrossRef]
21. Emami, N.; Sedaei, Z.; Ferdousi, R. Computerized cell tracking: Current methods, tools and challenges. *Visual Inform.* **2021**, *5*, 1–13. [CrossRef]
22. Ulman, V.; Maška, M.; Magnusson, K.E.G.; Ronneberger, O.; Haubold, C.; Harder, N.; Matula, P.; Matula, P.; Svoboda, D.; Radojevic, M.; et al. An objective comparison of cell-tracking algorithms. *Nat. Methods* **2017**, *14*, 1141–1152. [CrossRef]
23. Van Valen, D.A.; Kudo, T.; Lane, K.M.; Macklin, D.N.; Quach, N.T.; DeFelice, M.M.; Maayan, I.; Tanouchi, Y.; Ashley, E.A.; Covert, M.W. Deep Learning Automates the Quantitative Analysis of Individual Cells in Live-Cell Imaging Experiments. *PLoS Comput. Biol.* **2016**, *12*, e1005177. [CrossRef] [PubMed]
24. Lux, F.; Matula, P. Cell segmentation by combining marker-controlled watershed and deep learning. *arXiv* **2020**, arXiv:2004.01607.
25. Hilsenbeck, O.; Schwarzfischer, M.; Loeffler, D.; Dimopoulos, S.; Hastreiter, S.; Marr, C.; Theis, F.J.; Schroeder, T. fastER: A user-friendly tool for ultrafast and robust cell segmentation in large-scale microscopy. *Bioinformatics* **2017**, *33*, 2020–2028. [CrossRef] [PubMed]
26. Edlund, C.; Jackson, T.R.; Khalid, N.; Bevan, N.; Dale, T.; Dengel, A.; Ahmed, S.; Trygg, J.; Sjögren, R. LIVECell: A large-scale dataset for label-free live cell segmentation. *Nat. Methods* **2021**, *18*, 1038–1045. [CrossRef]
27. Caicedo, J.; Goodman, A.; Karhohs, K.; Cimini, B.; Ackerman, J.; Haghighi, M.; Heng, C.; Becker, T.; Doan, M.; McQuin, C.; et al. Nucleus segmentation across imaging experiments: The 2018 Data Science Bowl. *Nat. Methods* **2019**, *16*, 1247–1253. [CrossRef]
28. Casalino, L.; D'Ambra, P.; Guarracino, M.R.; Irpino, A.; Maddalena, L.; Maiorano, F.; Minchiotti, G.; Jorge Patriarca, E. Image Analysis and Classification for High-Throughput Screening of Embryonic Stem Cells. In *Proceedings of the Mathematical Models in Biology: Bringing Mathematics to Life*; Zazzu, V., Ferraro, M.B., Guarracino, M.R., Eds.; Springer International Publishing: Cham, Switzerland, 2015; pp. 17–31. [CrossRef]
29. Casalino, L.; Guarracino, M.R.; Maddalena, L. Imaging for High-Throughput Screening of Pluripotent Stem Cells, SIAM Conference on Imaging Science—IS18. 2018. Available online: https://www.siam-is18.dm.unibo.it/presentations/811.html (accessed on 3 August 2022).
30. de Haan, K.; Rivenson, Y.; Wu, Y.; Ozcan, A. Deep-Learning-Based Image Reconstruction and Enhancement in Optical Microscopy. *Proc. IEEE* **2020**, *108*, 30–50. [CrossRef]

31. Gregoretti, F.; Cesarini, E.; Lanzuolo, C.; Oliva, G.; Antonelli, L., An Automatic Segmentation Method Combining an Active Contour Model and a Classification Technique for Detecting Polycomb-group Proteinsin High-Throughput Microscopy Images. In *Polycomb Group Proteins: Methods and Protocols*; Lanzuolo, C., Bodega, B., Eds.; Springer New York: New York, NY, USA, 2016; pp. 181–197. [CrossRef]
32. Yi, J.; Wu, P.; Jiang, M.; Huang, Q.; Hoeppner, D.J.; Metaxas, D.N. Attentive neural cell instance segmentation. *Med. Image Anal.* **2019**, *55*, 228–240. [CrossRef]
33. Gregoretti, F.; Cortesi, A.; Oliva, G.; Bodega, B.; Antonelli, L., An Algorithm for the Analysis of the 3D Spatial Organization of the Genome. In *Capturing Chromosome Conformation: Methods and Protocols*; Bodega, B., Lanzuolo, C., Eds.; Springer US: New York, NY, USA, 2021; pp. 299–320. [CrossRef]
34. Antonelli, L.; De Simone, V.; di Serafino, D. A view of computational models for image segmentation. In *Annali dell'Università di Ferrara*; Springer: Cham, Switzerland, 2022. [CrossRef]
35. Arteta, C.; Lempitsky, V.S.; Noble, J.A.; Zisserman, A. Learning to Detect Cells Using Non-overlapping Extremal Regions. In Proceedings of the Medical Image Computing and Computer-Assisted Intervention—MICCAI 2012—15th International Conference, Nice, France, 1–5 October 2012; Proceedings, Part I; Ayache, N., Delingette, H., Golland, P., Mori, K., Eds.; Springer: Berlin/Heidelberg, Germany, 2012; Volume 751, pp. 348–356. [CrossRef]
36. Antonelli, L.; Guarracino, M.R.; Maddalena, L.; Sangiovanni, M. Integrating imaging and omics data: A review. *Biomed. Signal Process. Control.* **2019**, *52*, 264–280. [CrossRef]
37. Ronneberger, O.; Fischer, P.; Brox, T. U-Net: Convolutional Networks for Biomedical Image Segmentation. In Proceedings of the Medical Image Computing and Computer-Assisted Intervention—MICCAI 2015—18th International Conference, Munich, Germany, 5–9 October 2015; Proceedings, Part III; Navab, N., Hornegger, J., Wells, W.M., Frangi, A.F., Eds.; Springer, Cham, Switzerland, 2015; Volume 9351, pp. 234–241. [CrossRef]
38. Berg, S.; Kutra, D.; Kroeger, T.; Straehle, C.N.; Kausler, B.X.; Haubold, C.; Schiegg, M.; Ales, J.; Beier, T.; Rudy, M.; et al. ilastik: Interactive machine learning for (bio)image analysis. *Nat. Methods* **2019**, *16*, 1226–1232. [CrossRef]
39. Carpenter, A.; Jones, T.; Lamprecht, M.; Clarke, C.; Kang, I.; Friman, O.; Guertin, D.A.; Chang, J.H.; Lindquist, R.A.; Moffat, J.; et al. CellProfiler: Image analysis software for identifying and quantifying cell phenotypes. *Genome Biol.* **2006**, *7*, R100. [CrossRef]
40. Liu, W.; Anguelov, D.; Erhan, D.; Szegedy, C.; Reed, S.E.; Fu, C.; Berg, A.C. SSD: Single Shot MultiBox Detector. In Proceedings of the Computer Vision—ECCV 2016—14th European Conference, Amsterdam, The Netherlands, 11–14 October 2016; Proceedings, Part I; Leibe, B., Matas, J., Sebe, N., Welling, M., Eds.; Springer, Cham, Switzerland, 2016; Volume 9905, pp. 21–37. [CrossRef]
41. Beucher, S.; Meyer, F., The Morphological Approach to Segmentation: The Watershed Transformation. In *Mathematical Morphology in Image Processing*; Thompson, B.J., Dougherty, E., Eds.; CRC Press: Boca Raton, FL, USA, 1993; p. 49. [CrossRef]
42. Scherr, T.; Löffler, K.; Böhland, M.; Mikut, R. Cell segmentation and tracking using CNN-based distance predictions and a graph-based matching strategy. *PLoS ONE* **2020**, *15*, e0243219. [CrossRef] [PubMed]
43. Nishimura, K.; Wang, C.; Watanabe, K.; Fei Elmer Ker, D.; Bise, R. Weakly supervised cell instance segmentation under various conditions. *Med. Image Anal.* **2021**, *73*, 102182. [CrossRef] [PubMed]
44. Boykov, Y.; Kolmogorov, V. An experimental comparison of min-cut/max- flow algorithms for energy minimization in vision. *IEEE Trans. Pattern Anal. Mach. Intell.* **2004**, *26*, 1124–1137. [CrossRef] [PubMed]
45. Stringer, C.; Wang, T.; Michaelos, M.; Pachitariu, M. Cellpose: A generalist algorithm for cellular segmentation. *Nat. Methods* **2021**, *18*, 100–106. [CrossRef]
46. Stringer, C.; Pachitariu, M. Cellpose 2.0: How to train your own model. *bioRxiv* **2022**. [CrossRef]
47. Borensztejn, K.; Tyrna, P.; Gaweł, A.M.; Dziuba, I.; Wojcik, C.; Bialy, L.P.; Mlynarczuk-Bialy, I. Classification of Cell-in-Cell Structures: Different Phenomena with Similar Appearance. *Cells* **2021**, *10*, 2569. [CrossRef]
48. Su, Y.T.; Lu, Y.; Chen, M.; Liu, A.A. Spatiotemporal joint mitosis detection using CNN-LSTM network in time-lapse phase contrast microscopy images. *IEEE Access* **2017**, *5*, 18033–18041. [CrossRef]
49. Mao, Y.; Yin, Z. Two-Stream Bidirectional Long Short-Term Memory for Mitosis Event Detection and Stage Localization in Phase-Contrast Microscopy Images. In *Proceedings of the Medical Image Computing and Computer-Assisted Intervention—MICCAI 2017*; Descoteaux, M., Maier-Hein, L., Franz, A., Jannin, P., Collins, D., Duchesne, S., Eds.; Springer: Cham, Switzerland, 2017; pp. 56–64. [CrossRef]
50. Phan, H.T.H.; Kumar, A.; Feng, D.; Fulham, M.; Kim, J. Semi-supervised estimation of event temporal length for cell event detection. *arXiv* **2019**, arXiv:1909.09946. [CrossRef]
51. Nishimura, K.; Bise, R. Spatial-Temporal Mitosis Detection in Phase-Contrast Microscopy via Likelihood Map Estimation by 3DCNN. In Proceedings of the 2020 42nd Annual International Conference of the IEEE Engineering in Medicine & Biology Society (EMBC), Montreal, QC, Canada, 20–24 July 2020; pp. 1811–1815. [CrossRef]
52. Milletari, F.; Navab, N.; Ahmadi, S. V-Net: Fully Convolutional Neural Networks for Volumetric Medical Image Segmentation. In Proceedings of the 2016 Fourth International Conference on 3D Vision (3DV), Stanford, CA, USA, 25–28 October 2016; pp. 565–571. [CrossRef]
53. Su, Y.; Lu, Y.; Chen, M.; Liu, A. Deep Reinforcement Learning-Based Progressive Sequence Saliency Discovery Network for Mitosis Detection In Time-Lapse Phase-Contrast Microscopy Images. *IEEE ACM Trans. Comput. Biol. Bioinform.* **2022**, *19*, 854–865. [CrossRef] [PubMed]

54. Su, Y.T.; Lu, Y.; Liu, J.; Chen, M.; Liu, A.A. Spatio-Temporal Mitosis Detection in Time-Lapse Phase-Contrast Microscopy Image Sequences: A Benchmark. *IEEE Trans. Med. Imaging* **2021**, *40*, 1319–1328. [CrossRef]
55. Theagarajan, R.; Bhanu, B. DeephESC 2.0: Deep Generative Multi Adversarial Networks for improving the classification of hESC. *PLoS ONE* **2019**, *14*, 1–28. [CrossRef] [PubMed]
56. Guan, B.X.; Bhanu, B.; Talbot, P.; Lin, S. Bio-Driven Cell Region Detection in Human Embryonic Stem Cell Assay. *IEEE/ACM Trans. Comput. Biol. Bioinform.* **2014**, *11*, 604–611. [CrossRef] [PubMed]
57. Durugkar, I.; Gemp, I.M.; Mahadevan, S. Generative Multi-Adversarial Networks. *arXiv* **2017**, arXiv:1611.01673.
58. La Greca, A.D.; Pérez, N.; Castañeda, S.; Milone, P.M.; Scarafía, M.A.; Möbbs, A.M.; Waisman, A.; Moro, L.N.; Sevlever, G.E.; Luzzani, C.D.; et al. celldeath: A tool for detection of cell death in transmitted light microscopy images by deep learning-based visual recognition. *PLoS ONE* **2021**, *16*, e0253666. [CrossRef]
59. He, K.; Zhang, X.; Ren, S.; Sun, J. Deep Residual Learning for Image Recognition. In Proceedings of the 2016 IEEE Conference on Computer Vision and Pattern Recognition (CVPR), Las Vegas, NV, USA, 27–30 June 2016; pp. 770–778. [CrossRef]
60. Magnusson, K.E.G.; Jaldén, J.; Gilbert, P.M.; Blau, H.M. Global Linking of Cell Tracks Using the Viterbi Algorithm. *IEEE Trans. Med. Imaging* **2015**, *34*, 911–929. [CrossRef]
61. Grah, J.S.; Harrington, J.A.; Koh, S.B.; Pike, J.A.; Schreiner, A.; Burger, M.; Schönlieb, C.B.; Reichelt, S. Mathematical imaging methods for mitosis analysis in live-cell phase contrast microscopy. *Methods* **2017**, *115*, 91–99. Image Processing for Biologists, [CrossRef]
62. Rea, D.; Perrino, G.; di Bernardo, D.; Marcellino, L.; Romano, D. A GPU algorithm for tracking yeast cells in phase-contrast microscopy images. *Int. J. High Perform. Comput. Appl.* **2019**, *33*. [CrossRef]
63. Tsai, H.F.; Gajda, J.; Sloan, T.F.; Rares, A.; Shen, A.Q. Usiigaci: Instance-aware cell tracking in stain-free phase contrast microscopy enabled by machine learning. *SoftwareX* **2019**, *9*, 230–237. [CrossRef]
64. He, K.; Gkioxari, G.; Dollár, P.; Girshick, R. Mask R-CNN. In Proceedings of the 2017 IEEE International Conference on Computer Vision (ICCV), Venice, Italy, 22–29 October 2017; pp. 2980–2988. [CrossRef]
65. Allan, D.B.; Caswell, T.; Keim, N.C.; van der Wel, C.M. trackpy: Trackpy v0.4.1; Zenodo, 2018. [CrossRef]
66. Frank, E.; Hall, M.A.; Witten, I.H. *The WEKA Workbench. Online Appendix for Data Mining: Practical Machine Learning Tools and Techniques*, 3rd ed.; Morgan Kaufmann Series in Data Management Systems, Morgan Kaufmann: Amsterdam, The Netherlands, 2011.
67. Breiman, L. Random Forests. *Mach. Learn.* **2001**, *45*, 5–32. [CrossRef]
68. Arganda-Carreras, I.; Kaynig, V.; Rueden, C.; Eliceiri, K.W.; Schindelin, J.; Cardona, A.; Sebastian Seung, H. Trainable Weka Segmentation: A machine learning tool for microscopy pixel classification. *Bioinformatics* **2017**, *33*, 2424–2426. [CrossRef] [PubMed]
69. Von Chamier, L.; Laine, R.F.; Jukkala, J.; Spahn, C.; Krentzel, D.; Nehme, E.; Lerche, M.; Hernández-Pérez, S.; Mattila, P.K.; Karinou, E.; et al. ZeroCostDL4Mic: An open platform to use Deep-Learning in Microscopy. *BioRxiv* **2020**. [CrossRef]
70. Gómez-de Mariscal, E.; García-López-de Haro, C.; Ouyang, W.; Donati, L.; Lundberg, E.; Unser, M.; Muñoz-Barrutia, A.; Sage, D. DeepImageJ: A user-friendly environment to run deep learning models in ImageJ. *bioRxiv* **2021**. [CrossRef]
71. Ouyang, W.; Beuttenmueller, F.; Gómez-de Mariscal, E.; Pape, C.; Burke, T.; Garcia-López-de Haro, C.; Russell, C.; Moya-Sans, L.; de-la Torre-Gutiérrez, C.; Schmidt, D.; et al. BioImage Model Zoo: A Community-Driven Resource for Accessible Deep Learning in BioImage Analysis. *bioRxiv* **2022**. [CrossRef]
72. Aragaki, H.; Ogoh, K.; Kondo, Y.; K., A. LIM Tracker: A software package for cell tracking and analysis with advanced interactivity. *Sci. Rep.* **2022**, *12*, 2702. [CrossRef] [PubMed]
73. Ershov, D.; Phan, M.; Pylvänäinen, J.; Rigaud, S.; Le Blanc, L.; Charles-Orszag, A.; Conway, J.; Laine, R.; Roy, N.; Bonazzi, D.; et al. TrackMate 7: Integrating state-of-the-art segmentation algorithms into tracking pipelines. *Nat. Methods* **2022**, *19*, 829–832. [CrossRef]
74. Schmidt, U.; Weigert, M.; Broaddus, C.; Myers, G. Cell Detection with Star-Convex Polygons. In Proceedings of the Medical Image Computing and Computer Assisted Intervention—MICCAI 2018—21st International Conference, Granada, Spain, 16–20 September 2018; Proceedings, Part II, pp. 265–273. [CrossRef]
75. Weigert, M.; Schmidt, U.; Haase, R.; Sugawara, K.; Myers, G. Star-convex Polyhedra for 3D Object Detection and Segmentation in Microscopy. In Proceedings of the 2020 IEEE Winter Conference on Applications of Computer Vision (WACV), Snowmass Village, CO, USA, 2–5 March 2020; pp. 3655–3662. [CrossRef]
76. Ouyang, W.; Mueller, F.; Hjelmare, M.; Lundberg, E.; Zimmer, C. ImJoy: An open-source computational platform for the deep learning era. *Nat. Methods* **2019**, *16*, 1199–1200. [CrossRef]
77. Schindelin, J.; Arganda-Carreras, I.; Frise, E.; Kaynig, V.; Longair, M.; Pietzsch, T.; Preibisch, S.; Rueden, C.; Saalfeld, S.; Schmid, B.; et al. Fiji: An open-source platform for biological-image analysis. *Nat. Methods* **2012**, *9*, 676–682. [CrossRef]
78. Ouyang, W.; Winsnes, C.F.; Hjelmare, M.; Åkesson, L.; Xu, H.; Sullivan, D.P.; Lundberg, E. Analysis of the Human Protein Atlas Image Classification competition. *Nat. Methods* **2019**, *16*, 1254. [CrossRef]
79. Jaqaman, K.; Loerke, D.; Mettlen, M.; Kuwata, H.; Grinstein, S.; Schmid, S.; G., D. Robust single-particle tracking in live-cell time-lapse sequences. *Nat. Methods* **2008**, *5*, 695–702. [CrossRef]
80. Bolya, D.; Zhou, C.; Xiao, F.; Lee, Y.J. YOLACT++ Better Real-Time Instance Segmentation. *IEEE Trans. Pattern Anal. Mach. Intell.* **2022**, *44*, 1108–1121. [CrossRef] [PubMed]

81. Abdulla, W. Mask R-CNN for Object Detection and Instance Segmentation on Keras and TensorFlow. 2017. Available online: https://github.com/matterport/Mask_RCNN (accessed on 3 August 2022).
82. Wu, Y.; Kirillov, A.; Massa, F.; Lo, W.Y.; Girshick, R. Detectron2. 2019. Available online: https://github.com/facebookresearch/detectron2 (accessed on 3 August 2022).
83. Tinevez, J.Y.; Perry, N.; Schindelin, J.; Hoopes, G.M.; Reynolds, G.D.; Laplantine, E.; Bednarek, S.Y.; Shorte, S.L.; Eliceiri, K.W. TrackMate: An open and extensible platform for single-particle tracking. *Methods* **2017**, *115*, 80–90. Image Processing for Biologists. [CrossRef] [PubMed]
84. Lucas, A.M.; Ryder, P.V.; Li, B.; Cimini, B.A.; Eliceiri, K.W.; Carpenter, A.E. Open-source deep-learning software for bioimage segmentation. *Mol. Biol. Cell* **2021**, *32*, 823–829. [CrossRef] [PubMed]
85. Smith, K.; Piccinini, F.; Balassa, T.; Koos, K.; Danka, T.; Azizpour, H.; Horvath, P. Phenotypic Image Analysis Software Tools for Exploring and Understanding Big Image Data from Cell-Based Assays. *Cell Syst.* **2018**, *6*, 636–653. [CrossRef] [PubMed]
86. Roberts, B.; Haupt, A.; Tucker, A.; Grancharova, T.; Arakaki, J.; Fuqua, M.A.; Nelson, A.; Hookway, C.; Ludmann, S.A.; Mueller, I.A.; et al. Systematic gene tagging using CRISPR/Cas9 in human stem cells to illuminate cell organization. *Mol. Biol. Cell* **2017**, *28*, 2854–2874. [CrossRef]
87. Gurari, D.; Theriault, D.; Sameki, M.; Isenberg, B.; Pham, T.A.; Purwada, A.; Solski, P.; Walker, M.; Zhang, C.; Wong, J.Y.; et al. How to Collect Segmentations for Biomedical Images? A Benchmark Evaluating the Performance of Experts, Crowdsourced Non-experts, and Algorithms. In Proceedings of the 2015 IEEE Winter Conference on Applications of Computer Vision, Waikoloa, HI, USA, 5–9 January 2015; pp. 1169–1176. [CrossRef]
88. Schwendy, M.; Unger, R.E.; Parekh, S.H. EVICAN—A balanced dataset for algorithm development in cell and nucleus segmentation. *Bioinformatics* **2020**, *36*, 3863–3870. [CrossRef]
89. Maska, M.; Ulman, V.; Svoboda, D.; Matula, P.; Matula, P.; Ederra, C.; Urbiola, A.; España, T.; Venkatesan, S.; Balak, D.M.W.; et al. A benchmark for comparison of cell tracking algorithms. *Bioinformatics* **2014**, *30*, 1609–1617. [CrossRef]
90. Anjum, S.; Gurari, D. CTMC: Cell Tracking with Mitosis Detection Dataset Challenge. In Proceedings of the 2020 IEEE/CVF Conference on Computer Vision and Pattern Recognition Workshops (CVPRW), Seattle, WA, USA, 14–19 June 2020; pp. 4228–4237. [CrossRef]
91. Ker, D.; Eom, S.; Sanami, S.; Bise, R.; Pascale, C.; Yin, Z.; Huh, S.; Osuna-Highley, E.; Junkers, S.; Helfrich, C.; et al. Phase contrast time-lapse microscopy datasets with automated and manual cell tracking annotations. *Sci. Data* **2018**, *5*. [CrossRef]
92. Ljosa, V.; Sokolnicki, K.; Carpenter, A. Annotated high-throughput microscopy image sets for validation. *Nat. Methods* **2012**, *9*, 637. [CrossRef]
93. Tian, C.; Yang, C.; Spencer, S.L. EllipTrack: A Global-Local Cell-Tracking Pipeline for 2D Fluorescence Time-Lapse Microscopy. *Cell Rep.* **2020**, *32*, 107984. [CrossRef]
94. Lin, T.; Maire, M.; Belongie, S.J.; Hays, J.; Perona, P.; Ramanan, D.; Dollár, P.; Zitnick, C.L. Microsoft COCO: Common Objects in Context. In Proceedings of the Computer Vision—ECCV 2014—13th European Conference, Zurich, Switzerland, 6–12 September 2014; Proceedings, Part V; Fleet, D.J., Pajdla, T., Schiele, B., Tuytelaars, T., Eds.; Springer: Cham, Switzerland, 2014; Volume 8693, pp. 740–755. [CrossRef]
95. Matula, P.; Maška, M.; Sorokin, D.V.; Matula, P.; de Solórzano, C.O.; Kozubek, M. Cell tracking accuracy measurement based on comparison of acyclic oriented graphs. *PLoS ONE* **2015**, *10*, e0144959. [CrossRef]
96. Dendorfer, P.; Ošep, A.; Milan, A.; Schindler, K.; Cremers, D.; Reid, I.; Roth, S.; Leal-Taixé, L. MOTChallenge: A Benchmark for Single-Camera Multiple Target Tracking. *arXiv* **2020**, arXiv:2010.07548.
97. Bernardin, K.; Stiefelhagen, R. Evaluating Multiple Object Tracking Performance: The CLEAR MOT Metrics. *EURASIP J. Image Video Process.* **2008**, *2008*. [CrossRef]
98. Milan, A.; Leal-Taixe, L.; Reid, I.; Roth, S.; Schindler, K. MOT16: A Benchmark for Multi-Object Tracking. *arXiv* **2016**, arXiv:1603.00831.
99. Ristani, E.; Solera, F.; Zou, R.S.; Cucchiara, R.; Tomasi, C. Performance Measures and a Data Set for Multi-Target, Multi-Camera Tracking. *arXiv* **2016**, arXiv:1609.01775.
100. Luiten, J.; Osep, A.; Dendorfer, P.; Torr, P.; Geiger, A.; Leal-Taixé, L.; Leibe, B. HOTA: A Higher Order Metric for Evaluating Multi-Object Tracking. *Int. J. Comput. Vis.* **2020**, 1–31. [CrossRef]
101. Xing, F.; Xie, Y.; Su, H.; Liu, F.; Yang, L. Deep Learning in Microscopy Image Analysis: A Survey. *IEEE Trans. Neural Netw. Learn. Syst.* **2018**, *29*, 4550–4568. [CrossRef]

Review

Polymer Models of Chromatin Imaging Data in Single Cells

Mattia Conte [1,*], Andrea M. Chiariello [2], Alex Abraham [2], Simona Bianco [2], Andrea Esposito [2], Mario Nicodemi [1,2,3], Tommaso Matteuzzi [2] and Francesca Vercellone [2]

1. Berlin Institute for Medical Systems Biology, Max-Delbrück Centre (MDC) for Molecular Medicine, 10115 Berlin, Germany
2. Dipartimento di Fisica, Università di Napoli Federico II, and INFN Napoli, Complesso Universitario di Monte Sant'Angelo, 80126 Naples, Italy
3. Berlin Institute of Health (BIH), MDC-Berlin, 10178 Berlin, Germany
* Correspondence: mattia.conte@mdc-berlin.de

Abstract: Recent super-resolution imaging technologies enable tracing chromatin conformation with nanometer-scale precision at the single-cell level. They revealed, for example, that human chromosomes fold into a complex three-dimensional structure within the cell nucleus that is essential to establish biological activities, such as the regulation of the genes. Yet, to decode from imaging data the molecular mechanisms that shape the structure of the genome, quantitative methods are required. In this review, we consider models of polymer physics of chromosome folding that we benchmark against multiplexed FISH data available in human loci in IMR90 fibroblast cells. By combining polymer theory, numerical simulations and machine learning strategies, the predictions of the models are validated at the single-cell level, showing that chromosome structure is controlled by the interplay of distinct physical processes, such as active loop-extrusion and thermodynamic phase-separation.

Keywords: chromosome architecture; multiplexed FISH imaging; polymer physics; machine learning; computer simulations

1. Introduction

Mammalian genomes are folded into a complex three-dimensional (3D) architecture in the cell nucleus, including a large-scale structure of chromosomal interactions [1–4] that involves, for instance, DNA loops [5], topologically associated domains (TADs) [6,7] and higher-order contacts, such as meta-TADs [8] and A/B compartments [9]. Such a nested 3D organization serves important functional roles, as genes and their distal regulators form specific physical contacts to control transcriptional regulation [1,2]. Indeed, for example, disruption of TADs due to genomic structural rearrangements, such as deletions or inversions, has been linked to ectopic gene-regulator contacts, resulting in gene misexpression and disease [10–13].

In the last decade, powerful technologies based on super-resolution microscopy approaches enabled to probe the 3D conformation of the genome with nanometer-scale precision in single nuclei [14–17]. Those techniques revealed, for instance, that TADs exist at the single-cell level, they broadly vary from cell to cell and correspond to spatially segregated globular 3D conformations, confining, e.g., the activity of the regulators to their proper target genes [15].

Those recent experiments triggered questions on the nature of chromatin contacts and their origin: what are the mechanisms that shape genome 3D structure? What methods can be developed to identify them? In this review, we discuss the application of models from polymer physics to understand the machinery that establish chromosome architecture in the nucleus of the cells. In particular, we focus on two recently proposed models of folding that rely on two different physical processes, respectively, loop-extrusion and polymer phase-separation. In the first process, spatial proximity between distal DNA sites is achieved by

molecular motors that stochastically bind to DNA and extrude a polymer loop in an out-of-equilibrium, active (e.g., ATP-dependent) physical process [18–24], and in the second, distal genomic sites are tethered together by interactions mediated, e.g., by diffusing cognate molecular particles, such as transcription factors, or by direct interactions produced, for example, by DNA-bound histone molecules [12,25–40]. By taking as a case study a 2 Mb wide chromatin region in human IMR90 cells where super-resolution multiplexed FISH data are available [15], we combine those distinct physical mechanisms into polymer models that we investigate by massive computer simulations (see Methods). We show that both loop-extrusion and phase-separation significantly recapitulate microscopy data, hinting that both processes can reliably coexist to determine the structure of chromosomes at the single-cell level [28].

2. Methods

In the studied models, chromatin is represented as a polymer chain of non-overlapping beads, subject to standard physical potentials derived from classical studies of polymer simulations [41,42]. Specifically, adjacent beads along the polymer are tethered by an elastic FENE potential and their overlap is prevented by a repulsive Weeks–Chandler–Anderson (WCA) potential. In the loop-extrusion (LE) model, the extruding motors are modelled as harmonic springs that can extrude loops by a translocation along the polymer chain, i.e., at each simulation step the spring is updated from the bead pair (i,j) to (i − 1,j + 1). As broadly reported in the literature [18–23], those springs cannot pass through each other, their number is fixed and they halt translocation when they collide with another extruding motor or anchor sites with opposite orientation, or they stochastically unbind from the polymer. A typical parameter choice in the simulations is to set the LE spring energy constant equal to 10 k_BT (k_B is the Boltzmann constant and T the temperature) and its rest length to 1.1σ (σ is the bead diameter) [18,19,37]. Additionally, to unveil the roles of the LE ingredients beyond its minimal implementation, we examined a more refined version where LE boundaries are chosen to best reproduce population-averaged contact data and the model anchor sites are present with a specific, finite probability in a single-polymer molecule to model cell-to-cell variation [28,37]. The average domain structure of the model is thus reproduced from bulk data, but the ensemble of its single-molecule structures is validated against independent single-cell microscopy conformations (see below). Another key parameter controlling LE dynamics is the extruder processivity, i.e., the ratio between the extrusion velocity and the unbinding rate from the chain, whose values can range, e.g., from 80 kb up to 750 kb [19,23,37].

In the class of phase-separation based models, we focused on the strings and binders (SBS) model [30,39], in which a chromosome region is modeled as a self-avoiding polymer chain where different specific types of binding sites are located for diffusing cognate molecular particles (called binders). Binders and polymer sites are subject to a Brownian motion regulated by the Langevin equation with standard parameters (i.e., friction coefficient $\zeta = 0.5$ [41]). The binders, via specific attractive interactions represented by a truncated Lennard–Jones potential [34], can bridge their cognate sites on the chain, hence guiding a micro-phase-separation of the polymer into different globules. As the number of the binders (or their energy affinity) increases above a given threshold, the system undergoes a thermodynamic phase-transition from a coil (i.e., randomly folded) to a phase-separated globule state where the polymer self-assembles into distinct, spatially segregated globules via a phase-separation mechanism [39]. Critical binder concentrations, for weak biochemical affinities, fall in the fractions of µmol/L range [39], which is consistent with typical transcription factor concentrations. The genomic locations of the binding sites of the SBS model are inferred by a machine learning procedure based on the PRISMR algorithm [12]. In brief, PRISMR is a recursive Monte Carlo procedure that identifies the minimal set of binding sites to best match input bulk (e.g., ensemble-averaged Hi-C or microscopy) data, as fully detailed in [12,29,39]. Finally, we also discuss a model where the LE and SBS models are combined and act simultaneously in a single-polymer molecule (hereafter indicated as the LE+SBS model).

To generate a statistical ensemble of in silico single-molecule conformations, each model is investigated by massive molecular dynamics simulations until stationarity is fully reached (typically up to 10^8 MD time iteration steps [43]); Langevin dynamics is integrated via the Velocity–Verlet algorithm by using the free available LAMMPS [44] and HOOMD [45] software. All the scripts required to perform the simulations of the models are available at https://github.com/ehsanirani/PhaseSeparation-LoopExtrusion-MD (accessed on 1 August 2022) [28].

3. Results

In this section, we benchmark our polymer models against single-cell super-resolution microscopy data [15] available at 30 kb resolution in a 2 Mb wide genomic region (Chr21: 28–30 Mb) in human IMR90 cells. We show that the different models capture the complex pattern of chromatin contacts at the cell population-averaged level, as well as the observed 3D conformations of the imaged chromatin region in single DNA molecules [28].

3.1. The Models Recapitulate Ensemble-Averaged Microscopy Data

In a first validation of the models, we computed their median distance matrix that we compared against the corresponding map from multiplexed FISH data [15] (Figure 1).

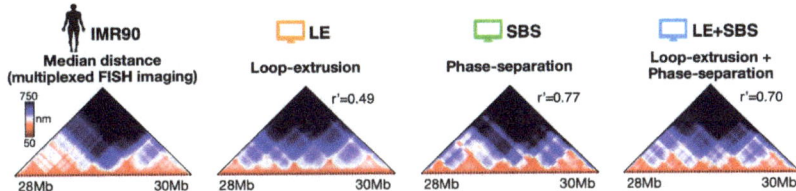

Figure 1. The median spatial distance matrix of the IMR90 locus (Chr21: 28–30 Mb) from multiplexed FISH microscopy [15] is compared against the corresponding in silico matrices of the considered polymer models [28]. Both loop-extrusion (LE) and phase-separation based models (SBS and LE + SBS) well recapitulate the complex experimental pattern of contacts. Adapted from [28].

The median distance map is the ensemble median of the single-molecule distance maps, which, by definition, are symmetric square matrices reporting the Euclidean distances between all pairs of polymer sites. Those matrices are visually represented as a 2D heatmap with a color bar scheme to highlight contacting regions that are closer in 3D space (e.g., TADs or loops, colored in red in Figure 1) or those that have no significant interactions (blue regions in Figure 1). To efficiently compute the distance matrices, we used built-in functions within the Python SciPy package [28]. To reduce the noise within imaging data, we applied a Gaussian filter on single-cell distance maps (standard deviation of the Gaussian kernel = 1) and excluded single-cell conformations whose 3D coordinates have >80% missing values. To quantitatively estimate the similarity between microscopy and model distance matrices, we used the genomic distance-corrected Pearson correlation coefficient, r', which corrects the usual Pearson coefficient for genomic distance effects [12]. In brief, r' is the Pearson coefficient computed on distance matrices where each entry is subtracted by the mean value of its diagonal. We found that the different models recapitulate the complex TAD patterns observed in microscopy data, as well as specific pointwise interactions, as highlighted by the high r' correlation values: $r' = 0.49$, $r' = 0.77$ and $r' = 0.70$, respectively, for LE, SBS and LE+SBS [28]. To substantiate the statistical significance of the r' correlations of the models, we considered as null control model a self-avoiding chain with the same number of beads as the imaged conformations and found that it returns a significantly lower correlation value ($r' = 0.11$, which is, respectively, four and seven times lower than the values found for LE and SBS/LE+SBS). That indicates that both active processes, like loop-extrusion, and passive mechanisms, e.g., thermodynamic polymer phase-separation, are consistent with the average structure of the considered IMR90 genomic region measured by bulk imaging data.

Next, we checked whether our models also explain local properties of chromatin structure. To this aim, we computed the boundary probability genomic function, i.e., the probability for each genomic position across the studied IMR90 locus to appear as boundary of a single-cell TAD domain [15] (Figure 2).

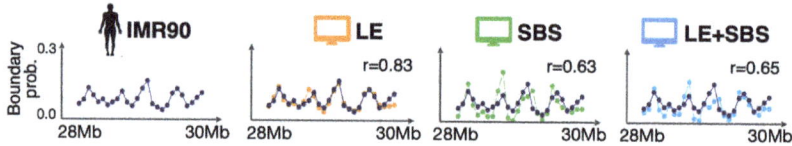

Figure 2. The genomic boundary probability function of the IMR90 locus is consistently recapitulated by the different models. Adapted from [28].

The boundary function has local peaks corresponding to the main TAD boundaries visible in the median distance map of the IMR90 locus and, interestingly, this function is non-zero across the entire imaged region, indicating a substantial cell-to-cell variability in the genomic position of TAD boundaries. We found that the different models return boundary probabilities with profiles consistent with imaging data, as quantified by the high Pearson correlations between models and experiment: r = 0.83, r = 0.63 and r = 0.65, respectively, for LE, SBS and LE + SBS [28].

Taken together, these analyses show that both loop-extrusion and phase-separation processes can quantitatively explain chromatin structure at the cell population-averaged level. In particular, loop-extrusion (LE) is the best to capture the boundary probability function, while phase-separation based models (SBS and LE + SBS) return overall higher correlation values with ensemble-averaged distance data.

3.2. All-against-All Comparison between Single-Molecule Imaged and Model-Derived 3D Structures

As a further step, we aimed to investigate the structural predictions of our polymer models at the single-molecule level. In particular, to assess whether our models do provide a bona-fide representation of the imaged chromatin structures, we used a computational method based on the root-mean-square deviation (RMSD) criterion [39,46]. In brief, the algorithm performs a roto-translational alignment of two conformations (e.g., experimental and model derived) by minimizing the RMSD of their particle positions; in this way, each experimental 3D structure from imaging is univocally associated to a corresponding best-matching conformation of the models by searching for the minimum RMSD of their coordinates. To fairly compare model and imaged 3D conformations, a z-score is performed on both sets of coordinates. To efficiently run the RMSD comparison, we used the MDAnalysis Python library, which employs the fast quaternion-based characteristic polynomial (QCP) algorithm to calculate the least RMSD between two structures [47]. In Figure 3 we report an example of best-matching conformations identified by the RMSD method: in this case, for instance, the single-cell imaged distance map is characterized by two main TAD-like structures, corresponding to distinct globules in 3D space, which are consistently recapitulated by the different models (Figure 3).

To check the statistical significance of the RMSD analysis, we considered as control the RMSD distribution between random pairs of imaged conformations (Figure 4). For each type of model, we found that the experiment-model best-match distribution is statistically distinguishable from the control (Figure 4a, two-sided Mann–Whitney test *p*-value = 0), with less than 5% of the entries of the former distribution that fall above the first decile of control (Figure 4b) [28]. Overall, the all-against-all RMSD analysis show that both loop-extrusion and phase-separation single-molecule conformations significantly represent the ensemble of single-cell imaged 3D structures of the studied IMR90 cell region.

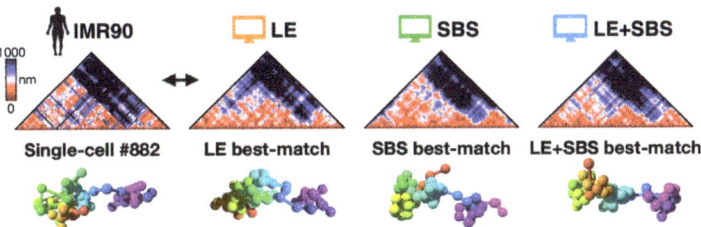

Figure 3. Example of experiment-model best-matching 3D structures, along with their corresponding single-molecule distance maps, as identified by the RMSD method. Adapted from [28].

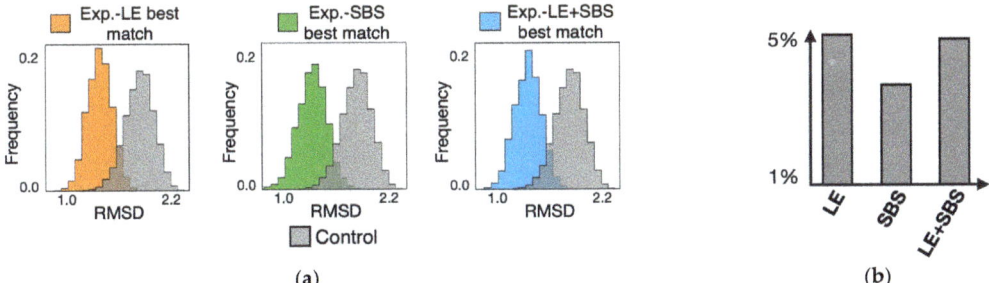

Figure 4. Statistical significance of the RMSD analysis: (**a**) the RMSD distribution of the experiment-model best-matches (for each type of model) is statistically distinguishable from a control made of random pairs of imaged conformations; (**b**) less than 5% of the entries of the experiment-model best-match distributions are within the first 10% of the control. Adapted from [28].

4. Discussion

In this work, we discussed the application of polymer physics models to investigate the mechanisms that establish the complex 3D structure of the genome as observed by recent single-cell imaging data [15]. We focused on two main, distinct physical processes that are supported by growing experimental evidence, i.e., loop-extrusion and phase-separation. In the first mechanism, an active motor (e.g., Cohesin or Condensin) extrudes DNA loops between specific anchor sites (envisaged as CTCF binding sites with opposite orientation) in an out-of-equilibrium process; in the second, chromatin contacts between distal genomic sites are established by diffusing molecular agents (such as transcription factors) or direct DNA interactions that, sustained by the thermal bath, spontaneously bridge their cognate sites.

By using as benchmark super-resolution microscopy data available for a 2 Mb wide chromosome region in human fibroblast cells, we showed that both mechanisms can quantitatively recapitulate single-cell imaged conformations, indicating that they can coexist in shaping chromosome folding [28]. By allowing a deeper understanding of the mechanisms driving the organization of the genome, models from polymer physics can be used for real-world applications in real experimental contexts [48]. For example, validated polymer models can be efficiently employed to impute missing values or reduce noise effects in large imaging datasets. Additionally, and importantly, they can be employed to predict in silico the structural effects of disease-associated mutations, linked, for instance, to congenital disorders [11,12] or cancer [13,49].

Overall, those studies show that novel data from microscopy can be complemented with quantitative models from physics to understand the mechanisms and function of genome structure, paving the way for important and useful applications, such as the prediction of genomic perturbations on chromosome 3D architecture.

Author Contributions: Conceptualization, M.C., A.M.C., A.A., S.B., A.E., M.N., T.M. and F.V.; writing—original draft preparation, M.C.; writing—review and editing, M.C. and M.N. All authors have read and agreed to the published version of the manuscript.

Funding: This research received no external funding.

Data Availability Statement: Data is contained within the article.

Conflicts of Interest: The authors declare no conflict of interest.

References

1. Dixon, J.R.; Gorkin, D.U.; Ren, B. Chromatin Domains: The Unit of Chromosome Organization. *Mol. Cell* **2016**, *62*, 668–680. [CrossRef] [PubMed]
2. Dekker, J.; Mirny, L. The 3D Genome as Moderator of Chromosomal Communication. *Cell* **2016**, *164*, 1110–1121. [CrossRef] [PubMed]
3. Bickmore, W.A.; van Steensel, B. Genome Architecture: Domain Organization of Interphase Chromosomes. *Cell* **2013**, *152*, 1270–1284. [CrossRef]
4. Finn, E.H.; Misteli, T. Molecular Basis and Biological Function of Variability in Spatial Genome Organization. *Science* **2019**, *365*, eaaw9498. [CrossRef] [PubMed]
5. Rao, S.S.P.; Huntley, M.H.; Durand, N.C.; Stamenova, E.K.; Bochkov, I.D.; Robinson, J.T.; Sanborn, A.L.; Machol, I.; Omer, A.D.; Lander, E.S.; et al. A 3D Map of the Human Genome at Kilobase Resolution Reveals Principles of Chromatin Looping. *Cell* **2014**, *159*, 1665–1680. [CrossRef] [PubMed]
6. Dixon, J.R.; Selvaraj, S.; Yue, F.; Kim, A.; Li, Y.; Shen, Y.; Hu, M.; Liu, J.S.; Ren, B. Topological Domains in Mammalian Genomes Identified by Analysis of Chromatin Interactions. *Nature* **2012**, *485*, 376–380. [CrossRef]
7. Nora, E.P.; Lajoie, B.R.; Schulz, E.G.; Giorgetti, L.; Okamoto, I.; Servant, N.; Piolot, T.; Van Berkum, N.L.; Meisig, J.; Sedat, J.; et al. Spatial Partitioning of the Regulatory Landscape of the X-Inactivation Centre. *Nature* **2012**, *485*, 381–385. [CrossRef]
8. Fraser, J.; Ferrai, C.; Chiariello, A.M.; Schueler, M.; Rito, T.; Laudanno, G.; Barbieri, M.; Moore, B.L.; Kraemer, D.C.; Aitken, S.; et al. Hierarchical Folding and Reorganization of Chromosomes Are Linked to Transcriptional Changes in Cellular Differentiation. *Mol. Syst. Biol.* **2015**, *11*, 852. [CrossRef]
9. Lieberman-Aiden, E.; Van Berkum, N.L.; Williams, L.; Imakaev, M.; Ragoczy, T.; Telling, A.; Amit, I.; Lajoie, B.R.; Sabo, P.J.; Dorschner, M.O.; et al. Comprehensive Mapping of Long-Range Interactions Reveals Folding Principles of the Human Genome. *Science* **2009**, *326*, 289–293. [CrossRef]
10. Lupiáñez, D.G.; Kraft, K.; Heinrich, V.; Krawitz, P.; Brancati, F.; Klopocki, E.; Horn, D.; Kayserili, H.; Opitz, J.M.; Laxova, R.; et al. Disruptions of Topological Chromatin Domains Cause Pathogenic Rewiring of Gene-Enhancer Interactions. *Cell* **2015**, *161*, 1012–1025. [CrossRef]
11. Spielmann, M.; Lupiáñez, D.G.; Mundlos, S. Structural Variation in the 3D Genome. *Nat. Rev. Genet.* **2018**, *19*, 453–467. [CrossRef] [PubMed]
12. Bianco, S.; Lupiáñez, D.G.; Chiariello, A.M.; Annunziatella, C.; Kraft, K.; Schöpflin, R.; Wittler, L.; Andrey, G.; Vingron, M.; Pombo, A.; et al. Polymer Physics Predicts the Effects of Structural Variants on Chromatin Architecture. *Nat. Genet.* **2018**, *50*, 662–667. [CrossRef] [PubMed]
13. Valton, A.-L.; Dekker, J. TAD Disruption as Oncogenic Driver. *Curr. Opin. Genet. Dev.* **2016**, *36*, 34–40. [CrossRef] [PubMed]
14. Huang, B.; Wang, W.; Bates, M.; Zhuang, X. Three-Dimensional Super-Resolution Imaging by Stochastic Optical Reconstruction Microscopy. *Science* **2008**, *319*, 810–813. [CrossRef] [PubMed]
15. Bintu, B.; Mateo, L.J.; Su, J.-H.; Sinnott-Armstrong, N.A.; Parker, M.; Kinrot, S.; Yamaya, K.; Boettiger, A.N.; Zhuang, X. Super-Resolution Chromatin Tracing Reveals Domains and Cooperative Interactions in Single Cells. *Science* **2018**, *362*, eaau1783. [CrossRef]
16. Boettiger, A.N.; Bintu, B.; Moffitt, J.R.; Wang, S.; Beliveau, B.J.; Fudenberg, G.; Imakaev, M.; Mirny, L.A.; Wu, C.T.; Zhuang, X. Super-Resolution Imaging Reveals Distinct Chromatin Folding for Different Epigenetic States. *Nature* **2016**, *529*, 418–422. [CrossRef]
17. Finn, E.H.; Pegoraro, G.; Brandão, H.B.; Valton, A.L.; Oomen, M.E.; Dekker, J.; Mirny, L.; Misteli, T. Extensive Heterogeneity and Intrinsic Variation in Spatial Genome Organization. *Cell* **2019**, *176*, P1502–P1515. [CrossRef]
18. Sanborn, A.L.; Rao, S.S.P.; Huang, S.C.; Durand, N.C.; Huntley, M.H.; Jewett, A.I.; Bochkov, I.D.; Chinnappan, D.; Cutkosky, A.; Li, J.; et al. Chromatin Extrusion Explains Key Features of Loop and Domain Formation in Wild-Type and Engineered Genomes. *Proc. Natl. Acad. Sci. USA* **2015**, *112*, E6456. [CrossRef]
19. Fudenberg, G.; Imakaev, M.; Lu, C.; Goloborodko, A.; Abdennur, N.; Mirny, L.A. Formation of Chromosomal Domains by Loop Extrusion. *Cell Rep.* **2016**, *15*, 2038–2049. [CrossRef]

20. Racko, D.; Benedetti, F.; Dorier, J.; Stasiak, A. Transcription-Induced Supercoiling as the Driving Force of Chromatin Loop Extrusion during Formation of TADs in Interphase Chromosomes. *Nucleic Acids Res.* **2018**, *46*, 1648–1660. [CrossRef]
21. Brackley, C.A.; Johnson, J.; Michieletto, D.; Morozov, A.N.; Nicodemi, M.; Cook, P.R.; Marenduzzo, D. Nonequilibrium Chromosome Looping via Molecular Slip Links. *Phys. Rev. Lett.* **2017**, *119*, 138101. [CrossRef] [PubMed]
22. Banigan, E.J.; Mirny, L.A. Loop Extrusion: Theory Meets Single-Molecule Experiments. *Curr. Opin. Cell Biol.* **2020**, *64*, 124–138. [CrossRef] [PubMed]
23. Goloborodko, A.; Marko, J.F.; Mirny, L.A. Chromosome Compaction by Active Loop Extrusion. *Biophys. J.* **2016**, *110*, 2162–2168. [CrossRef]
24. Goloborodko, A.; Imakaev, M.V.; Marko, J.F.; Mirny, L. Compaction and Segregation of Sister Chromatids via Active Loop Extrusion. *eLife* **2016**, *5*, e14864. [CrossRef]
25. Jost, D.; Carrivain, P.; Cavalli, G.; Vaillant, C. Modeling Epigenome Folding: Formation and Dynamics of Topologically Associated Chromatin Domains. *Nucleic Acids Res.* **2014**, *42*, 9553–9561. [CrossRef] [PubMed]
26. Conte, M.; Fiorillo, L.; Annunziatella, C.; Esposito, A.; Musella, F.; Abraham, A.; Bianco, S.; Chiariello, A.M. Dynamic and Equilibrium Properties of Finite-Size Polymer Models of Chromosome Folding. *Phys. Rev. E* **2021**, *104*, 054402. [CrossRef]
27. Nuebler, J.; Fudenberg, G.; Imakaev, M.; Abdennur, N.; Mirny, L.A. Chromatin Organization by an Interplay of Loop Extrusion and Compartmental Segregation. *Proc. Natl. Acad. Sci. USA* **2018**, *115*, E6697–E6706. [CrossRef] [PubMed]
28. Conte, M.; Irani, E.; Chiariello, A.M.; Abraham, A.; Bianco, S.; Esposito, A.; Nicodemi, M. Loop-Extrusion and Polymer Phase-Separation Can Co-Exist at the Single-Molecule Level to Shape Chromatin Folding. *Nat. Commun.* **2022**, *13*, 4070. [CrossRef]
29. Esposito, A.; Bianco, S.; Chiariello, A.M.; Abraham, A.; Fiorillo, L.; Conte, M.; Campanile, R.; Nicodemi, M. Polymer Physics Reveals a Combinatorial Code Linking 3D Chromatin Architecture to 1D Chromatin States. *Cell Rep.* **2022**, *38*, 110601. [CrossRef]
30. Barbieri, M.; Chotalia, M.; Fraser, J.; Lavitas, L.-M.; Dostie, J.; Pombo, A.; Nicodemi, M. Complexity of Chromatin Folding Is Captured by the Strings and Binders Switch Model. *Proc. Natl. Acad. Sci. USA* **2012**, *109*, 16173–16178. [CrossRef]
31. Di Pierro, M.; Zhang, B.; Aiden, E.L.; Wolynes, P.G.; Onuchic, J.N. Transferable Model for Chromosome Architecture. *Proc. Natl. Acad. Sci. USA* **2016**, *113*, 12168–12173. [CrossRef]
32. Plewczynski, D.; Kadlof, M. Computational Modelling of Three-Dimensional Genome Structure. *Methods* **2020**, *181–182*, 1–4. [CrossRef] [PubMed]
33. Zhang, B.; Wolynes, P.G. Topology, Structures, and Energy Landscapes of Human Chromosomes. *Proc. Natl. Acad. Sci. USA* **2015**, *112*, 6062–6067. [CrossRef] [PubMed]
34. Chiariello, A.M.; Annunziatella, C.; Bianco, S.; Esposito, A.; Nicodemi, M. Polymer Physics of Chromosome Large-Scale 3D Organisation. *Sci. Rep.* **2016**, *6*, 29775. [CrossRef] [PubMed]
35. Brackley, C.A.; Brown, J.M.; Waithe, D.; Babbs, C.; Davies, J.; Hughes, J.R.; Buckle, V.J.; Marenduzzo, D. Predicting the Three-Dimensional Folding of Cis-Regulatory Regions in Mammalian Genomes Using Bioinformatic Data and Polymer Models. *Genome Biol.* **2016**, *17*, 59. [CrossRef]
36. Di Stefano, M.; Paulsen, J.; Lien, T.G.; Hovig, E.; Micheletti, C. Hi-C-Constrained Physical Models of Human Chromosomes Recover Functionally-Related Properties of Genome Organization. *Sci. Rep.* **2016**, *6*, 35985. [CrossRef]
37. Buckle, A.; Brackley, C.A.; Boyle, S.; Marenduzzo, D.; Gilbert, N. Polymer Simulations of Heteromorphic Chromatin Predict the 3D Folding of Complex Genomic Loci. *Mol. Cell* **2018**, *72*, 786–797.e11. [CrossRef]
38. Shi, G.; Liu, L.; Hyeon, C.; Thirumalai, D. Interphase Human Chromosome Exhibits out of Equilibrium Glassy Dynamics. *Nat. Commun.* **2018**, *9*, 3161. [CrossRef]
39. Conte, M.; Fiorillo, L.; Bianco, S.; Chiariello, A.M.; Esposito, A.; Nicodemi, M. Polymer Physics Indicates Chromatin Folding Variability across Single-Cells Results from State Degeneracy in Phase Separation. *Nat. Commun.* **2020**, *11*, 3289. [CrossRef]
40. Bohn, M.; Heermann, D.W. Diffusion-Driven Looping Provides a Consistent Provides a Consistent Framework for Chromatin Organization. *PLoS ONE* **2010**, *5*, e12218. [CrossRef]
41. Kremer, K.; Grest, G.S. Dynamics of Entangled Linear Polymer Melts: A Molecular-Dynamics Simulation. *J. Chem. Phys.* **1990**, *92*, 5057–5086. [CrossRef]
42. Rosa, A.; Everaers, R. Structure and Dynamics of Interphase Chromosomes. *PLoS Comput. Biol.* **2008**, *4*, e1000153. [CrossRef] [PubMed]
43. Conte, M.; Esposito, A.; Fiorillo, L.; Campanile, R.; Annunziatella, C.; Corrado, A.; Chiariello, M.G.; Bianco, S.; Chiariello, A.M. Efficient Computational Implementation of Polymer Physics Models to Explore Chromatin Structure. *Int. J. Parallel, Emergent Distrib. Syst.* **2019**, *37*, 91–102. [CrossRef]
44. Plimpton, S. Fast Parallel Algorithms for Short-Range Molecular Dynamics. *J. Comput. Phys.* **1995**, *117*, 1–19. [CrossRef]
45. Anderson, J.A.; Glaser, J.; Glotzer, S.C. HOOMD-Blue: A Python Package for High-Performance Molecular Dynamics and Hard Particle Monte Carlo Simulations. *Comput. Mater. Sci.* **2020**, *173*, 109363. [CrossRef]
46. Stevens, T.J.; Lando, D.; Basu, S.; Atkinson, L.P.; Cao, Y.; Lee, S.F.; Leeb, M.; Wohlfahrt, K.J.; Boucher, W.; O'Shaughnessy-Kirwan, A.; et al. 3D Structures of Individual Mammalian Genomes Studied by Single-Cell Hi-C. *Nature* **2017**, *544*, 59–64. [CrossRef]
47. Theobald, D.L. Rapid Calculation of RMSDs Using a Quaternion-Based Characteristic Polynomial. *Acta Crystallogr. Sect. A Found. Crystallogr.* **2005**, *61*, 478–480. [CrossRef]

48. Fiorillo, L.; Musella, F.; Conte, M.; Kempfer, R.; Chiariello, A.M.; Bianco, S.; Kukalev, A.; Irastorza-Azcarate, I.; Esposito, A.; Abraham, A.; et al. Comparison of the Hi-C, GAM and SPRITE Methods Using Polymer Models of Chromatin. *Nat. Methods* **2021**, *18*, 482–490. [CrossRef]
49. Weischenfeldt, J.; Dubash, T.; Drainas, A.P.; Mardin, B.R.; Chen, Y.; Stütz, A.M.; Waszak, S.M.; Bosco, G.; Halvorsen, A.R.; Raeder, B.; et al. Pan-Cancer Analysis of Somatic Copy-Number Alterations Implicates IRS4 and IGF2 in Enhancer Hijacking. *Nat. Genet.* **2017**, *49*, 65–74. [CrossRef]

 *algorithms*

Article

Smart(Sampling)Augment: Optimal and Efficient Data Augmentation for Semantic Segmentation

Misgana Negassi [1,2,*,†], Diane Wagner [1,†] and Alexander Reiterer [1,2]

1 Institute for Sustainable Systems Engineering INATECH, Albert Ludwigs University of Freiburg, 79110 Freiburg, Germany; wagnerd@cs.uni-freiburg.de (D.W.); alexander.reiterer@ipm.fraunhofer.de (A.R.)
2 Fraunhofer Institute for Physical Measurement Techniques IPM, 79110 Freiburg, Germany
* Correspondence: misgana.negassi@ipm.fraunhofer.de
† These authors contributed equally to this work.

Abstract: Data augmentation methods enrich datasets with augmented data to improve the performance of neural networks. Recently, automated data augmentation methods have emerged, which automatically design augmentation strategies. The existing work focuses on image classification and object detection, whereas we provide the first study on semantic image segmentation and introduce two new approaches: *SmartAugment* and *SmartSamplingAugment*. SmartAugment uses Bayesian Optimization to search a rich space of augmentation strategies and achieves new state-of-the-art performance in all semantic segmentation tasks we consider. SmartSamplingAugment, a simple parameter-free approach with a fixed augmentation strategy, competes in performance with the existing resource-intensive approaches and outperforms cheap state-of-the-art data augmentation methods. Furthermore, we analyze the impact, interaction, and importance of data augmentation hyperparameters and perform ablation studies, which confirm our design choices behind SmartAugment and SmartSamplingAugment. Lastly, we will provide our source code for reproducibility and to facilitate further research.

Keywords: data augmentation; hyperparameter optimization; semantic segmentation

1. Introduction

In many real-world applications, only a limited amount of annotated data is available, which is particularly pronounced in medical imaging applications, where expert knowledge is indispensable to annotate data accurately [1,2]. Given insufficient training data, deep learning methods frequently overfit and fail to learn a discriminative function that generalizes well to unseen examples [3]. *Data augmentation* is an established approach that improves the generalization of neural networks by adjusting the limited available data to achieve more and diverse samples for the network to train on. In most cases, additional data are constructed by simply applying label-preserving transformations to the original data. In image processing, for instance, these can be simple geometric transformations (e.g., rotation), color transformations (e.g., contrast adjustments), or more complex approaches such as CutMix [4], Cutout [5], and Mixup [6]. Data augmentation has been applied to various areas, such as image classification [6], object detection [7], and semi-supervised learning [8] and segmentation [9]. This work provides a first and extensive study on automated data augmentation for semantic segmentation on different and diverse datasets.

Data augmentations used in practice are mostly simple and easy to implement. Despite this simplicity, the choice of augmentations is crucial and requires domain knowledge. Recently, automated data augmentation methods were proposed that learn optimal augmentation policies from data without the need for domain knowledge. These approaches improve performance over manually designed data augmentation strategies commonly used across different domains and datasets [10–13].

Citation: Negassi, M.; Wagner, D.; Reiterer, A. Smart(Sampling)Augment: Optimal and Efficient Data Augmentation for Semantic Segmentation. *Algorithms* 2022, 15, 165. https://doi.org/10.3390/a15050165

Academic Editor: Laura Antonelli

Received: 8 April 2022
Accepted: 9 May 2022
Published: 16 May 2022

Publisher's Note: MDPI stays neutral with regard to jurisdictional claims in published maps and institutional affiliations.

Copyright: © 2022 by the authors. Licensee MDPI, Basel, Switzerland. This article is an open access article distributed under the terms and conditions of the Creative Commons Attribution (CC BY) license (https://creativecommons.org/licenses/by/4.0/).

The main focus of existing research in automated data augmentation is image classification [10,12], with a particular blind spot being dense prediction tasks such as semantic segmentation. Furthermore, these methods either use complicated proxy tasks to learn an optimal augmentation strategy [10] or optimize the augmentation operations without taking the type of augmentation applied and the probability of their application into account [12].

In this work, we introduce two novel data augmentation methods, *SmartAugment* and *SmartSamplingAugment* with key focus on diverse semantic segmentation applications: medical imaging (RaVeNNa, EM), bridge inspection (ErFASst), and autonomous driving (KITTI). SmartAugment uses Bayesian Optimization [14,15] to optimize data augmentation strategies and outperforms the previous state-of-the-art methods (see Table 1) across all semantic segmentation tasks we consider. In contrast to existing approaches, we define a separate set of each color and geometric data augmentation operations, search for their optimal number of operations and magnitudes, and further optimize a probability P of applying these augmentations.

Table 1. Test mean Intersection over Union (IoU) in percentage for different algorithms on semantic segmentation datasets. SmartAugment outperforms all other data augmentation strategies across all datasets. SmartSamplingAugment competes with the previous state-of-the-art approaches and outperforms TrivialAugment, a comparably cheap method. For DefaultAugment, TrivialAugment, and SmartSamplingAugment, we evaluated each experiment three times using different seeds to obtain the mean performance. For RandAugment++ (an extended version of RandAugment) and SmartAugment, we took the mean test IoU over the three best performing validation configurations. Please note that DefaultAugment represents the baseline, and the higher the value, the better the performance. # iterations refers to the number of BO iterations completed to find best configuration.

Dataset	Default	Rand++	Trivial	Smart	SmartSampling
KITTI	65.07	67.19	64.82	**68.84**	66.53
RaVeNNa	88.37	90.71	90.53	**91.00**	90.72
EM	77.25	78.83	78.15	**79.04**	78.42
ErfASst	67.01	68.75	66.79	**73.72**	70.24
# Iterations	1	50	1	50	1

SmartAugment performs well compared to existing approaches in performance and computational budget. However, it still requires multiple iterations to find the best augmentation strategy, which can be expensive for researchers with computational constraints. With this in mind, we develop a fast and efficient data augmentation method, SmartSamplingAugment, that has a competitive performance to current best methods and outperforms TrivialAugment [16], a previous state-of-the-art simple augmentation method. SmartSamplingAugment is a parameter-free approach that samples augmentation operations according to their weights, and the probability of application is annealed during training. We summarize our contributions in the following points:

- We provide a first and extensive study of data augmentation on different and diverse datasets for semantic segmentation.
- We introduce a new state-of-the-art automated data augmentation algorithm for semantic segmentation that outperforms previous methods with half of the computational budget. It optimizes the number of applied geometric and color augmentations and their magnitude separately. Furthermore, it optimizes the probability of augmentation, which is crucial according to our hyperparameter importance analysis.
- We present a novel parameter-free data augmentation approach that weighs the applied data augmentation operations and anneals their probability of application. Our method is competitive with the previous automated data augmentation approaches and outperforms TrivialAugment, a cheap-to-evaluate method.

We will provide our source code: https://github.com/mvg-inatech/SmartAugment. (accessed on 1 April 2022).

2. Related Work

Data augmentation has been shown to have a considerable impact, particularly on computer vision tasks. Simple augmentation methods such as random cropping, horizontal flipping, random scaling, rotation, and translation have been effective and popular for image classification datasets [17–20]. Other approaches add noise or erase part of an image [5,21] or apply a convex combination of pairs of images and their labels [6]. Other approaches use generative adversarial networks to generate new training data [22,23].

Automated augmentation methods focus on learning an optimal data augmentation strategy from data [10,12]. Many recent methods define a set of data augmentations and their magnitude, where the best augmentation strategy is automatically selected. AutoAugment [10] uses a search algorithm based on reinforcement learning to find the best data augmentation policy with a validation accuracy as the reward. The search space consists of policies which in turn, have many sub-policies. Each sub-policy contains two augmentation operations, their magnitude, and a probability of application. A sub-policy is selected uniformly at random and applied to an image from a mini-batch. This process has high computational demands; therefore, it is applied on a proxy task with a smaller dataset and model. The best-found augmentation policy is then applied to the target task.

Population-Based Augmentation (PBA) [24] uses a population-based training algorithm [13] to learn a schedule of augmentation policies at every epoch during training. The policies are parameterized to consist of the magnitude and probability values for each augmentation operation. PBA randomly initializes and trains a model with these different policies in parallel. The weights of the better-performing models are cloned and perturbed with noise to make an exploration and exploitation trade-off. The schedule is learned with a child model and applied to a larger model on the same dataset.

Fast AutoAugment [25] speeds up the search for the best augmentation strategy with density matching. This method directly learns augmentation policies on inference time and tries to maximize the match of the distribution between augmented and non-augmented data without the need for child models. The idea is that if a network trained on real data generalizes well on augmented validation data, then the policy that produces these augmented data will be optimal. In other words, the policy preserves the label of the images, thus the distribution of the real data.

Adversarial AutoAugment [26] optimizes a target network and augmentation policy network jointly on target task in an adversarial fashion. The augmentation policy network generates data augmentations policies that produce hard examples, therefore increasing the target network's training loss. The hard examples force the target network to learn more robust features that improve its generalization and overall performance.

RandAugment [12] uses a much reduced search space than AutoAugment and optimizes two hyperparameters: the number of applied augmentations and the magnitude. RandAugment tunes these parameters with a simple Grid Search [27] on the target task, therefore, removes the need for a proxy task as is the case in AutoAugment [10]. The authors argue that this simplification helped the strong performance and efficiency of their approach.

TrivialAugment [16] samples one augmentation from a given set of augmentations and its magnitude uniformly at random and applies on a given image. This method is efficient, parameter-free, and competes with RandAugment [12] in performance for image classification.

In this work, we introduce two novel (automated) data augmentation methods for semantic segmentation: SmartAugment and SmartSamplingAugment. With hyperparameter optimization, SmartAugment finds optimal data augmentation strategy and SmartSamplingAugment's efficient and parameter-free approach competes with the previous state-of-the-art methods.

3. Methods

In this section, we present our data augmentation algorithms: SmartAugment and SmartSamplingAugment. Similar to previous methods, namely RandAugment and TrivialAugment, we define a set of color and geometric augmentations along with their magnitudes as shown in Table 2. We describe our algorithms in detail in the following subsections.

Table 2. Detailed overview of data augmentation operations and their magnitude ranges. We use the same augmentations as in RandAugment paper [12]. * The Identity operation only belongs to this list for the RandAugment and TrivialAugment approaches.

Color Ops	Range	Geometric Ops	Range
Sharpness	(0.1, 1.9)	Rotate	(0, 30)
AutoContrast	(0, 1)	ShearX	(0.0, 0.3)
Equalize	(0, 1)	ShearY	(0.0, 0.3)
Solarize	(0, 256)	TranslateX	(0.0, 0.33)
Color	(0.1, 1.9)	TranslateY	(0.0, 0.33)
Contrast	(0.1, 1.9)	Identity *	
Brightness	(0.1, 1.9)		

3.1. Smartaugment

SmartAugment optimizes the number of sampled color and geometric augmentations and their magnitude separately (see Figure 1b and Algorithm 1). Having these distinct sets of augmentations allows control over the type of applied augmentation instead of optimizing the total number of sampled augmentations and their magnitude collectively. SmartAugment also optimizes a parameter that determines the probability of applying data augmentations P instead of having the Identity operation in the augmentation list, as done by recent approaches.

SmartAugment uses Bayesian Optimization (BO) [15] to search for the best augmentation strategy. The space of augmentation strategies include the following parameters: number of color augmentations N_C, number of geometric augmentations N_G, color magnitude M_C, geometric magnitude M_G, and probability of applying augmentations P. These hyperparameters are optimized with the BO algorithm until a given budget is exhausted. Once BO chooses the augmentation parameters, the augmentations are sampled randomly without replacement for each epoch and image from the given list of augmentation operations as listed in Table 2. RandAugment, in contrast, samples with replacement and therefore allows sampling the same augmentation several times for the same image.

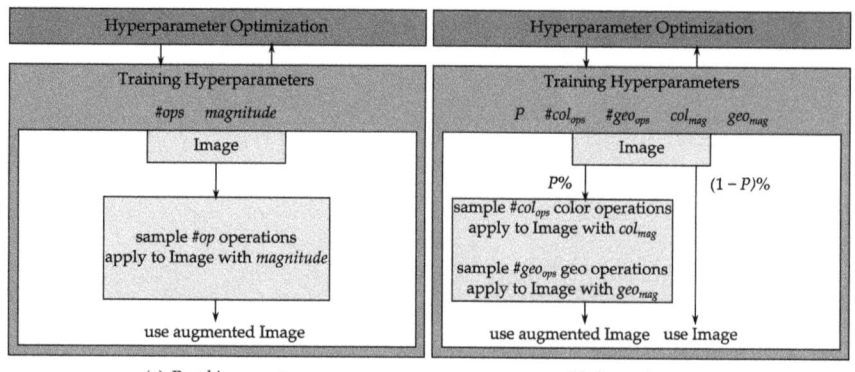

Figure 1. Comparison of RandAugment and SmartAugment.

Algorithm 1: Pseudocode for SmartAugment.

Input: Data D,
List of color augmentations C_{LIST},
List of geometric augmentations G_{LIST}

1 **for** *each configuration* **do**
2   Select 5 hyperparameters via BO:
3   1) # Color augmentations N_C to sample,
4   2) # Geometric augmentations N_G to sample,
5   3) Color magnitude M_C,
6   4) Geometric magnitude M_G,
7   5) Probability P of applying augmentations
8   **for** *each epoch* **do**
9   **for** *each image I in D* **do**
10   Sample *var* uniformly from [0, 1]
11   **if** *var > P* **then**
12   use I ;   // do not augment
13   **else**
14   C := random sample N_C ops from C_{LIST}
15   G := random sample N_G ops from G_{LIST}
16   I_{AUG} := apply C with M_C
17   and G with M_G to I
18   use I_{AUG}

3.2. SmartSamplingAugment

The number of sampled augmentations in SmartSamplingAugment, a tuning-free and computationally efficient algorithm, is fixed to two augmentation operations, and the magnitude is sampled randomly from the interval [5, 30] (see Figure 2b and Algorithm 2). These design choices are based on our preliminary experiments and seem to generalize well to unseen datasets. SmartSamplingAugment samples augmentations with a probability derived from the weights, which we set based on an ablation study for image classification on CIFAR10 from RandAugment [12]. In this study [12], the average improvement in performance is computed when a particular augmentation operation is added to a random subset of augmentations. We selected the augmentations with a positive average improvement and transformed this value into probabilities, by which we define the weights.

In SmartSamplingAugment, we linearly anneal the parameter P, that determines the probability of applying data augmentations, from 0 to 1, increasing the percentage of applying augmentation over the whole training epochs. That way, the model first sees the original data in the early epochs and encounters more variations as the training progresses.

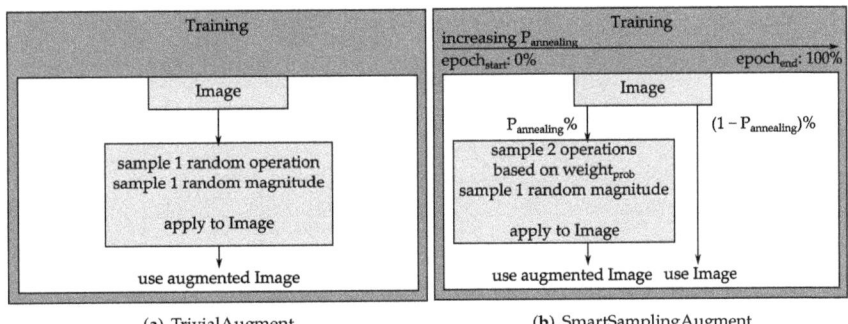

Figure 2. Comparison of TrivialAugment and SmartSamplingAugment.

Algorithm 2: Pseudocode for SmartSamplingAugment.

Input: Data D,
List of augmentations $A := [a_1, a_2, \ldots, a_{-1}]$,
Weights $W := [w_{a_1}, w_{a_2}, \ldots, w_{a_{-1}}]$

1 **for** *each epoch* **do**
2   Update P ;   `// P is linearly annealed`
3   **for** *each image I in D* **do**
4   Sample *var* from $[0,1]$
5   **if** *var > P* **then**
6   use I ;   `// do not augment`
7   **else**
8           $A_W :=$ random sample 2 ops $a_i, a_j \in A$ with weights $w_i, w_j \in W$
9           $M :=$ random sample magnitude from $[5,28]$
10           $I_{AUG} :=$ apply A_W with M to I
11   use I_{AUG}

4. Experiments and Results

In this section, we empirically evaluate and analyze the performance of SmartAugment and SmartSamplingAugment on several datasets and compare it to the previous state-of-the-art approaches. Furthermore, we investigate the impact, interaction, and importance of the optimized data augmentation hyperparameters.

4.1. Experimental Setup

4.1.1. Default and TrivialAugment

For completeness, we include in our experiments a "standard" augmentation strategy, a strategy based on augmentations often manually selected by researchers , we dubbed *DefaultAugment* and use it as our baseline. This default augmentation strategy is inspired by semantic segmentation literature [28,29] and uses the following standard augmentations: horizontal flipping ($p_{flip} = 0.5$), random rotation ($range = [-45, 45]$), random scaling ($range = [-0.35, 0.35]$), where p_{flip} represents the probability of applying this particular augmentation. Furthermore, we extended another recent method, TrivialAugment (see Figure 2a), for semantic segmentation and integrated it in our experiments.

4.1.2. RandAugment++

Classical RandAugment [12] uses simple Grid Search [27] to optimize its hyperparameters. Evaluating the full grid of classical RandAugment would lead to evaluate nearly 100 iterations (31 × 3 iterations: magnitude in the range of $[0, 30]$ and the number of operations in the range of $[1, 3]$) which is computationally very expensive. Therefore, we decided to implement an updated version of RandAugment, which we call *RandAugment++* (see Figure 1a) that uses the same algorithm but optimizes its hyperparameters with Random Search. Random Search is known to perform better than Grid Search [30] and its number of iterations is not limited to the size of the grid in the search space. Furthermore, using Random Search enabled us to reduce the number of iterations and increase the search space for RandAugment++ with less computational costs. We analyzed the performance of RandAugment++ with different operations on the EM dataset and found out that constraining the number of applied operations to three is not optimal (see Figure 3). From this observation, we increase the upper limit for the number of applied operations from 3 to 16, which denotes the total number of augmentations in the list we sample from. To ensure comparability between RandAugment++ and SmartAugment, we use the same computational budget of 50 iterations for both methods. We show in an ablation study (see Section 4.4) that RandAugment++ is a better choice than the classical RandAugment.

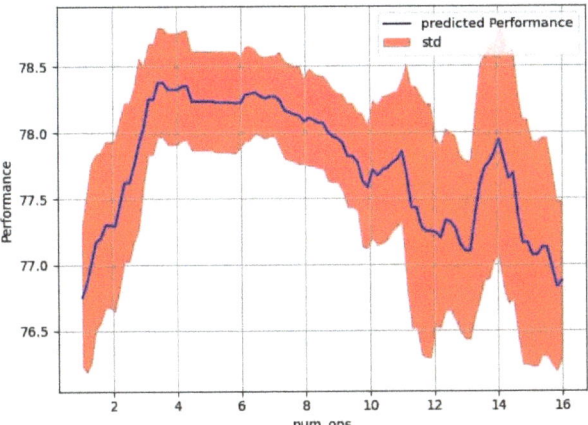

Figure 3. Performance (mean IoU) analysis for different numbers of operations for RandAugment++ on EM. These results indicate that the number of applied operations should optimally not be limited to three, as in classical RandAugment.

4.1.3. Training Setup

For all experiments, we use the U-Net architecture [31] to train the models and split the datasets into training, validation, and test set. To find good fitting training hyperparameters (e.g., learning rate and weight decay) for our in-house datasets, we performed Random Search over ten configurations until model convergence. As a preprocessing step, we apply with 50% probability either random crop or downsize operations before passing the data to the different augmentation strategies for efficient memory and computing use. For KITTI and EM datasets, we use a similar training setup as in [28]. To speed up memory intensive processes, we use mixed precision training with 16 bits. For our experiments, we made use of four GeForce GTX 1080 GPUs. For better reproducibility, we list the training parameters for each of the datasets for a detailed view in Table 3.

Table 3. Training parameters for each dataset. Train, val, test denote the data split used during training.

Dataset	Resolution	Batch Size	Learning Rate	Epochs	# Data	#Train	#Val	#Test
KITTI	185 × 612	4	0.001	4000	200	140	30	30
RaVeNNa	180 × 180	3	0.001	2000	1684	1107	216	361
EM	512 × 512	2	0.01	500	30	20	5	5
ErfASst	864 × 864	2	0.05	5000	50	30	10	10

Furthermore, we performed early stopping on the validation set. To save computing and still obtain enough samples on the validation set for early stopping, we evaluate every 10% of the total epochs on the validation set. This ensures that for each dataset, independent of the number of epochs needed until convergence, the number of epochs evaluated on the validation set is proportional to the total number of epochs. We run these experiments three times for the different data augmentation approaches and take the mean of the test IoU to ensure a fair comparison. In the case of RandAugment and SmartAugment, we evaluated 50 configurations for each method and report the mean test IoU of the three best performing configurations on the validation set.

For all our experiments, we use Stochastic Gradient Descent (SGD) optimizer [32] and Cosine Annealing [33] as our learning rate scheduler, and anneal the learning rate over the total number of epochs.

4.1.4. Datasets

We evaluate all approaches on four datasets with pixel-level annotated images from diverse semantic segmentation applications. ErFASst is a bridge inspection dataset with 50 images and two classes used for crack detection (Figure 4a). We use KITTI [34], a popular autonomous driving dataset consisting of 200 images with 19 classes (Figure 4b). RaVeNNa [1], is a cystoscopic medical imaging dataset comprises 1684 images with seven classes that is used in detecting artifacts such as tumors in human bladder (Figure 5a). EM [35] is a brain electron microscopy dataset of 30 images derived from a 2D segmentation challenge dataset and consists of two classes (Figure 5b). To achieve meaningful results, these datasets differ in size, resolutions, and type of images (RGB natural images, Grayscale, see Table 3). Since RaVeNNa and ErFASst are highly class-imbalanced datasets, we use a weighted cross-entropy loss during training. The weights are computed beforehand with inverse frequency of the number of pixels belonging to a specific class in the training set.

(a) ErFASst   (b) KITTI

Figure 4. Infrastructure mapping datasets.

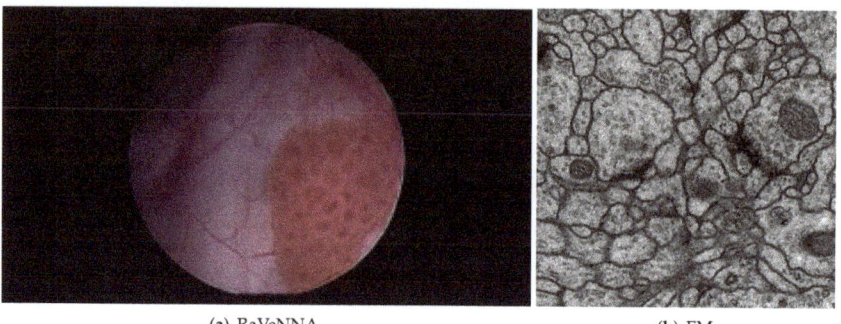

(a) RaVeNNA   (b) EM

Figure 5. Biomedical datasets.

4.2. Comparison to the State-of-the-Art

In Table 1, we compare our methods, SmartAugment and SmartSamplingAugment, to the aforementioned data augmentation methods as well as to our baseline, DefaultAugment, a basic augmentation strategy that is commonly used in semantic segmentation literature [28,29]. SmartAugment outperforms the previous state-of-the-art methods across all datasets, while SmartSamplingAugment competes with the previous state-of-the-art methods and outperforms the comparably cheap augmentation method, TrivialAugment. Moreover, SmartSamplingAugment outperforms RandAugment++ on half of the datasets, even though the latter has 50 times more budget.

Approximate Analysis of Compute Costs

We calculate the computing costs for each dataset for all the experiments done with GeForce GTX 1080. In Table 4 we list our cost estimates that each method requires until convergence.

Table 4. Approximate estimate of computing costs (in hours) for each dataset and augmentation approach. The costs are the time required until the maximum number of epochs is reached. Due to computational resource constraints, we run Smart, Rand++, $Rand_{classic}$ with four GPUs in parallel. $Rand_{classic}$ is RandAugment that uses GridSearch for optimization.

Dataset	Default	Rand++	Trivial	Smart	Smart Sampling	$Rand_{classic}$
KITTI	12 h	150 h	12 h	150 h	12 h	276 h
RaVeNNa	13 h	163 h	13 h	13 h	163 h	302 h
EM	0.5 h	6 h	0.5 h	6 h	0.5 h	11.6 h
ErfASst	23 h	287 h	23 h	287 h	23 h	537 h
# Iterations	1	50	1	50	1	93

4.3. Analysis with fANOVA

We analyze the impact, interaction, and importance of augmentation hyperparameters across different datasets with fANOVA [36]. Moreover, we quantify and visualize the effect of different augmentation configurations on the overall model performance on the validation mean IoU metric.

4.3.1. Impact of Hyperparameters across Different Datasets

The results in Figures 6 and 7 show that the optimal strategy of augmentation hyperparameters is dataset-specific and predominantly impacts the overall performance: As shown in Figure 6, applying many color operations with a high color magnitude to the data can be good for the EM dataset, but can have a detrimental effect on the performance of the KITTI dataset. There are areas in the augmentation space where it is sub-optimal to sample from for a particular dataset but are good for another one. Furthermore, Figure 7 indicates that the probability hyperparameter of applying data augmentations strongly varies across the datasets.

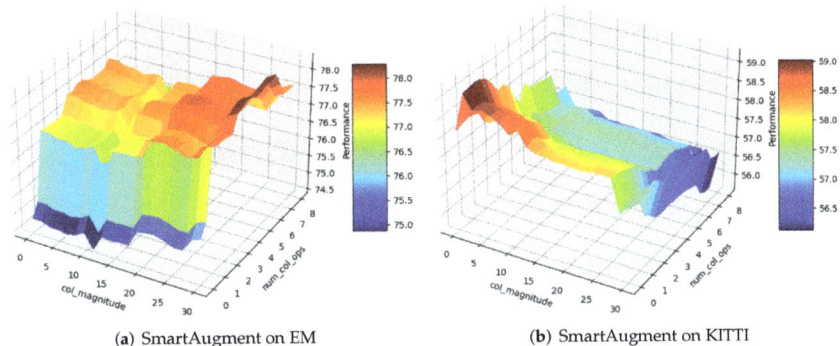

(a) SmartAugment on EM   (b) SmartAugment on KITTI

Figure 6. The impact of hyperparameters on different datasets based on performance metric mean IoU. This figure shows that the good values for each hyperparameter depend on the dataset. In this example, higher number of color ops and color magnitude is optimal for EM dataset but detrimental for KITTI dataset.

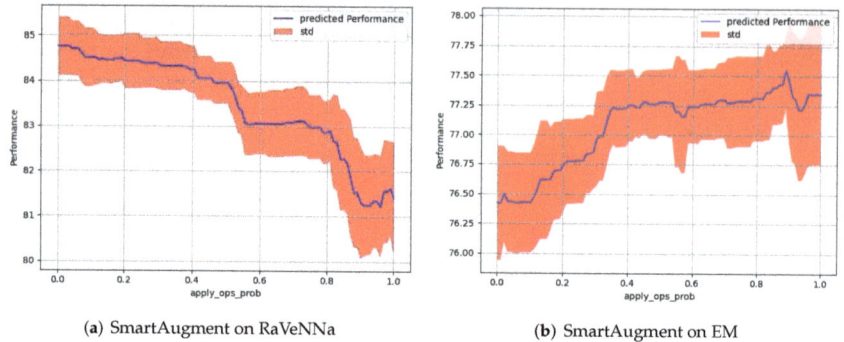

(**a**) SmartAugment on RaVeNNa

(**b**) SmartAugment on EM

Figure 7. Comparison of the probability hyperparameter of applying data augmentations. These results indicate that the EM dataset needs much more data augmentation than the RaVeNNa dataset. MeanIoU is used as performance metric.

4.3.2. Hyperparameter Interaction Analysis

Furthermore, we analyze the interaction of hyperparameters and their effect on the performance. As mentioned in Section 3, SmartAugment optimizes the color and geometric augmentations separately. The results in Table 1 and Figure 8 confirm our hypothesis that this is a good design choice. Looking more closely, the figure shows that for optimal performance, it does not suffice to optimize the total number of applied augmentations; rather, it is crucial to sample the right type of augmentation from the augmentation list carefully. For instance, according to Figure 8b, choosing four operations from the total number of augmentation seems to be the optimal choice for the KITTI dataset. However, according to Figure 8a, just sampling "blindly" four augmentation operations from the entire augmentation list might not always be a good choice. If we would pick four color augmentation operations and zero geometric augmentation operations, the performance would be significantly sub-optimal.

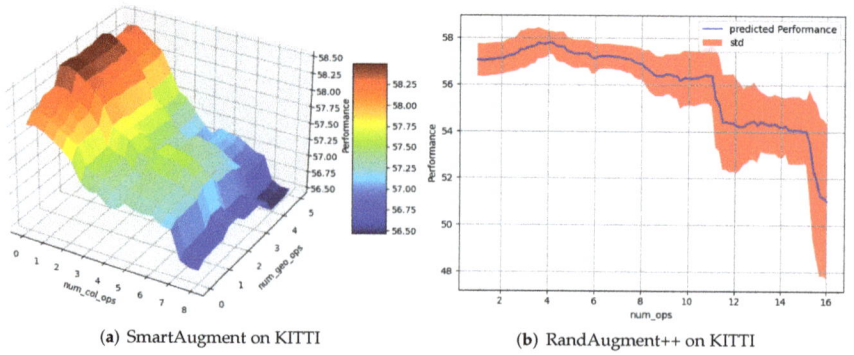

(**a**) SmartAugment on KITTI

(**b**) RandAugment++ on KITTI

Figure 8. Comparison considering the number of applied augmentations: RandAugment++ optimizes the total number of augmentations, whereas SmartAugment differs between the number of color augmentations and geometric augmentations. This figure shows that the performance of a total number of augmentations depends on the types of augmentations. Please note that mean IoU is used as a performance metric.

4.3.3. Hyperparameter Importance Study

In many algorithms that have a large hyperparameter space, only a few parameters are usually responsible for most of the performance improvement [36]. In this study, we use fANOVA to quantify how much each hyperparameter contributes to the overall variance in performance. As we observe in Table 5, the importance of a specific hyperparameter strongly depends on the dataset. For instance, the geometric magnitude has a much higher impact on the KITTI dataset than other datasets. Moreover, the results from Table 5 show that optimizing the probability of application is an important design choice since this parameter is the most important one in half of the datasets studied in these experiments.

Table 5. Hyperparameter importance study for different hyperparameters across different datasets on SmartAugment experiments. For instance, for the RaVeNNa dataset, the probability of applying a data augmentation strategy is responsible for 46% of mean IoU's variability across the configuration space. The higher the importance value, the more potential it has to improve the performance for a given dataset.

Dataset	p(aug)	col_mag	geo_mag	#col_ops	#geo_ops
KITTI	0.13	0.12	**0.24**	0.14	0.03
RaVeNNa	**0.46**	0.04	0.06	0.06	0.05
EM	**0.25**	0.14	0.09	0.04	0.03
ErFASst	0.1	0.12	0.04	**0.22**	0.04

4.4. Ablation Studies

In addition to comparing our methods to the state-of-the-art approaches and the baseline, we report some ablation studies that give deeper insights into the impact of our methods.

4.4.1. RandAugment(++) Ablation Studies

To confirm that the improvement of SmartAugment over RandAugment++ comes from the method differences, we study RandAugment with different optimization methods. For this purpose, we compare classical RandAugment with Grid Search, RandAugment++ with Random Search, and RandAugment with Bayesian Optimization as optimization algorithms. We chose a cheap-to-evaluate dataset (EM) for this ablation study. As the results in Table 6 confirm, SmartAugment outperforms RandAugment, independent of the selected hyperparameter optimization algorithm. An interesting observation from the study is that RandAugment++ improves over the classical RandAugment as shown in Table 6. It is worthy to note that these improvement gains were achieved with fewer iterations and less computational costs.

Furthermore, Figure 3 shows that it can be sub-optimal to limit the number of applied augmentations to three, as is done in classical RandAugment. Therefore, increasing the search space as in RandAugment++ allows finding a better number of augmentation operations.

Table 6. Comparison of RandAugment variants with SmartAugment on the EM dataset. For each of the results, we took the test mean IoU of the best three performing configurations evaluated on the validation set. The results show that SmartAugment outperforms RandAugment(++), independent of the hyperparameter optimization algorithm.

Method	HPO Algorithm	EM Dataset	# Iterations
Rand	Grid Search (classic approach)	78.54	93
Rand++	Random Search	78.83	50
Rand++	Bayesian Optimization	78.84	50
Smart	Bayesian Optimization	**79.04**	50

4.4.2. SmartSamplingAugment Ablation Studies

In these ablation studies, we analyze the impact of annealing the probability hyperparameter over epochs and weighting the augmentation operations. For the experiments without annealing, we set the probability of augmentation P to 1.

The results in Table 7 show that for three out of four datasets, annealing as well as weighting the augmentations are good design choices. Additionally, Table 7 shows that the combination of annealing the probability of augmentation and weighting the augmentations for RaVeNNa and ErFASst datasets improves the performance. Overall, SmartSamplingAugment does comparatively well and outperforms DefaultAugment and TrivialAugment across all datasets (see Table 1).

In the following, we give some possible explanations as to why annealing the augmentations for the EM dataset and weighting the augmentations for the KITTI dataset might not perform well. According to the hyperparameter importance study in Table 5, which quantifies the effect of how the values of these parameters affects the overall performance, the probability of augmenting data is the most important one for the EM dataset. Figure 7b, indicates that the EM dataset benefits from a high percentage of data augmentation; and therefore setting the probability of augmentation to 1 over the whole training yields better results rather than slowly increasing the probability of applied augmentations over the total number of epochs can be suboptimal. In contrast to the RaVeNNa dataset, where the probability of augmenting data is also an important hyperparameter (see Table 5), always augmenting data ($P = 1$) hurts performance. Figure 7a shows that annealing or progressively increasing the probability of augmentation for this particular dataset does seem to be a better alternative since we do early stopping.

Table 7. SmartSamplingAugment ablation study analyzing the impact of weighting the augmentations and annealing the probability hyperparameter over the whole epochs for different datasets. We evaluated each experiment three times using different seeds to obtain the mean IoU. For the experiments without annealing, we set the probability P of applying augmentations to 1.

Dataset	Weighting		Without Weighting	
	Annealing	No-Annealing	Annealing	No-Annealing
KITTI	66.53	67.15	**67.49**	67.13
RaVeNNa	**90.72**	87.07	85.65	85.68
EM	78.52	**79.26**	77.94	78.47
ErFASst	**70.24**	68.27	64.99	64.51

Furthermore, for the KITTI dataset, the geometric magnitude is the most important hyperparameter and Figure 9 shows that sampling a high geometric magnitude can hurt performance. In SmartSamplingAugment, rotation is strongly weighted, and there is a considerable probability that a higher magnitude for this operation is sampled. Figure 10 visualizes three KITTI and EM images, each rotated with a different magnitude, and gives an intuition why augmenting the KITTI dataset with high geometric operations can have a detrimental effect on performance. We note that we select the weights based on a study performed on a classification dataset, which probably is sub-optimal for semantic segmentation. However, this gives insight that studies focusing on optimizing the weights for augmentation operations can be a next step for further research.

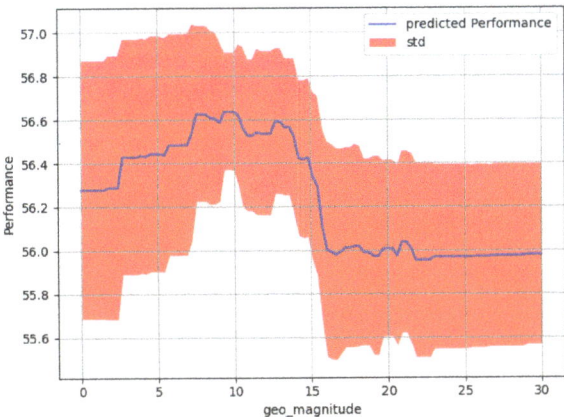

Figure 9. Results from SmartAugment on the KITTI dataset indicate that the geometric magnitude, which is the most important hyperparameter for this particular dataset, should be low. Taking this into account gives a possible explanation for why weighting the data augmentation with weights that focus on geometric augmentations might hurt performance (mean IoU) for the KITTI dataset.

Rotation with magnitude 10

Rotation with magnitude 30

2× Rotation with magnitude 30

Figure 10. Visualization of three images from the KITTI (left) and EM (right) datasets, each rotated with a different magnitude.

5. Conclusions

In this work, we provide a first and extensive study of data augmentation for segmentation and introduce two novel approaches: SmartAugment, a new state-of-the-art method that finds the best configuration for data augmentation with hyperparameter optimization, and SmartSamplingAugment, a parameter-free, resource-efficient approach that performs competitively with the previous state-of-the-art approaches. Both methods achieve excellent results on different and diverse datasets.

With SmartAugment, we show that Bayesian Optimization can effectively find an optimal augmentation strategy from a search space where the number of color and geometric augmentations and their magnitudes are optimized separately, along with a probability hyperparameter for applying data augmentations. Our results show that the type of applied augmentation is essential in making good decisions for improved performance. Furthermore, a hyperparameter importance study indicates that the probability of applying a data augmentation strategy could have considerable responsibility for the mean IoU's variability across the configuration space.

With SmartSamplingAugment, we develop a simple and cheap-to-evaluate algorithm that weighs the augmentations and anneals augmentations to increase the percentage of augmented images systematically. The results show that this is a powerful and efficient approach that is competitive to the more resource-intensive approaches and outperforms TrivialAugment, a comparably cheap-to-evaluate method. Furthermore, SmartSamplingAugment opens the gate for more research on weighting and annealing data augmentation. A possible future work will study an extension of our methods to image classification, detection and 3D segmentation, particularly for biomedical applications.

Author Contributions: Conceptualization, M.N., D.W.; methodology, M.N., D.W.; software, M.N., D.W.; validation, M.N., D.W. and A.R.; investigation, M.N., D.W.; resources, A.R.; data curation, M.N.; writing—original draft preparation, M.N., D.W.; writing—review and editing, M.N., D.W. and A.R.; visualization, M.N., D.W.; supervision, A.R.; project administration, M.N., A.R.; funding acquisition, A.R. All authors have read and agreed to the published version of the manuscript.

Funding: This research was funded by the German Federal Ministry of Education and Research (13GW0203A) and approved by the local Ethical Committee of the University of Freiburg, Germany.

Institutional Review Board Statement: Not applicable.

Informed Consent Statement: Not applicable.

Data Availability Statement: The data used are referenced in the article.

Acknowledgments: The authors would like to thank the Department of Urology of the Faculty of Medicine in University of Freiburg for annotation of cystoscopic images that were used to build the RaVeNNA (Ravenna 4pi) dataset. Furthermore, thanks to Dominik Merkle for providing us with the ErfAsst dataset.

Conflicts of Interest: The authors declare no conflict of interest.

Abbreviations

The following abbreviations are used in this manuscript:

BO	Bayesian Optimization
IoU	Intersection over Union
SGD	Stochastic Gradient Descent
N_C	Number of color augmentations
N_G	Number of geometric augmentations
M_C	Color magnitude
M_G	Geometric magnitude
P	Probability of applying augmentations

References

1. Negassi, M.; Suarez-Ibarrola, R.; Hein, S.; Miernik, A.; Reiterer, A. Application of artificial neural networks for automated analysis of cystoscopic images: A review of the current status and future prospects. *World J. Urol.* **2020**, *38*, 2349–2358. [CrossRef] [PubMed]
2. Péntek, Q.; Hein, S.; Miernik, A.; Reiterer, A. Image-based 3D surface approximation of the bladder using structure-from-motion for enhanced cystoscopy based on phantom data. *Biomed. Eng. Biomed. Tech.* **2018**, *63*, 461–466. [CrossRef] [PubMed]
3. Goodfellow, I.; Bengio, Y.; Courville, A. *Deep Learning*; MIT Press: Cambridge, MA, USA, 2016. Available online: http://www.deeplearningbook.org (accessed on 1 April 2022).
4. Yun, S.; Han, D.; Oh, S.J.; Chun, S.; Choe, J.; Yoo, Y. CutMix: Regularization Strategy to Train Strong Classifiers with Localizable Features. *arXiv* **2019**, arXiv:1905.04899.
5. Devries, T.; Taylor, G.W. Improved Regularization of Convolutional Neural Networks with Cutout. *arXiv* **2017**, arXiv:1708.04552.
6. Zhang, H.; Cissé, M.; Dauphin, Y.N.; Lopez-Paz, D. mixup: Beyond Empirical Risk Minimization. *arXiv* **2017**, arXiv:1710.09412.
7. Girshick, R.; Radosavovic, I.; Gkioxari, G.; Dollár, P.; He, K. Detectron. 2018. Available online: https://github.com/facebookresearch/detectron (accessed on 1 April 2022).
8. Chen, T.; Kornblith, S.; Norouzi, M.; Hinton, G.E. A Simple Framework for Contrastive Learning of Visual Representations. *arXiv* **2020**, arXiv:2002.05709.
9. Nishio, M.; Noguchi, S.; Fujimoto, K. Automatic Pancreas Segmentation Using Coarse-Scaled 2D Model of Deep Learning: Usefulness of Data Augmentation and Deep U-Net. *Appl. Sci.* **2020**, *10*, 3360. [CrossRef]
10. Cubuk, E.D.; Zoph, B.; Mané, D.; Vasudevan, V.; Le, Q.V. AutoAugment: Learning Augmentation Policies from Data. *arXiv* **2018**, arXiv:1805.09501.
11. Zoph, B.; Cubuk, E.D.; Ghiasi, G.; Lin, T.; Shlens, J.; Le, Q.V. Learning Data Augmentation Strategies for Object Detection. *arXiv* **2019**, arXiv:1906.11172.
12. Cubuk, E.D.; Zoph, B.; Shlens, J.; Le, Q.V. RandAugment: Practical data augmentation with no separate search. *arXiv* **2019**, arXiv:1909.13719.
13. Jaderberg, M.; Dalibard, V.; Osindero, S.; Czarnecki, W.M.; Donahue, J.; Razavi, A.; Vinyals, O.; Green, T.; Dunning, I.; Simonyan, K.; et al. Population Based Training of Neural Networks. *arXiv* **2017**, arXiv:1711.09846.
14. Snoek, J.; Larochelle, H.; Adams, R.P. Practical Bayesian Optimization of Machine Learning Algorithms. In *Advances in Neural Information Processing Systems*; Pereira, F., Burges, C.J.C., Bottou, L., Weinberger, K.Q., Eds.; Curran Associates, Inc.: Sussex, NB, Canada, 2012; Volume 25.
15. Falkner, S.; Klein, A.; Hutter, F. BOHB: Robust and Efficient Hyperparameter Optimization at Scale. *arXiv* **2018**, arXiv:1807.01774.
16. Müller, S.G.; Hutter, F. TrivialAugment: Tuning-free Yet State-of-the-Art Data Augmentation. *arXiv* **2021**, arXiv:2103.10158.
17. Krizhevsky, A.; Sutskever, I.; Hinton, G.E. ImageNet Classification with Deep Convolutional Neural Networks. In *Advances in Neural Information Processing Systems*; Pereira, F., Burges, C.J.C., Bottou, L., Weinberger, K.Q., Eds.; Curran Associates, Inc.: Sussex, NB, Canada, 2012; Volume 25.
18. He, K.; Zhang, X.; Ren, S.; Sun, J. Deep Residual Learning for Image Recognition. *arXiv* **2015**, arXiv:1512.03385.
19. Han, D.; Kim, J.; Kim, J. Deep Pyramidal Residual Networks. *arXiv* **2016**, arXiv:1610.02915.
20. Wan, L.; Zeiler, M.; Zhang, S.; Cun, Y.L.; Fergus, R. Regularization of Neural Networks using DropConnect. In Proceedings of the 30th International Conference on Machine Learning, Atlanta, GA, USA, 17–19 June 2013; Dasgupta, S., McAllester, D., Eds.; PMLR: Chicago, IL, USA, 2013; Volume 28, pp. 1058–1066.
21. Zhong, Z.; Zheng, L.; Kang, G.; Li, S.; Yang, Y. Random Erasing Data Augmentation. *arXiv* **2017**, arXiv:1708.04896.
22. Antoniou, A.; Storkey, A.; Edwards, H. Data Augmentation Generative Adversarial Networks. *arXiv* **2018**, arXiv:1711.04340.
23. Perez, L.; Wang, J. The Effectiveness of Data Augmentation in Image Classification using Deep Learning. *arXiv* **2017**, arXiv:1712.04621.
24. Ho, D.; Liang, E.; Chen, X.; Stoica, I.; Abbeel, P. Population Based Augmentation: Efficient Learning of Augmentation Policy Schedules. In Proceedings of the 36th International Conference on Machine Learning, Long Beach, CA, USA, 10–15 June 2019; Chaudhuri, K., Salakhutdinov, R., Eds.; PMLR: Chicago, USA, 2019; Volume 97, pp. 2731–2741.
25. Lim, S.; Kim, I.; Kim, T.; Kim, C.; Kim, S. Fast AutoAugment. *arXiv* **2019**, arXiv:1905.00397.
26. Zhang, X.; Wang, Q.; Zhang, J.; Zhong, Z. Adversarial AutoAugment. *arXiv* **2019**, arXiv:1912.11188.
27. LeCun, Y.; Bottou, L.; Orr, G.B.; Müller, K.R. Efficient BackProp. In *Neural Networks: Tricks of the Trade*, 2nd ed.; Montavon, G., Orr, G.B., Müller, K.R., Eds.; Lecture Notes in Computer Science; Springer: Berlin/Heidelberg, Germany, 2012; Volume 7700, pp. 9–48.
28. Chen, L.; Papandreou, G.; Schroff, F.; Adam, H. Rethinking Atrous Convolution for Semantic Image Segmentation. *arXiv* **2017**, arXiv:1706.05587.
29. Tao, A.; Sapra, K.; Catanzaro, B. Hierarchical Multi-Scale Attention for Semantic Segmentation. *arXiv* **2020**, arXiv:2005.10821.
30. Bergstra, J.; Bengio, Y. Random Search for Hyper-Parameter Optimization. *J. Mach. Learn. Res.* **2012**, *13*, 281–305.
31. Ronneberger, O.; P.Fischer.; Brox, T. U-Net: Convolutional Networks for Biomedical Image Segmentation. In *Medical Image Computing and Computer-Assisted Intervention (MICCAI)*; Lecture Notes in Computer Science; Springer: Berlin/Heidelberg, Germany, 2015; Volume 9351, pp. 234–241.
32. Ruder, S. An overview of gradient descent optimization algorithms. *arXiv* **2016**, arXiv:1609.04747.
33. Loshchilov, I.; Hutter, F. SGDR: Stochastic Gradient Descent with Restarts. *arXiv* **2016**, arXiv:1608.03983.

34. Geiger, A.; Lenz, P.; Stiller, C.; Urtasun, R. Vision meets Robotics: The KITTI Dataset. *Int. J. Robot. Res.* **2013**, *32*, 1231–1237. [CrossRef]
35. Cardona, A.; Saalfeld, S.; Preibisch, S.; Schmid, B.; Cheng, A.; Pulokas, J.; Tomancak, P.; Hartenstein, V. An integrated micro-and macroarchitectural analysis of the Drosophila brain by computer-assisted serial section electron microscopy. *PLoS Biol.* **2010**, *8*, e1000502. [CrossRef]
36. Hutter, F.; Hoos, H.; Leyton-Brown, K. An Efficient Approach for Assessing Hyperparameter Importance. In Proceedings of the 31st International Conference on Machine Learning, Bejing, China, 21–26 June 2014; Xing, E.P., Jebara, T., Eds.; PMLR: Chicago, IL, USA, 2014; Volume 32, pp. 754–762.

 algorithms

Article

Machine Learning and rs-fMRI to Identify Potential Brain Regions Associated with Autism Severity

Igor D. Rodrigues [1,*], Emerson A. de Carvalho [1,2], Caio P. Santana [1,†] and Guilherme S. Bastos [1]

1. Institute of Systems Engineering and Information Technology, Federal University of Itajubá, Itajubá 37500-903, Brazil; emerson.carvalho@ifsuldeminas.edu.br (E.A.d.C.); caiopsantana@unifei.edu.br (C.P.S.); sousa@unifei.edu.br (G.S.B.)
2. IFSULDEMINAS, Computer Department, Machado 37750-000, Brazil
* Correspondence: igordrodrigues@gmail.com
† Current address: Department of Computer Engineering and Industrial Automation, University of Campinas, Campinas 13083-970, Brazil.

Abstract: Autism Spectrum Disorder (ASD) is a neurodevelopmental disorder characterized primarily by social impairments that manifest in different severity levels. In recent years, many studies have explored the use of machine learning (ML) and resting-state functional magnetic resonance images (rs-fMRI) to investigate the disorder. These approaches evaluate brain oxygen levels to indirectly measure brain activity and compare typical developmental subjects with ASD ones. However, none of these works have tried to classify the subjects into severity groups using ML exclusively applied to rs-fMRI data. Information on ASD severity is frequently available since some tools used to support ASD diagnosis also include a severity measurement as their outcomes. The aforesaid is the case of the Autism Diagnostic Observation Schedule (ADOS), which splits the diagnosis into three groups: 'autism', 'autism spectrum', and 'non-ASD'. Therefore, this paper aims to use ML and fMRI to identify potential brain regions as biomarkers of ASD severity. We used the ADOS score as a severity measurement standard. The experiment used fMRI data of 202 subjects with an ASD diagnosis and their ADOS scores available at the ABIDE I consortium to determine the correct ASD sub-class for each one. Our results suggest a functional difference between the ASD sub-classes by reaching 73.8% accuracy on cingulum regions. The aforementioned shows the feasibility of classifying and characterizing ASD using rs-fMRI data, indicating potential areas that could lead to severity biomarkers in further research. However, we highlight the need for more studies to confirm our findings.

Keywords: ABIDE; ASD; autism spectrum disorder severity classification; fMRI; machine learning

Citation: Rodrigues, I.D.; de Carvalho, E.A.; Santana, C.P.; Bastos, G.S. Machine Learning and rs-fMRI to Identify Potential Brain Regions Associated with Autism Severity. *Algorithms* **2022**, *15*, 195. https://doi.org/10.3390/a15060195

Academic Editor: Lucia Maddalena

Received: 15 April 2022
Accepted: 28 May 2022
Published: 7 June 2022

Publisher's Note: MDPI stays neutral with regard to jurisdictional claims in published maps and institutional affiliations.

Copyright: © 2022 by the authors. Licensee MDPI, Basel, Switzerland. This article is an open access article distributed under the terms and conditions of the Creative Commons Attribution (CC BY) license (https://creativecommons.org/licenses/by/4.0/).

1. Introduction

Autism Spectrum Disorder (ASD) is a neurodevelopmental disorder characterized mainly by social impairments, commonly followed by communication challenges or restricted and repetitive patterns of behavior [1]. ASD is a substantially heterogeneous disorder in which two diagnosed subjects may have a completely different set of symptoms. Some researchers estimated that approximately one in 44 children aged eight years are in the spectrum [2]. Despite a possible gender bias regarding diagnosis, ASD seems to be a sex-related disorder, with a male-to-female ratio close to 3–4:1 [2–4]. Current research points to ASD as a primarily hereditary disorder. Approximately 80–83% of ASD cases are due to genetic inheritance. Close to 17–20% are due to environmental risk factors, including problems during the gestation period and the parents' age [5–7].

Children and adolescents with an ASD diagnosis have medical expenses up to 6.2 times greater than those with typical development (TD), with general costs from 8.4 to 9.5 times greater than the average [8]. In addition to medical expenses, intensive behavioral interventions needed for ASD treatment have costs from USD 40,000 to USD 60,000 per child per year [9]. Moreover, most ASD individuals live in low- or middle-income countries and receive no proper support from health or social care systems, suffering from the high costs of (1) proprietary tools for diagnosis; (2) evidence-based intervention techniques, and (3) training of parents and professionals to conduct the ASD treatment process [10].

Early diagnosis and proper interventions are critical factors in reversing the impairments generated by ASD in children. Unfortunately, there are no low-cost automated tests to identify the disorder. Instead, the ASD diagnosis is performed through clinical observation, which is challenging to accomplish in young children, especially in the early years of life [11]. Early treatments may result in improved cognitive, behavioral, and social functioning, allowing, for a subset of people, an evolution that may lead to healthy adult life, as well as significant long-term societal cost reductions [12]. However, most technological tools proposed to assist the ASD intervention process showed some common limitations [13].

It is critical to comprehend the severity of each individual with ASD to plan personalized treatments and conduct more effective intervention processes. Nowadays, there are many protocols used to support diagnosis, such as the Autism Diagnostic Observation Schedule (ADOS), Autism Diagnostic Interview—Revised (ADI-R), and Social Communication Questionnaire (SCQ). However, ADOS is currently one of the most used worldwide. ADOS divides ASD classification between autism—the ones with more severe symptoms—autism spectrum—the ones with less severe symptoms—and as non-spectrum—those diagnosed outside of the spectrum [14].

An ADOS diagnosis consists of standard evaluation on three main domains: communication, social relations, and behavior. Each domain has a set of tasks to be evaluated, with different total scores. The ADOS diagnosis comprises four modules for a specific range of ages and language skills, each with different cut-offs for each of the three classes [15]. Furthermore, current ASD diagnosis is performed by trained professionals, with the help of tools such as ADOS, which has both sensibility and specificity above 80% [16]. It is important to note that the current ADOS version mainly used is the ADOS-2 [14], but due to our available samples, we used the ADOS in its classic version.

The last decade was marked by research looking for methods to take advantage of the recent evolution of machine learning (ML) to build automated ASD diagnosis processes [17–20]. The first works in this field date from mid-2010 [21]. Since then, there has been an increase in the number of papers and improved outcomes. Many of these works used magnetic resonance imaging (MRI) and ML combined, aiming for a positive or negative ASD diagnosis by classifying subjects between ASD and TD [21], as in [18–20,22–24].

One of MRI's advantages is that it is a non-invasive procedure, being a prevalent method to scan the brain in living human beings [25]. There are two main uses for brain MRI: (1) the structural scan, which scans brain tissues and assesses their differences; and (2) the functional scan, which tracks the oxygen flow in the brain. This second method is usually called functional MRI (fMRI) and allows the indirect measurement of brain activities in regions of interest (ROIs). From the measured oxygen levels, it is possible to determine which regions are more activated than others [25,26].

There are many tasks applied to a subject for an fMRI scan; they range from resting state to very narrow activities, such as watching a video. The resting-state fMRI is usually called rs-fMRI, which is a means to delimitate the activity for scan acquisition. However, the other activities, in general, do not have a specific nomination. The rs-fMRI is easiest to apply and is also easy to compare between multiple studies, as it is easier to reproduce in the same setup than any other activity.

Additionally, other medical images are also combined with ML to diagnose ASD, as is the case of electroencephalograms (EEG), which try to measure brain activity by scanning magnetic signals originating from the brain. There are many different setups, but as in fMRI, many papers using resting-state scans are available, such as [27–30]. However, some other setups, such as during the ADOS test [31] or while watching videos [32], are also available. However, there are few EEG data with ASD diagnosis that are publicly available.

Meanwhile, on the fMRI side, some universities have worked together and created the Autism Brain Imaging Data Exchange (ABIDE) [33], an initiative that makes available more than 2000 brain fMRI scans for research purposes. In addition, all fMRI subjects gave consent to use their images. This initiative facilitates autism investigation by providing access to a database that otherwise would not be easily acquired. Moreover, the preprocessed data available on ABIDE I PREPROCESSED also contribute in this sense.

Therefore, we take into account the following true propositions: (1) early diagnosis and interventions lead to better outcomes for autism treatment, as well as long-term cost reduction; (2) ADOS scores allow a rating of the ASD severity; (3) promising results of ML techniques classifying ASD vs. neurotypical through the use of rs-fMRI; and (4) the ADOS scores and ASD rs-fMRI data available at ABIDE. This work aims to investigate the functional differences between autism spectrum and autistic individuals, looking for potential brain regions that may be associated with autism severity. We used ML applied to brain segments from rs-fMRI data to classify individuals from the two groups to identify these regions, selecting the ones with the greatest differences as potential biomarkers that should be more deeply investigated in future works.

The remainder of this paper is structured as follows: Section 2 presents the methodology employed. Sections 3 and 4 present and discuss our results, while Section 5 concludes this work.

2. Methodology

This section presents this work's methodology. It starts by describing the materials used in Section 2.1, followed by a presentation of the ADOS sub-classes for ASD classification in Section 2.2 and the region selection process in Section 2.3. Then, we explain both the ML used to classify the samples in Section 2.4 and the validation process in Section 2.5. Finally, we present the final data source in Section 2.6 and the accuracy, sensitivity, and sensibility cut-off points in Section 2.7.

2.1. Materials

In this work, we used the rs-fMRI data provided by ABIDE [33]. The ABIDE I consortium currently offers 1100 rs-fMRI scans from subjects with and without ASD diagnosis. Since our work was not an ASD vs. TD classification, all rs-fMRI data of neurotypical subjects were discarded, leaving 505 preprocessed fMRI scans from subjects with ASD diagnosis. From these ASD data, only 202 had information concerning ADOS scores for communication, social interaction, and repetitive behavior, which are essential data in our classification approach. Thus, the final data comprised 202 ASD subjects.

The original data from fMRI are 3D images over time. Therefore, applying an atlas and a preprocessing pipeline is necessary to transform the 3D images into matrices representing the brain regions (columns) and their respective activities over time (rows). The preprocessing pipeline also removes noises and other undesirable artifacts, which allows better results.

2.1.1. Automated Anatomical Labeling (AAL)

An atlas is a brain mapping that allows us to evaluate brain activity through its regions. We used the AAL atlas [34] available at ABIDE, as it is the most used atlas in the literature for ASD classification using fMRI and ML [21], reaching meaningful outcomes in [18,20,35–37].

In its third version, AAL segments the human brain into 116 ROIs. A detailed explanation of these regions can be seen in [34]. Table 1 presents the AAL's labels.

Table 1. Automated anatomical labeling (ID and name).

ID	Label Name	ID	Label Name	ID	Label Name
0	Precentral.L	39	ParaHippocampal.R	78	Heschl.L
1	Precentral.R	40	Amygdala.L	79	Heschl.R
2	Frontal.S.L	41	Amygdala.R	80	Temporal.S.L
3	Frontal.S.R	42	Calcarine.L	81	Temporal.S.R
4	Frontal.S.Orb.L	43	Calcarine.R	82	Temporal.Pole.S.L
5	Frontal.S.Orb.R	44	Cuneus.L	83	Temporal.Pole.S.R
6	Frontal.Mid.L	45	Cuneus.R	84	Temporal.Mid.L
7	Frontal.Mid.R	46	Lingual.L	85	Temporal.Mid.R
8	Frontal.Mid.Orb.L	47	Lingual.R	86	Temporal.Pole.Mid.L
9	Frontal.Mid.Orb.R	48	Occipital.S.L	87	Temporal.Pole.Mid.R
10	Frontal.Inf.Oper.L	49	Occipital.S.R	88	Temporal.Inf.L
11	Frontal.Inf.Oper.R	50	Occipital.Mid.L	89	Temporal.Inf.R
12	Frontal.Inf.Tri.L	51	Occipital.Mid.R	90	Cerebelum.Crus1.L
13	Frontal.Inf.Tri.R	52	Occipital.Inf.L	91	Cerebelum.Crus1.R
14	Frontal.Inf.Orb.L	53	Occipital.Inf.R	92	Cerebelum.Crus2.L
15	Frontal.Inf.Orb.R	54	Fusiform.L	93	Cerebelum.Crus2.R
16	Rolandic.Oper.L	55	Fusiform.R	94	Cerebelum.3.L
17	Rolandic.Oper.R	56	Postcentral.L	95	Cerebelum.3.R
18	Sp.Motor.Area.L	57	Postcentral.R	96	Cerebelum.4.5.L
19	Sp.Motor.Area.R	58	Parietal.S.L	97	Cerebelum.4.5.R
20	Olfactory.L	59	Parietal.S.R	98	Cerebelum.6.L
21	Olfactory.R	60	Parietal.Inf.L	99	Cerebelum.6.R
22	Frontal.S.Medial.L	61	Parietal.Inf.R	100	Cerebelum.7b.L
23	Frontal.S.Medial.R	62	SraMarginal.L	101	Cerebelum.7b.R
24	Frontal.Med.Orb.L	63	SraMarginal.R	102	Cerebelum.8.L
25	Frontal.Med.Orb.R	64	Angular.L	103	Cerebelum.8.R
26	Rectus.L	65	Angular.R	104	Cerebelum.9.L
27	Rectus.R	66	Precuneus.L	105	Cerebelum.9.R
28	Insula.L	67	Precuneus.R	106	Cerebelum.10.L
29	Insula.R	68	Paracentral.Lobule.L	107	Cerebelum.10.R
30	Cingulum.Ant.L	69	Paracentral.Lobule.R	108	Vermis.1.2
31	Cingulum.Ant.R	70	Caudate.L	109	Vermis.3
32	Cingulum.Mid.L	71	Caudate.R	110	Vermis.4.5
33	Cingulum.Mid.R	72	Putamen.L	111	Vermis.6
34	Cingulum.Post.L	73	Putamen.R	112	Vermis.7
35	Cingulum.Post.R	74	Pallidum.L	113	Vermis.8
36	Hippocampus.L	75	Pallidum.R	114	Vermis.9
37	Hippocampus.R	76	Thalamus.L	115	Vermis.10
38	ParaHippocampal.L	77	Thalamus.R		

2.1.2. Preprocessing Pipeline

Different machines across multiple sites acquired the fMRI data available at ABIDE. Moreover, some sites used different total time acquisition. Thus, some rs-fMRI scans have more frames than others.

The ABIDE offers 884 preprocessed rs-fMRI scans in four pipeline options:

- Connectome Computation System (CCS);
- Configurable Pipeline for the Analysis of Connectomes (CPAC);
- Data Processing Assistant for rs-fMRI (DPARSF);
- Neuroimaging Analysis Kit (NIAK).

These pipelines have different methods and sequences to manage fMRI data, removing noise such as head motion, skull, and magnetic interference. We only used the DPARSF pipeline in this work [26,38,39]. The criteria used for choosing DPARSF were analogous to those employed in the atlas definition process. Except for works where the authors create their preprocessing pipeline, DPARSF is the prevailing pipeline in a number of papers [21], reaching meaningful outcomes in ASD classification using rs-fMRI and ML [37,40–42].

The DPARSF final product is a matrix (X, Y), where X is the number of columns, and Y is the number of rows. Each table column represents one ROI, according to the chosen atlas, and each table row represents the elapsed time during the scan. The number of rows (Y) could differ for each fMRI, even using the same atlas. However, the X value must be the same for all fMRI using the same atlas. For example, in a DPARSF matrix, a value (X_i, Y_j) represents the oxygen level of ROI i at time j.

2.2. ADOS Classification

We used the ADOS standard division for ASD diagnosis to investigate any functional differences in the severity of ASD. The ADOS standard division has previously defined cut-off points to classify subjects as autistic, ASD, or non-ASD. Table 2 shows the maximum scores and the ASD and autism cut-off points for each module (ASD score groups according to the individual's age) and domain areas. For each ADOS module, the first line indicates the maximum value; the second line shows the ASD cut-off point, and the third line indicates the autism cut-off point, according to the domain area.

Table 2. ADOS maximum score and cut off points for ASD [15].

		Comm	SI	IS + Comm	RB
Module 1	*Maximum score*	10	14	24	6
	ASD cut off	2	4	7	-
	Autism cut off	4	7	12	-
Module 2		10	14	24	6
		3	4	8	-
		5	6	12	-
Module 3		8	14	22	8
		2	4	7	-
		3	6	10	-
Module 4		8	14	22	8
		2	4	7	-
		3	6	10	-

Comm (Communication); SI (Social Interaction); IS + Comm (Communication + Social Interaction); RB (Repetitive Behavior).

We adopted the cut-off points from [15] to determine into which class a given subject should be classified, based on their scores available on ABIDE. This way, if a subject scored in at least one domain above the "autism cut-off", they were classified as Class 2 (autism). If the subject did not score above the "autism cut-off" but had at least one domain scoring above the "ASD cut-off", they were classified as Class 1 (ASD). We classified the remaining subjects as non-ASD, discarding them. Tables 3 and 4 show the ABIDE subjects' distribution according to the ADOS class; the complete phenotypes of each subject are available on [33].

Table 3. ASD subjects group.

Subject Index from ABIDE									
51457	50145	50995	51470	50152	51007	50803	50056	51011	50499
50960	50182	51019	50976	51211	51026	50983	51229	50142	50991
50993	51461	50146	51001	51471	50025	51008	50958	50057	51034
51018	50967	51210	51021	50981	51224				

Table 4. Autistic subjects group.

Subject index from ABIDE									
51456	51458	51459	51460	51462	51463	51464	51465	51466	51467
51468	51469	51472	51474	50649	50653	50651	50791	50792	50795
50798	50799	50800	50802	50804	50823	50824	50825	50954	50955
50956	50961	50962	50964	50965	50966	50968	50969	50970	50972
50973	50974	50977	50978	50979	50982	50984	50985	50986	50987
50988	50989	50990	50992	50994	50996	50997	50998	50999	51000
51002	51003	51006	51009	51010	51012	51014	51015	51016	51017
51020	51023	51024	51025	51027	51028	51029	51032	51033	51035
50143	50144	50148	50150	50153	50004	50005	50006	50007	50012
50014	50016	50022	50024	50027	50029	50183	50184	50186	50187
50188	50189	50190	50191	50212	51206	51208	51212	51214	51216
51217	51218	51221	51222	51223	51226	51234	51235	51236	51237
51239	51240	51241	51248	51249	51291	51293	51294	51295	51298
51301	51302	50477	50480	50482	50483	50486	50487	50488	50490
50491	50492	50493	50494	50496	50497	50498	50500	50502	50503
50504	50505	50507	50514	50515	50516	50518	50519	50520	50521
50524	50525	50526	50528	50529	50530				

Tables 5–7 present the phenotype information of the selected subjects.

Table 5. Sex distribution.

Group	Total	Male	Female
ASD	36	32	4
Autistic	166	152	14

Table 6. Age distribution.

Group	AVG	MAX	MIN	Standard Deviation
ASD	16.47	38.76	8.0	7.90
Autistic	17.63	55.4	7.13	8.91

Table 7. FIQ distribution.

Group	AVG	MAX	MIN	Standard Deviation
ASD	108.35	132.0	76.0	13.66
Autistic	104.81	148.0	65.0	16.76

2.3. Region Selection

We grouped the ROIs from AAL by macro regions, considering the region name. The result was a set of regions (SoRs) (e.g., precentral left and right as one SoRs, angular left and right as one SoRs). This process resulted in 35 SoRs containing the ROIs grouped by brain region. We also included one SoRs with all the ROIs.

Table 8 presents the resulting SoRs, where the set ID is the SoRs' identification, and the RoIs IDs match the RoIs used in Table 1.

Table 8. SoRs IDs and their respective RoIs IDs from AAL.

Set ID	ROIs IDs	Set ID	ROIs IDs	Set ID	ROIs IDs	Set ID	ROIs IDs
0	[0, 1]	9	[26, 27]	18	[48, ...,53]	27	[72, 73]
1	[2, ..., 5]	10	[28, 29]	19	[54, 55]	28	[74, 75]
2	[6, ..., 9]	11	[30, ..., 35]	20	[56, 57]	29	[76, 77]
3	[10, ..., 15]	12	[36, 37]	21	[58, ..., 61]	30	[78, 79]
4	[16, 17]	13	[38, 39]	22	[62, 63]	31	[80, ..., 89]
5	[18, 19]	14	[40, 41]	23	[64, 65]	32	[90, ..., 107]
6	[20, 21]	15	[42, 43]	24	[66, 67]	33	[108, ..., 115]
7	[22, 23]	16	[44, 45]	25	[68, 69]	34	ALL
8	[24, 25]	17	[46, 47]	26	[70, 71]		

$[X, ..., Y]$ is a one-to-one incremental sequence where X is the lower limit and Y the superior (e.g., $[1, ..., 4]$ is the same as $[1, 2, 3, 4]$).

This approach aimed: (1) to simplify the SVC classification; and (2) to give a more generic location of the functional differences between ASD classes in a manner that would allow better comparison between existing studies that use different atlases.

2.4. SVC Classifying Algorithm

We used a supervised learning method, support vector machine (SVM), specifically the C-Support Vector Classification (SVC), to check the differences between ASD sub-classes. This method has three steps: training, validation, and test [43,44].

Based on an in-depth systematic review and meta-analysis available in [21], we selected SVM as our ML method. SVM was the most used AI tool for solving ASD classification problems, showing some reliable results when applied in similar situations [18,20,37,45,46]. The second most used method was the artificial neural network (ANN) [21]. Both approaches have similar results in the literature, with SVM slightly better in terms of sensitivity [21]. As our goal was to find potential regions of a biomarker, and due to the complexity of the problem, we decided to adopt SVM given its more direct comparison, facilitating the interpretability of the results. We used the SVM from the scikit-learn library available at [47].

SVM creates a multidimensional plane, where each object (in our case, each subject) will be positioned according to the selected features' value. First, the sample part used for training will determine a curve to split the plane, as shown in Figure 1, where each area corresponds to one class. Then, the validation sample part will verify the accuracy of the curve, and this process will be repeated until the SVM reaches the best angle given the features, training sample, and validation sample. After this, the test sample is used to measure the SVM generalization.

Figure 1. Classification curve generated by SVM with two features.

We hypothesized that higher accuracy would reflect the existence of an interpretative way to differ each class. In other words, SoRs with higher accuracy potentially contain the regions where classes are more distinct regarding the features used. These findings can highlight the areas to consider for further investigations on functional brain activity and ASD severity.

As the main goal was to find regions where there is a functional brain difference in the ASD severity level, and there is a lack of data about SVM setups in previews works on fMRI related to ASD investigations, as observed in [21], we chose a few educated-guess setups in our experiment. The setup was related to the variables *gamma*, *coef0*, *kernel*, *class_weight*, *degree*, and *max_iter*.

The *gamma* delimitates how close the final classification should be regarding the training sample, with more significant values given to more rigid solutions and lower values to given more flexible solutions.

The *coef0* is an independent value related to the scale of the sample. Meanwhile, the *kernel* is the mathematical equation used to solve the problem, and the ones available from [47] are *linear, poly, rbf, sigmoid*.

The *class_weight* option considers the size of each class in the training step, adjusting the weight accordingly. For example, regarding training, if Class 1 has three subjects and Class 2 has nine subjects, Class 1 will weigh three while Class 2 will weigh one. This process is meant to avoid the algorithm taking into account only the dominant class from training, which can jeopardize the SVM's generalization capacity.

The *degree* will define the curve degree of the equation that splits the SVM classification plane. Finally, *max_iter* is the total training iterations allowed to be used by the algorithm, stopping the training when the value is reached, regardless of the gain.

Here, we used the following values for each variable:

- *gamma* = [2,4],
- *coef0* = [1.0],
- *kernel* = [poly],
- *class_weight* = [balanced],
- *degree* = [2,3],
- *max_iter* = [400000].

2.5. Validation Process

We performed a k-fold cross-validation model to validate our process [48–50]. We selected k = 10, which is recommended for samples larger than 200 objects. The SVM automatically split the sample into training and test; in this case, we used the standard 70% to training and 30% for test. Therefore, the 9 folds were sent to the SVM and then split into 7/3 for training and test, and then applied in the 10th fold for validation; the process was repeated until all 10 folds were used as the validation sample.

We adopted the following division criteria to avoid bias noise:

- Amount of subjects of a specific ADOS subclass in each fold, avoiding any fold having only subjects of the same subclass. For example, a fold without autistic subjects could bias the SVC always to answer ASD due to the lack of autistic subjects on training or validation.

We first divided our sample into two groups, ASD and autistic, one for each ADOS subclass. Then, we ordered them by subject ID, and for each group, we designated one subject at a time for each fold: $\{Subject\ 1\ to\ Fold\ 1,\ Subject\ 2\ to\ Fold\ 2,\ Subject\ n\ to\ Fold\ (n\ mod\ 10)\}$.

Thus, each fold had a balanced subclass distribution at the end of this process. Given our sample's limitations, this process aimed to produce the most adaptive learning for our SVC.

2.6. Final Data Source

The resultant data were composed of two files for each subject. The first file contained a matrix where each column represented one of the 116 ROIs from the AAL atlas, and each row represented a picture of the brain over time. The second file was a vector with the subject's phenotype data, including the ADOS score. Since the first row of each fMRI placed the ROI label, we removed it from the file sent to the SVM.

SVM only accept vectors as its input. Therefore, we converted the resulting matrix from DPARSF into a vector. We considered two conversion options: (1) construct a vector from the matrix where the matrix position (X_i, Y_j) is placed on the vector position (Z_{i+i*j}); and (2) acquire the maximum, minimum, median, and average values for each ROI from each SoRs and create a vector $(Z_{a^{max}}, Z_{a^{min}}, Z_{a^{med}}, Z_{a^{avg}}, ..., Z_{b^{max}}, Z_{b^{min}}, Z_{b^{med}}, Z_{b^{avg}})$, where a and b are, respectively, the first and the last ROI ID of a SoRs.

Both conversion options have advantages and drawbacks. The first option has the simplest preprocessing but a more significant need for computer power for the SVC to process all data. On the other hand, the second option has the drawback of a preprocessing pipeline, which will acquire the data from each subject to transform in the four values mentioned above, with loss of information due to transformation. However, due to the size reduction, the SVC requires less computer power to analyze all the data from all subjects. Thus, aiming for better scalability and facilitating human understanding of the results, we chose the second option for this paper.

2.7. Accuracy, Sensitivity, and Specificity Restrictions, and Post-Hoc Tests

We imposed restrictions on the minimum accuracy, sensitivity, and sensibility required to consider a functional difference between the two ASD sub-classes. The cut-off point was 60%, based on values achieved by other ASD vs. non-ASD classification studies [22–24,51–53]. Thus, we discarded results with accuracy (ACC), specificity (SPC), or sensibility (SNS) less than 60%.

Finally, we applied three post-hoc tests on the features from the SoRs that achieved the cut-off: addition of phenotype data, t-test, and p-value. The addition of phenotype data aimed to investigate the effect of sex, age, and FIQ on SVM accuracy for each SoRs, while t-test and p-value aimed to investigate the separability of the sample used, to investigate how they differed from both groups.

3. Results

This section presents the results of our ASD vs. autism classification experiments. All SoRs can be seen in Table 8 and each ROI used by these sets can be seen in Table 1. In this paper, we used specificity (SPC) related to the ASD classification and sensitivity (SNS) associated with the autistic classification.

Our experiments worked with a total of 202 subjects, which comprised 36 with ASD and 166 with autism, according to the ADOS scores. Table 9 shows the SoRs with the ACC, SNS, and SPC greater than or equal to 60%.

Table 9. SoRs above the required threshold.

SoRs ID	ACC	SNS	SPC
11	73.85%	76.50%	60.83%
23	66.28%	67.38%	60.83%
1	64.88%	65.69%	63.33%
30	63.38%	61.47%	70.83%
27	60.90%	60.84%	60.00%

ACC ranged from 60.9% (SoRs 27) to 73.8% (SoRs 11). SNS ranged from 60.8% (SoRs 27) to 76.5% (SoRs 11). SPC ranged from 60.0% (SoRs 27) to 70.8% (SoRs 30). This shows the existence of a non-random separation when considering five brain regions.

The t-test of each feature allows us to understand the difference between the ASD and autistic groups. The t-test results are a statistical difference between any two given groups, and positive values mean that the group 1 average is larger than group 2, while negative values mean that the group 2 average is larger than group 1. Table 10 shows the t-test result for each feature on each SoRs for which SVM had above threshold results, and the positive values mean that the ASD group average is larger than the autistic group for that feature, while negative values mean that the autistic group average is higher.

Table 10. The t-test for features on SoRs with values above required threshold.

Feature	SoRs				
	1	11	23	27	30
1st ROI max	−2.2285	−1.7574	−1.3936	−2.0293	−1.9078
1st ROI min	2.0665	1.9254	1.7192	2.2895	1.8749
1st ROI mean	−0.2457	−0.3619	−0.1699	0.4010	−0.4500
1st ROI STD	0.2434	0.2758	0.0988	−0.4227	0.4915
2nd ROI max	−1.6051	−1.7618	−1.4630	−1.8003	−1.9181
2nd ROI min	1.9787	1.6766	1.4059	2.0074	1.8686
2nd ROI mean	0.3057	−0.4697	−0.0915	−0.8066	0.8104
2nd ROI STD	−0.2794	0.4066	0.0596	0.8234	−0.6772
3rd ROI max	−1.8155	−1.7295	-	-	-
3rd ROI min	1.7308	1.6808	-	-	-
3rd ROI mean	0.0548	0.4520	-	-	-
3rd ROI STD	−0.2010	−0.5442	-	-	-
4th ROI max	−1.6348	−1.7266	-	-	-
4th ROI min	1.8527	1.9396	-	-	-
4th ROI mean	−0.1745	1.8407	-	-	-
4th ROI STD	0.1780	−1.9850	-	-	-

Table 10. Cont.

Feature	SoRs				
	1	11	23	27	30
5th ROI max	-	−1.8367	-	-	-
5th ROI min	-	1.3644	-	-	-
5th ROI mean	-	−0.5116	-	-	-
5th ROI STD	-	0.5581	-	-	-
6th ROI max	-	−1.5904	-	-	-
6th ROI min	-	1.3676	-	-	-
6th ROI mean	-	0.5552	-	-	-
6th ROI STD	-	−0.5744	-	-	-

Furthermore, reinforcing the *t*-test result, the *p*-value (scale [0,1]) of each feature from SoRs above the required threshold is plotted in Table 11. The higher *p*-value was 0.96 for the mean on ROI 4 (Frontal Sup. Orb. Left), the third ROI from SoRs 1, with high values indicating a risk of not being able to distinguish the two groups from each other. On the other hand, lower values indicate a high possibility of discerning the two groups using the feature. The lower *p*-value was 0.02 from the min on ROI 72 (Putamen Left), the first ROI from SoRs 27. The SoRs 1 has a mean *p*-value of 0.45 (0.43 STD), while SoRs 11 has a mean *p*-value of 0.32 (0.14 STD); for SoRs 23, 27, and 30, the mean *p*-value is 0.53 (0.51 STD), 0.30 (0.24 STD), and 0.30 (0.24 STD), respectively. Therefore, SoRs 11 has the lowest *p*-value STD and one of the lowest *p*-value means, which indicates a high probability of containing the largest set of features to classify ASD severity. It is worth noting that these values reflect only our sample and should not be used as a diagnostic tool as further research is needed to either confirm or deny our findings.

Table 11. *p*-values for features on SoRs with values above required threshold.

Feature	SoRs				
	1	11	23	27	30
1st ROI max	**0.02696**	0.08038	0.16498	**0.04375**	0.05785
1st ROI min	**0.04007**	0.05560	0.08713	**0.02309**	0.06227
1st ROI mean	0.80617	0.71784	0.86524	0.68888	0.65319
1st ROI STD	0.80794	0.78296	0.92141	0.67295	0.62359
2nd ROI max	0.11005	0.07963	0.14504	0.07332	0.05652
2nd ROI min	**0.04922**	0.09519	0.16131	**0.04605**	0.06314
2nd ROI mean	0.76015	0.63907	0.92717	0.42088	0.41870
2nd ROI STD	0.78026	0.68474	0.95254	0.41129	0.49906
3rd ROI max	0.07095	0.08527	-	-	-
3rd ROI min	0.08502	0.09437	-	-	-
3rd ROI mean	0.95639	0.65175	-	-	-
3rd ROI STD	0.84090	0.58691	-	-	-
4th ROI max	0.10366	0.08578	-	-	-

Table 11. *Cont.*

Feature	SoRs				
	1	11	23	27	30
4th ROI min	0.06540	0.05384	-	-	-
4th ROI mean	0.86167	0.06715	-	-	-
4th ROI STD	0.85890	**0.04852**	-	-	-
5th ROI max	-	0.06773	-	-	-
5th ROI min	-	0.17396	-	-	-
5th ROI mean	-	0.60950	-	-	-
5th ROI STD	-	0.57737	-	-	-
6th ROI max	-	0.11332	-	-	-
6th ROI min	-	0.17297	-	-	-
6th ROI mean	-	0.57936	-	-	-
6th ROI STD	-	0.56635	-	-	-

Moreover, we performed other trials adding phenotype information (age, sex, and full IQ). We used the same features and added the phenotype data in the vector sent to the ML algorithm. We executed the test for the three phenotypes together, one at a time, and all combinations of two phenotypes. We used the same process for the main experiment; the results that reached the threshold defined in Section 2.7, as well as the ACC gain, using the phenotype for each SoRs are shown in Table 12. However, as shown by [21], these features did not show a significant improvement, if any, in the sample.

Table 12. Results adding phenotype data to the SoRs.

SoRS ID + Phenotype Data	ACC	SNS	SPC	ACC Gain
23 + Sex	68, 88%	70, 58%	62, 5%	2, 595%
27 + Sex	62, 45%	62, 2%	63, 3%	1, 546%
30 + Age	69, 3%	68, 74%	71, 66%	5, 920%
30 + Age and Sex	66, 28%	65, 69%	69, 16%	2, 900%

The missing combinations did not reach the cut-offs in at least one of ACC, SNS, or SPC.

Finally, we show the mean result for each of the features with high ACC both for ASD and autistic in Tables 13 and 14, respectively.

Table 13. Mean values for features on SoRs from ASD sample.

Feature	SoRs				
	1	11	23	27	30
1st ROI max	0.9605	1.6019	2.6961	1.5552	3.0939
1st ROI min	−1.0676	−1.5430	−2.5440	−1.4001	−3.0682
1st ROI mean	0.0000	0.0009	−0.0004	0.0005	−0.0019
1st ROI STD	−0.0341	−0.4287	0.1747	−0.2329	0.9709
2nd ROI max	1.1802	2.8490	2.5306	1.3805	2.3672

Table 13. Cont.

Feature	SoRs				
	1	11	23	27	30
2nd ROI min	−1.0081	−2.8490	−2.5677	−1.3228	−2.3113
2nd ROI mean	0.0000	0.0013	0.0001	−0.0002	0.0000
2nd ROI STD	−0.0025	−0.6258	−0.0893	0.1171	0.0720
3rd ROI max	1.7238	0.9808	-	-	-
3rd ROI min	−1.8015	−1.0159	-	-	-
3rd ROI mean	0.0010	0.0005	-	-	-
3rd ROI STD	−0.5470	−0.2449	-	-	-
4th ROI max	1.7880	1.6496	-	-	-
4th ROI min	−1.6441	−1.5445	-	-	-
4th ROI mean	0.0003	0.0021	-	-	-
4th ROI STD	−0.1568	−1.0049	-	-	-
5th ROI max	-	1.6627	-	-	-
5th ROI min	-	−1.8507	-	-	-
5th ROI mean	-	−0.0001	-	-	-
5th ROI STD	-	0.0597	-	-	-
6th ROI max	-	2.9188	-	-	-
6th ROI min	-	−3.2137	-	-	-
6th ROI mean	-	0.0013	-	-	-
6th ROI STD	-	−0.6678	-	-	-

Table 14. Mean values for features on SoRs from autistic sample.

Feature	SoRs				
	1	11	23	27	30
1st ROI max	1.7303	2.7176	4.1538	2.8470	5.9894
1st ROI min	−1.7637	−2.7257	−4.4038	−2.7160	−5.8292
1st ROI mean	0.0002	0.0013	−0.0002	0.0001	−0.0008
1st ROI STD	−0.1171	−0.5762	0.1041	−0.0193	0.3691
2nd ROI max	1.9003	4.5360	4.1990	2.3653	4.1346
2nd ROI min	−1.8646	−4.4891	−4.0994	−2.3611	−3.9732
2nd ROI mean	−0.0002	0.0021	0.0003	0.0003	−0.0011
2nd ROI STD	0.0790	−0.9468	−0.1331	−0.1156	0.4724
3rd ROI max	2.8208	1.6436	-	-	-
3rd ROI min	−2.8687	−1.6166	-	-	-
3rd ROI mean	0.0010	0.0003	-	-	-

Table 14. Cont.

Feature	SoRs				
	1	11	23	27	30
3rd ROI STD	−0.4340	−0.1223	-	-	-
4th ROI max	2.8618	2.8466	-	-	-
4th ROI min	−2.8870	−2.6779	-	-	-
4th ROI mean	0.0006	0.0001	-	-	-
4th ROI STD	−0.2536	−0.0148	-	-	-
5th ROI max	-	2.6724	-	-	-
5th ROI min	-	−2.6525	-	-	-
5th ROI mean	-	0.0003	-	-	-
5th ROI STD	-	−0.1597	-	-	-
6th ROI max	-	4.6039	-	-	-
6th ROI min	-	−4.9155	-	-	-
6th ROI mean	-	0.0003	-	-	-
6th ROI STD	-	−0.1874	-	-	-

4. Discussion

This paper assessed brain functional differences between ASD and autism using rs-fMRI and SVM classification (SVC). The measure used to distinguish ASD from autism was the ADOS score and cut-off points, as seen in Table 2.

Our results highlight some brain regions that potentially can distinguish functional differences between both groups (ASD vs. autism). The main finding in distinguishing the two ASD sub-classes reached up to 73.8% accuracy (SoRs 11). These results need to be taken with caution due to the limitations mentioned and given its Matthews Correlation Coefficient of 0.31 (scale [−1,1]), which is better than a random selection but still not ideal. However, our results show a promising path to investigate the functional difference between both ASD sub-classes.

The best ACC was reached for SoRs 11, consisting of the cingulate gyrus (cingulum), and both left and right sides of the brain for the anterior, median, and posterior. We can conjecture that brain regions such as the cingulum (73.8% ACC, 76.5% SNS, 60.8% SPC) and angular (SoRs 23) (66.3% ACC, 67.4% SNS, 60.8% SPC) have the potential to differentiate the severity of ASD subjects taking into consideration the ACC reached on this experiment. These SoRs applied together with methods such as ADOS may in the future allow professionals to classify individuals. The frontal lobe (SoRs 1) (64.9% ACC, 65.7% SNS, 63.3% SPC) also should be considered for further investigations as it shows reasonable ACC.

Our results support previous studies [54–56] that point to the cingulum region functions differences between ASD vs. TD. Likewise, [19,40] detected the thalamus as a key region for classifying ASD vs. TD, and [57–60] pointed to the frontal lobe as a region where ASD vs. TD can be differentiated from each other. Angular (SoRs 23) [61,62], Heschl (SoRs 30) [63,64], and putamen (SoRs 27) [65,66] also have consistently been linked to ASD.

Since these brain regions are commonly pointed to as an ASD vs. TD differential, we can also suppose, based on our results, that such regions have the potential to describe areas where functional activity may be a biomarker for ASD severity, supporting previous investigations [64]. Therefore, we can presume the potential functional difference between subjects from the ASD group and the autism group using these ROIs.

5. Conclusions

Firstly, and most importantly, the field lacks sample data to strengthen the recent outcomes. We believe that all published studies have insufficient samples to ensure definitive conclusions on ML applied to fMRI for ASD diagnoses. For example, the ADOS used hundreds of thousands of subjects to validate its algorithm, while the sum of all subjects from all published papers regarding ML applied to fMRI (discounting the subjects duplicated for multiple studies) is not even close to this value. Therefore, any claim to solve the issue tends to be premature. Nevertheless, it is mandatory to research possible biomarkers while waiting for more available data to validate the findings.

We investigated the functional brain activity difference between ADOS ASD subclasses (autism and ASD) using fMRI data from subjects previously diagnosed and available at ABIDE. The differences between each ASD sub-class were the ADOS score and cut-off points. We applied these data to train an ML classification algorithm (SVC) to classify the disorder severity, investigating the existence of functional brain differences across regions between both ASD sub-classes.

Our main contribution was the identification of five SoRs that potentially have discriminating patterns for ASD severity. Additionally, the suggested use of SoRs can help to improve investigations by allowing more clarity in interpreting and comparing the results, aiming to enable physicians to look up the same markers found by the ML. In this same aspect, opting to explore approaches using features more easily observed by human analyses, such as the maximum, minimum, mean, and standard deviation from each ROI, is also another contribution. These contributions can improve further research to give tools for physicians to utilize these signals when evaluating a subject, more than simply finding an ML to aid the ASD evaluation.

Our findings are consistent with previous studies on autism and brain development, bringing a promising approach to evaluating ASD subtypes. A computational aid system could improve medical diagnosis by delivering more tools for physicians' evaluation, reducing analysis ambiguity. Further research, applied to a younger sample, can allow a computational system to assess individuals early, before the most severe symptoms begin. Distinguishing the severity of a subject can help in intervention selection, and earlier diagnosis can help set proper interventions to improve the individual's quality of life.

Our study limitations lie mainly in the reduced sample size, which may not generalize our outcomes for all populations. However, we can speculate about these functional differences between the ASD subtypes.

Another limitation of the study was the mean age of the subjects ($\approx$16 years old), which does not correspond to early diagnosis. Therefore, an additional experiment with younger subjects will be required to improve the results' reliability.

For further works, an increase in the available subjects, including younger ones, would help to raise the accuracy as it would help to clarify how many of our results can be generalized to all populations. In addition, the research community would benefit from more available fMRI data with the respective phenotype data (such as ADOS score, age at scan, sex, FIQ), allowing more accurate investigations.

Author Contributions: Conceptualization, I.D.R., E.A.d.C., C.P.S. and G.S.B.; methodology, I.D.R. and E.A.d.C.; software, I.D.R.; validation, I.D.R., E.A.d.C. and C.P.S.; formal analysis, I.D.R.; investigation, I.D.R. and E.A.d.C.; resources, I.D.R. and G.S.B.; data curation, I.D.R.; writing—original draft preparation, I.D.R.; writing—review and editing, I.D.R., E.A.d.C. and C.P.S.; visualization, I.D.R. and E.A.d.C.; supervision, G.S.B. and E.A.d.C.; project administration, G.S.B.; funding acquisition, G.S.B. All authors have read and agreed to the published version of the manuscript.

Funding: This study was financed in part by the Coordenação de Aperfeiçoamento de Pessoal de Nível Superior—Brazil (CAPES)—Finance Code 001, and the Fundação de Amparo à Pesquisa do Estado de Minas Gerais (FAPEMIG) (APQ-01565-18).

Institutional Review Board Statement: Ethical review and approval were waived for this study due to the use of publicly available, previously published data.

Informed Consent Statement: This study use of publicly available, previously published data from ABIDE.

Data Availability Statement: Not applicable.

Conflicts of Interest: The authors declare no conflict of interest.

References

1. American Psychiatric Association. *DSM-5: Diagnostic and Statistical Manual of Mental Disorders*; Artmed Editora: Porto Alegre, RS, Brazil, 2014.
2. Maenner, M.J.; Shaw, K.A.; Bakian, A.V.; Bilder, D.A.; Durkin, M.S.; Esler, A.; Furnier, S.M.; Hallas, L.; Hall-Lande, J.; Hudson, A.; et al. Prevalence and characteristics of autism spectrum disorder among children aged 8 years—Autism and developmental disabilities monitoring network, 11 sites, United States, 2018. *MMWR Surveill. Summ.* **2021**, *70*, 1–16. [CrossRef]
3. Maenner, M.J.; Shaw, K.A.; Baio, J.; Washington, A.; Patrick, M.; DiRienzo, M.; Christensen, D.L.; Wiggins, L.D.; Pettygrove, S.; Andrews, G.; et al. Prevalence of autism spectrum disorder among children aged 8 years—Autism and developmental disabilities monitoring network, 11 sites, United States, 2016. *MMWR Surveill. Summ.* **2020**, *69*, 1–12. [CrossRef] [PubMed]
4. Loomes, R.; Hull, L.; Mandy, W.P.L. What is the male-to-female ratio in autism spectrum disorder? A systematic review and meta-analysis. *J. Am. Acad. Child Adolesc. Psychiatry* **2017**, *56*, 466–474. [CrossRef] [PubMed]
5. Bai, D.; Yip, B.H.K.; Windham, G.C.; Sourander, A.; Francis, R.; Yoffe, R.; Glasson, E.; Mahjani, B.; Suominen, A.; Leonard, H.; et al. Association of genetic and environmental factors with autism in a 5-country cohort. *JAMA Psychiatry* **2019**, *76*, 1035–1043. [CrossRef] [PubMed]
6. Sandin, S.; Lichtenstein, P.; Kuja-Halkola, R.; Hultman, C.; Larsson, H.; Reichenberg, A. The heritability of autism spectrum disorder. *JAMA* **2017**, *318*, 1182–1184. [CrossRef] [PubMed]
7. Carvalho, E.A.; Santana, C.P.; Rodrigues, I.D.; Lacerda, L.; Bastos, G.S. Hidden Markov Models to Estimate the Probability of Having Autistic Children. *IEEE Access* **2020**, *8*, 99540–99551. [CrossRef]
8. Shimabukuro, T.T.; Grosse, S.D.; Rice, C. Medical expenditures for children with an autism spectrum disorder in a privately insured population. *J. Autism Dev. Disord.* **2008**, *38*, 546–552. [CrossRef]
9. Amendah, D.; Grosse, S.; Peacock, G.; Mandell, D. The economic costs of autism: A review. *Autism Spectr. Disord.* **2011**, *168*, 1347–1360.
10. Durkin, M.S.; Elsabbagh, M.; Barbaro, J.; Gladstone, M.; Happe, F.; Hoekstra, R.A.; Lee, L.C.; Rattazzi, A.; Stapel-Wax, J.; Stone, W.L.; et al. Autism screening and diagnosis in low resource settings: Challenges and opportunities to enhance research and services worldwide. *Autism Res.* **2015**, *8*, 473–476. [CrossRef]
11. Brazil's Ministry of Health. *Diretrizes de Atenção à Reabilitação da Pessoa com Transtorno do Espectro Autista (TEA)*; Brazil's Ministry of Health: Brasilia, Brazil, 2014.
12. Hazlett, H.C.; Gu, H.; Munsell, B.C.; Kim, S.H.; Styner, M.; Wolff, J.J.; Elison, J.T.; Swanson, M.R.; Zhu, H.; Botteron, K.N.; et al. Early brain development in infants at high risk for autism spectrum disorder. *Nature* **2017**, *542*, 348. [CrossRef]
13. Alves, F.J.; De Carvalho, E.A.; Aguilar, J.; De Brito, L.L.; Bastos, G.S. Applied behavior analysis for the treatment of autism: A systematic review of assistive technologies *IEEE Access* **2020**, *8*, 118664–118672. [CrossRef]
14. McCrimmon, A.; Rostad, K. Test Review: Autism Diagnostic Observation Schedule, (ADOS-2) Manual (Part II): Toddler Module. *J. Psychoeduc. Assess.* **2014**, *32*, 88–92.
15. Lord, C.; Risi, S.; Lambrecht, L.; Cook, E.H.; Leventhal, B.L.; DiLavore, P.C.; Pickles, A.; Rutter, M. The Autism Diagnostic Observation Schedule–Generic: A standard measure of social and communication deficits associated with the spectrum of autism. *J. Autism Dev. Disord.* **2000**, *30*, 205–223. [CrossRef] [PubMed]
16. Falkmer, T.; Anderson, K.; Falkmer, M.; Horlin, C. Diagnostic procedures in autism spectrum disorders: A systematic literature review. *Eur. Child Adolesc. Psychiatry* **2013**, *22*, 329–340. [CrossRef]
17. Ghiassian, S.; Greiner, R.; Jin, P.; Brown, M. Learning to classify psychiatric disorders based on fMR images: Autism vs healthy and ADHD vs healthy. In Proceedings of the 3rd NIPS Workshop on Machine Learning and Interpretation in NeuroImaging, Chico, CA, USA, 5 December 2013; pp. 9–10.
18. Mahanand, B.S.; Vigneshwaran, S.; Suresh, S.; Sundararajan, N. An enhanced effect-size thresholding method for the diagnosis of Autism Spectrum Disorder using resting state functional MRI. In Proceedings of the 2016 Second International Conference on Cognitive Computing and Information Processing (CCIP), Mysuru, India, 12–13 August 2016; pp. 1–6. [CrossRef]
19. Iidaka, T. Resting state functional magnetic resonance imaging and neural network classified autism and control. *Cortex* **2015**, *63*, 55–67. [CrossRef] [PubMed]
20. Bi, X.A.; Wang, Y.; Shu, Q.; Sun, Q.; Xu, Q. Classification of Autism Spectrum Disorder Using Random Support Vector Machine Cluster. *Front. Genet.* **2018**, *9*, 18. [CrossRef] [PubMed]
21. Santana, C.P.; Carvalho, E.A.D.; Rodrigues, I.D.; Bastos, G.S.; Souza, A.D.D.; Brito, L.L.D. rs-fMRI and machine learning for ASD diagnosis: A systematic review and meta-analysis. *Sci. Rep.* **2022**, *12*, 6030. [CrossRef]
22. Chaitra, N.; Vijaya, P.A. Comparing univalent and bivalent brain functional connectivity measures using machine learning. In Proceedings of the 2017 Fourth International Conference on Signal Processing, Communication and Networking (ICSCN), Chennai, India, 16–18 March 2017; pp. 1–5.

23. Abraham, A.; Milham, M.P.; Di Martino, A.; Craddock, R.C.; Samaras, D.; Thirion, B.; Varoquaux, G. Deriving reproducible biomarkers from multi-site resting-state data: An Autism-based example. *NeuroImage* **2017**, *147*, 736–745. [CrossRef] [PubMed]
24. Zu, C.; Gao, Y.; Munsell, B.; Kim, M.; Peng, Z.; Zhu, Y.; Gao, W.; Zhang, D.; Shen, D.; Wu, G. Identifying High Order Brain Connectome Biomarkers via Learning on Hypergraph. In Proceedings of the Machine Learning in Medical Imaging, Athens, Greece, 17 October 2016; Wang, L., Adeli, E., Wang, Q., Shi, Y., Suk, H.I., Eds.; Springer International Publishing: Cham, Switzerland, 2016; pp. 1–9.
25. Heeger, D.J.; Ress, D. What does fMRI tell us about neuronal activity? *Nat. Rev. Neurosci.* **2002**, *3*, 142–151. [CrossRef] [PubMed]
26. Yan, C.; Zang, Y. DPARSF: A MATLAB toolbox for "pipeline" data analysis of resting-state fMRI. *Front. Syst. Neurosci.* **2010**, *4*, 13. [CrossRef]
27. Grossi, E.; Olivieri, C.; Buscema, M. Diagnosis of autism through EEG processed by advanced computational algorithms: A pilot study. *Comput. Methods Programs Biomed.* **2017**, *142*, 73–79. [CrossRef]
28. Ibrahim, S.; Djemal, R.; Alsuwailem, A. Electroencephalography (EEG) signal processing for epilepsy and autism spectrum disorder diagnosis. *Biocybern. Biomed. Eng.* **2018**, *38*, 16–26. [CrossRef]
29. Kang, J.; Han, X.; Song, J.; Niu, Z.; Li, X. The identification of children with autism spectrum disorder by SVM approach on EEG and eye-tracking data. *Comput. Biol. Med.* **2020**, *120*, 103722. [CrossRef] [PubMed]
30. Peya, Z.J.; Akhand, M.; Ferdous Srabonee, J.; Siddique, N. EEG Based Autism Detection Using CNN Through Correlation Based Transformation of Channels' Data. In Proceedings of the 2020 IEEE Region 10 Symposium (TENSYMP), Dhaka, Bangladesh, 5–7 June 2020; pp. 1278–1281. [CrossRef]
31. Jayawardana, Y.; Jaime, M.; Jayarathna, S. Analysis of temporal relationships between ASD and brain activity through EEG and machine learning. In Proceedings of the 2019 IEEE 20th International Conference on Information Reuse and Integration for Data Science (IRI), Los Angeles, CA, USA, 30 July–1 August 2019; pp. 151–158.
32. Bajestani, G.S.; Behrooz, M.; Khani, A.G.; Nouri-Baygi, M.; Mollaei, A. Diagnosis of autism spectrum disorder based on complex network features. *Comput. Methods Programs Biomed.* **2019**, *177*, 277–283. [CrossRef] [PubMed]
33. Craddock, C.; Benhajali, Y.; Chu, C.; Chouinard, F.; Evans, A.; Jakab, A.; Khundrakpam, B.S.; Lewis, J.D.; Li, Q.; Milham, M.; et al. The Neuro Bureau Preprocessing Initiative: Open sharing of preprocessed neuroimaging data and derivatives. In Proceedings of the Neuroinformatics 2013, Stockholm, Sweden, 27 August–29 August 2013. [CrossRef]
34. Rolls, E.T.; Huang, C.C.; Lin, C.P.; Feng, J.; Joliot, M. Automated anatomical labelling atlas 3. *NeuroImage* **2019**, *206*, 116–189. [CrossRef]
35. Zhu, Y.; Zhu, X.; Kim, M.; Yan, J.; Wu, G. A Tensor Statistical Model for Quantifying Dynamic Functional Connectivity. In Proceedings of the Information Processing in Medical Imaging, Boone, NC, USA, 25–30 June 2017; Niethammer, M., Styner, M., Aylward, S., Zhu, H., Oguz, I., Yap, P.T., Shen, D., Eds.; Springer International Publishing: Cham, Switzerland, 2017; pp. 398–410.
36. Crimi, A.; Dodero, L.; Murino, V.; Sona, D. Case-control discrimination through effective brain connectivity. In Proceedings of the 2017 IEEE 14th International Symposium on Biomedical Imaging (ISBI 2017), Melbourne, Australia, 18–21 April 2017; pp. 970–973.
37. Bi, X.A.; Chen, J.; Sun, Q.; Liu, Y.; Wang, Y.; Luo, X. Analysis of Asperger Syndrome Using Genetic-Evolutionary Random Support Vector Machine Cluster. *Front. Physiol.* **2018**, *9*, 1646. [CrossRef]
38. Ashburner, J. A fast diffeomorphic image registration algorithm. *NeuroImage* **2007**, *38*, 95–113. [CrossRef]
39. Ashburner, J.; Friston, K.J. Unified segmentation. *NeuroImage* **2005**, *26*, 839–851. [CrossRef]
40. Subbaraju, V.; Suresh, M.B.; Sundaram, S.; Narasimhan, S. Identifying differences in brain activities and an accurate detection of autism spectrum disorder using resting state functional-magnetic resonance imaging: A spatial filtering approach. *Med. Image Anal.* **2017**, *35*, 375–389. [CrossRef]
41. Jun, E.; Suk, H.I. Region-Wise Stochastic Pattern Modeling for Autism Spectrum Disorder Identification and Temporal Dynamics Analysis. In Proceedings of the International Workshop on Connectomics in Neuroimaging, Quebec City, QC, Canada, 14 September 2017; Springer: Berlin/Heidelberg, Germany, 2017; pp. 143–151.
42. Zhu, Y.; Zhu, X.; Zhang, H.; Gao, W.; Shen, D.; Wu, G. Reveal consistent spatial-temporal patterns from dynamic functional connectivity for autism spectrum disorder identification. In Proceedings of the International conference on Medical Image Computing and Computer-Assisted Intervention, Athens, Greece, 17 October 2016; Springer: Berlin/Heidelberg, Germany, 2016; pp. 106–114.
43. Chang, C.C.; Lin, C.J. LIBSVM: A library for support vector machines. *ACM Trans. Intell. Syst. Technol. (TIST)* **2011**, *2*, 27. [CrossRef]
44. Platt, J.C. Probabilistic outputs for support vector machines and comparisons to regularized likelihood methods. *Adv. Large Margin Classif.* **1999**, *10*, 61–74.
45. Sartipi, S.; Kalbkhani, H.; Shayesteh, M.G. Ripplet II transform and higher order cumulants from R-fMRI data for diagnosis of autism. In Proceedings of the 2017 10th International Conference on Electrical and Electronics Engineering (ELECO), Bursa, Turkey, 30 November–2 December 2017; pp. 557–560.
46. Ren, Y.; Hu, X.; Lv, J.; Quo, L.; Han, J.; Liu, T. Identifying autism biomarkers in default mode network using sparse representation of resting-state fMRI data. In Proceedings of the 2016 IEEE 13th International Symposium on Biomedical Imaging (ISBI), Prague, Czech Republic, 13–16 April 2016; pp. 1278–1281. [CrossRef]

47. Pedregosa, F.; Varoquaux, G.; Gramfort, A.; Michel, V.; Thirion, B.; Grisel, O.; Blondel, M.; Prettenhofer, P.; Weiss, R.; Dubourg, V.; et al. Scikit-learn: Machine Learning in Python. *J. Mach. Learn. Res.* **2011**, *12*, 2825–2830.
48. Bengio, Y.; Grandvalet, Y. No unbiased estimator of the variance of k-fold cross-validation. *J. Mach. Learn. Res.* **2004**, *5*, 1089–1105.
49. Rodriguez, J.D.; Perez, A.; Lozano, J.A. Sensitivity analysis of k-fold cross validation in prediction error estimation. *IEEE Trans. Pattern Anal. Mach. Intell.* **2009**, *32*, 569–575. [CrossRef] [PubMed]
50. Fushiki, T. Estimation of prediction error by using K-fold cross-validation. *Stat. Comput.* **2011**, *21*, 137–146. [CrossRef]
51. Dodero, L.; Sambataro, F.; Murino, V.; Sona, D. Kernel-Based Analysis of Functional Brain Connectivity on Grassmann Manifold. In Proceedings of the Medical Image Computing and Computer-Assisted Intervention—MICCAI 2015, Munich, Germany, 5–9 October 2015; Navab, N., Hornegger, J., Wells, W.M., Frangi, A.F., Eds.; Springer International Publishing: Cham, Switzerland, 2015; pp. 604–611.
52. Dodero, L.; Minh, H.Q.; Biagio, M.S.; Murino, V.; Sona, D. Kernel-based classification for brain connectivity graphs on the Riemannian manifold of positive definite matrices. In Proceedings of the 2015 IEEE 12th International Symposium on Biomedical Imaging (ISBI), Brooklyn, NY, USA, 16–19 April 2015; pp. 42–45.
53. Bhaumik, R.; Pradhan, A.; Das, S.; Bhaumik, D. Predicting Autism Spectrum Disorder Using Domain-Adaptive Cross-Site Evaluation. *Neuroinformatics* **2018**, *16*, 197–205. [CrossRef]
54. Hau, J.; Aljawad, S.; Baggett, N.; Fishman, I.; Carper, R.A.; Müller, R.A. The cingulum and cingulate U-fibers in children and adolescents with autism spectrum disorders. *Hum. Brain Mapp.* **2019**, *40*, 3153–3164. [CrossRef]
55. Ikuta, T.; Shafritz, K.M.; Bregman, J.; Peters, B.D.; Gruner, P.; Malhotra, A.K.; Szeszko, P.R. Abnormal cingulum bundle development in autism: A probabilistic tractography study. *Psychiatry Res. Neuroimaging* **2014**, *221*, 63–68. [CrossRef]
56. Ameis, S.; Fan, J.; Rockel, C.; Soorya, L.; Wang, A.; Anagnostou, E. Altered cingulum bundle microstructure in autism spectrum disorder. *Acta Neuropsychiatr.* **2013**, *25*, 275–282. [CrossRef]
57. Sundaram, S.K.; Kumar, A.; Makki, M.I.; Behen, M.E.; Chugani, H.T.; Chugani, D.C. Diffusion Tensor Imaging of Frontal Lobe in Autism Spectrum Disorder. *Cereb. Cortex* **2008**, *18*, 2659–2665. [CrossRef]
58. Carper, R.A.; Courchesne, E. Localized enlargement of the frontal cortex in early autism. *Biol. Psychiatry* **2005**, *57*, 126–133. [CrossRef]
59. Zilbovicius, M.; Garreau, B.; Samson, Y.; Remy, P.; Barthélémy, C.; Syrota, A.; Lelord, G. Delayed maturation of the frontal cortex in childhood autism. *Am. J. Psychiatry* **1995**, *152*, 248–252. [CrossRef] [PubMed]
60. Carper, R.A.; Courchesne, E. Inverse correlation between frontal lobe and cerebellum sizes in children with autism. *Brain* **2000**, *123*, 836–844. [CrossRef] [PubMed]
61. Long, Z.; Huang, J.; Li, B.; Li, Z.; Li, Z.; Chen, H.; Jing, B. A Comparative Atlas-Based Recognition of Mild Cognitive Impairment With Voxel-Based Morphometry. *Front. Neurosci.* **2018**, *12*, 916. [CrossRef] [PubMed]
62. Liu, J.; Yao, L.; Zhang, W.; Xiao, Y.; Liu, L.; Gao, X.; Shah, C.; Li, S.; Tao, B.; Gong, Q.; et al. Gray matter abnormalities in pediatric autism spectrum disorder: A meta-analysis with signed differential mapping. *Eur. Child Adolesc. Psychiatry* **2017**, *26*, 933–945. [CrossRef]
63. Prigge, M.D.; Bigler, E.D.; Fletcher, P.T.; Zielinski, B.A.; Ravichandran, C.; Anderson, J.; Froehlich, A.; Abildskov, T.; Papadopolous, E.; Maasberg, K.; et al. Longitudinal Heschl's Gyrus Growth During Childhood and Adolescence in Typical Development and Autism. *Autism Res.* **2013**, *6*, 78–90. [CrossRef]
64. Kaku, S.M.; Jayashankar, A.; Girimaji, S.C.; Bansal, S.; Gohel, S.; Bharath, R.D.; Srinath, S. Early childhood network alterations in severe autism. *Asian J. Psychiatry* **2019**, *39*, 114–119. [CrossRef]
65. Sato, W.; Kubota, Y.; Kochiyama, T.; Uono, S.; Yoshimura, S.; Sawada, R.; Sakihama, M.; Toichi, M. Increased putamen volume in adults with autism spectrum disorder. *Front. Hum. Neurosci.* **2014**, *8*, 957. [CrossRef]
66. Hollander, E.; Anagnostou, E.; Chaplin, W.; Esposito, K.; Haznedar, M.M.; Licalzi, E.; Wasserman, S.; Soorya, L.; Buchsbaum, M. Striatal volume on magnetic resonance imaging and repetitive behaviors in autism. *Biol. Psychiatry* **2005**, *58*, 226–232. [CrossRef]

Article

Semi-Automatic Multiparametric MR Imaging Classification Using Novel Image Input Sequences and 3D Convolutional Neural Networks

Bochong Li [1,*], Ryo Oka [2], Ping Xuan [3], Yuichiro Yoshimura [4] and Toshiya Nakaguchi [5]

1. Graduate School of Science and Technology, Chiba University, Chiba-shi 263-8522, Japan
2. Department of Urology, Toho University Sakura Medical Center, Sakura-shi 285-8741, Japan; ryou.oka@med.toho-u.ac.jp
3. School of Computer Science and Technology, Heilongjiang University, Harbin 150080, China; xuanpinghdu@gmail.com
4. School of Medicine, Toyama University, Toyama 930-8555, Japan; yysmr13@gmail.com
5. Center for Frontier Medical Engineering, Chiba University, Chiba-shi 263-8522, Japan; nakaguchi@faculty.chiba-u.jp
* Correspondence: li.bochong@chiba-u.jp

Citation: Li, B.; Oka, R.; Xuan, P.; Yoshimura, Y.; Nakaguchi, T. Semi-Automatic Multiparametric MR Imaging Classification Using Novel Image Input Sequences and 3D Convolutional Neural Networks. *Algorithms* 2022, 15, 248. https://doi.org/10.3390/a15070248

Academic Editor: Lucia Maddalena

Received: 21 May 2022
Accepted: 16 July 2022
Published: 18 July 2022

Publisher's Note: MDPI stays neutral with regard to jurisdictional claims in published maps and institutional affiliations.

Copyright: © 2022 by the authors. Licensee MDPI, Basel, Switzerland. This article is an open access article distributed under the terms and conditions of the Creative Commons Attribution (CC BY) license (https://creativecommons.org/licenses/by/4.0/).

Abstract: The role of multi-parametric magnetic resonance imaging (mp-MRI) is becoming increasingly important in the diagnosis of the clinical severity of prostate cancer (PCa). However, mp-MRI images usually contain several unaligned 3D sequences, such as DWI image sequences and T2-weighted image sequences, and there are many images among the entirety of 3D sequence images that do not contain cancerous tissue, which affects the accuracy of large-scale prostate cancer detection. Therefore, there is a great need for a method that uses accurate computer-aided detection of mp-MRI images and minimizes the influence of useless features. Our proposed PCa detection method is divided into three stages: (i) multimodal image alignment, (ii) automatic cropping of the sequence images to the entire prostate region, and, finally, (iii) combining multiple modal images of each patient into novel 3D sequences and using 3D convolutional neural networks to learn the newly composed 3D sequences with different modal alignments. We arrange the different modal methods to make the model fully learn the cancerous tissue features; then, we predict the clinical severity of PCa and generate a 3D cancer response map for the 3D sequence images from the last convolution layer of the network. The prediction results and 3D response map help to understand the features that the model focuses on during the process of 3D-CNN feature learning. We applied our method to Toho hospital prostate cancer patient data; the AUC (=0.85) results were significantly higher than those of other methods.

Keywords: prostate cancer; computer-aided detection; magnetic resonance imaging; machine learning

1. Introduction

Prostate cancer [1] is currently one of the deadliest cancers in men, with a very high incidence and death rate each year. According to the World Health Organization, in 2020, about 1.41 million people suffered from prostate cancer and 380,000 died from it [2]. Early diagnosis and treatment of prostate cancer can be highly effective in preventing the development of cancerous tissue and metastasis into advanced prostate cancer, effectively improving the five-year survival rate of prostate cancer patients and reducing patients' suffering. The diagnosis of PCa is currently made clinically with a prostate-specific antigen (PSA) [3] blood test and digital rectal examination (DRE) [2], followed by a transrectal ultrasound (TRUS) biopsy if the PSA test result is positive. However, due to the limited number of biopsy samples and/or the low ultrasound resolution of TRUS [4], lesions may be missed or the Gleason score (GS) determined from the biopsy sample may differ in repeat biopsies and, sometimes, from the score determined by radical prostatectomy.

Moreover, prostate cancer is classified as clinically severe or clinically non-severe based on the GS, which is currently ≤ 7 for clinically non-severe prostate cancer and ≥ 8 for clinically severe prostate cancer. According to recent studies [3,5], the diagnosis of prostate cancer using PSA and biopsy has low sensitivity and specificity, which can lead to underdiagnoses and overtreatment, thus causing unnecessary suffering to patients. According to a recent study [6], the positive predictive values of DRE, TRUS, mpMRI, and TPSA levels for PCa were 39.91%, 39.38%, 64.14%, and 41.57%, respectively; the sensitivity of these parameters was 37.35%, 51.41%, 74.69%, and 57.43%, respectively; the specificity of these parameters was 62.26%, 46.90%, 71.97%, and 45.82%, respectively. Recent studies have demonstrated that multi-parametric magnetic resonance imaging (mp-MRI) [7–9] can provide a simpler, non-invasive, and more accurate method of detecting prostate cancer. By combining images different MRI modalities, these previous studies showed that mp-MRI images have a higher detection rate and better sensitivity and specificity for prostate cancer; because of the non-invasive and highly detectable nature of MRI, more and more studies are focusing on the classification of the clinical severity of prostate cancer under multiple modalities [10]. However, it is very difficult to manually perform operations such as classification and judgment of mp-MRI because there is a large number of images for each patient, thus requiring much time and expertise on the part of the radiologist for judging and interpretation analysis. In addition, due to the subjectiveness of the radiologist, there will be low sensitivity and specificity in analyzing and judging the images [11], especially in the articulation of different regions of the prostate. Therefore, there is a need for a computer-assisted prostate cancer classification method that can reduce the time required to classify prostate cancer and improve the specificity and sensitivity of prostate cancer diagnosis. In recent studies [6,12–21], methods were developed for automatic prostate cancer detection, diagnosis, and classification. Currently, the prostate cancer diagnosis method consists of three main parts: first, data pre-processing (cropping the overall prostate image to the prostate region or specific cancer site region); second, inputting the pre-processed image into a deep learning network for feature learning to obtain a feature map of the prostate; finally, outputting the results of the cancer grade according to the voxels in the learned feature map. The first computer-aided diagnosis system for prostate cancer, which was designed by Chen et al. [22], extracts pixel features from T2-weighted images (T2) with a matrix and discrete cosine transform, and then uses an SVM classifier to classify the peripheral regions of the prostate. In addition, Langer et al. [23] classified the peripheral zone (PZ) of the prostate using a dynamic contrast-enhanced (DCE) map, and Tiwari et al. [24] designed a classification system using semi-supervised multi-modal data. However, these studies separated different regions of the prostate, causing cancer at the junction of different regions to be easily missed and global features of the prostate to be ignored. Many recent studies focused on improving neural network models, but it is known that deep learning is still almost a black-box [25] system, and the intermediate learning process is difficult to understand. Therefore, there is the field of explainable deep learning, including CAM (class activation mapping) [26] technology, which uses feature visualization to explore the working mechanisms of deep convolutional neural networks and the basis of judgment. However, when implementing CAM, it is necessary to change the structure of the network itself; thus, Grad-cam was investigated on the basis of CAM [27]. Grad-cam can be implemented without changing the structure of the network itself and can extract the heat map of features of any layer, and a recent study investigated Grad-cam++ [28] in order to optimize the results of Grad-cam and make the positioning more accurate.

In this paper, we design a novel method for prostate cancer classification based on fusing image features under multiple modalities to enable the classification of the clinical severity of prostate cancer with a single input rather than using a costly multiple-input method with complex training. Specifically, we align the T2 and DWI images of the same patient to align the prostate region in space, crop the whole MRI image to the prostate region, fuse the aligned images with the T2 and DWI images to form a new 3D image sequence ("sequence" is used in this article to refer to the "input sequence" of a neural network, not to refer to an MRI acquisition sequence), and then input the new 3D sequence into the 3D-CNN for feature learning. Finally, we output the features for prostate cancer severity classification and visualize the learning interest points of the network using the improved 3D-Grad-cam.

In this study, there are three main contributions:

(a) We developed a novel 3D-CNN input method that maintains the advantage of a low training cost for a single input and the advantage of multi-modal feature fusion of previous multi-input models, such that the model can fully fuse multi-modal features and facilitate network prediction with a single input.
(b) We improve the category activation map based on CAM by using the category activation map in a 3D image sequence to obtain a 3D-Grad-cam to facilitate our visualization of the network learning process.
(c) We performed an extensive experimental evaluation and comparison and used different 3D-CNN models and different sampling methods for 3D-CNN models, and the AUC, sensitivity, and specificity of this method on a test dataset were 0.85, 0.88, and 0.88, respectively.

The rest of the paper is structured as follows. The following section focuses on the proposed method and the dataset used for the experiments, the Section 3 presents the experimental results and compares the baseline with the latest methods, the discussion is presented in the Section 4, and, finally, the conclusions are presented.

2. Methods

We predominantly used DWI and T2 image sequences from mp-MRI images in this study. Our main goal was to classify patients with prostate cancer as clinically severe and clinically less severe. Figure 1 illustrates the main framework of our proposed method, which has 3 main parts. First, we rigidly aligned [29,30] the T2 images with the DWI images in the planar spatial domain to correct the misalignment of the prostate region due to image sequences and biases with different MRI contrasts in the acquisition process. We then cropped out each T2 image with the DWI image containing the entire prostate region using an automatic method used for prostate region boundary detection, and then the cropped images were pixel-normalized. Third, we used the aligned and cropped T2 and DWI images to create a new 3D image sequence of the prostate, and we fed the new 3D image sequence into the 3D-CNN and obtained two outputs. The details of each step are presented in the following sections.

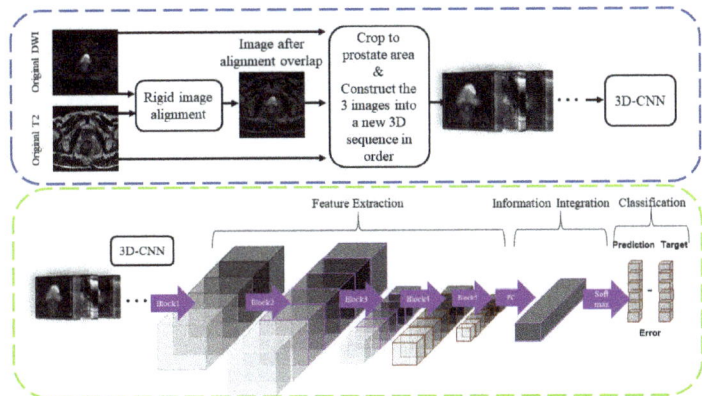

Figure 1. The framework of the proposed method consists of four key steps: (1) rigid multiparameter (DWI, T2) image alignment, (2) prostate region cropping, and (3) building a new 3D image sequence for input into a 3D-CNN.

2.1. Rigid Alignment of DWI and T2 Images

In previous studies [6,8,13], it was demonstrated that, in prostate mp-MRI, different MRI sequences are deterministic for prostate cancer detection and classification results, but the sensitivity of detection results under single-modality images is limited, so there is a need to use multiple MRI sequences to make judgments and fully utilize the characteristics of cancerous tissues under different MRI contrasts. Among all mp-MRI sequences, T2 images are more favorable for prostate cancer detection and diagnosis based on previous studies, but the sensitivity of T2 images is low [4,31]. DWI images show the extent of water diffusion in the prostate due to the tight accumulation of cancer cells, and any changes in the prostate cancer can be detected more easily in DWI images; thus, DWI is another type of image recommended for use in diagnosis. However, DWI does not completely represent prostate lesions [31,32], so there are many studies combining DWI with T2 images to achieve better sensitivity and specificity [6,8,33]. As shown in Figure 2, in the present study, we use DWI and T2 sequences in mp-MRI for prostate cancer classification. One of the keys to accurately combining the DWI and T2 image features is to align the DWI and T2 sequences, which can effectively eliminate the small variations between different sequences caused by external factors during mp-MRI acquisition [11]. In this study, no drugs were used in the MR acquisition protocol to reduce and prevent motion. In order to ensure that the shape of the cancer lesion in the image is maintained without changing so that the model can acquire the actual features of the shape of the cancer lesion, we use a rigid 2D medical image alignment algorithm based on mutual information to maximize the mutual information between the reference image and the target image without changing the shape information of the cancerous region, and we use DWI as the target image and T2 as the reference image. In this study, we use DWI as the target image and T2 as the reference image. We use the best available medical image alignment algorithm, ANTs SyN [34], to align the images. The image alignment strategy generally starts with an initial globally aligned linear transformation, and the linear changes available in ANTs are optimized for the mean squared deviation and correlated similarity measures, each of which are optimized for translation and rotation. To ensure the accuracy of the alignment process, we checked each image after alignment.

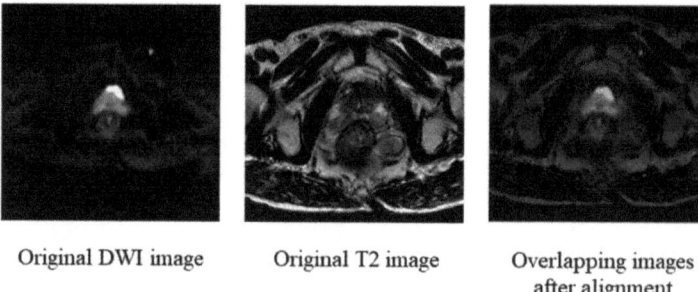

Original DWI image   Original T2 image   Overlapping images after alignment

Figure 2. Examples of the alignment of DWI and T2 images are shown: (1) original T2 image, (2) original DWI image, and (3) aligned T2 image after being overlaid with the DWI image.

2.2. Prostate Area Cropping

After alignment, we used a basic regression CNN to crop each image into a square region containing the prostate region. Figure 3 shows the architecture of our CNN model for automatically cropping the prostate region. We took the original image for training; the bounding box of the prostate region was marked manually, and the model output three parameters: the center coordinates of the square region (x, y) and the length l. The activation functions of all layers were tan h functions, and the corresponding loss function of our model was:

$$loss = 1/3(|\tan h(o_1) - x_t| + |\tan h(o_2) - y_t| + |\tan h(o_3) - l_t|) \qquad (1)$$

o_1, o_2 are the x and y coordinates, respectively, and o_3 is the length. In the present study, though there have been more complex target detection networks, such as R-CNN [35] or automatic segmentation networks [36], in our experiments, a simple regression CNN was able to achieve the detection of the square prostate area more accurately, and the surrounding tissues outside the square prostate area did not have any effects on the detection of prostate cancer.

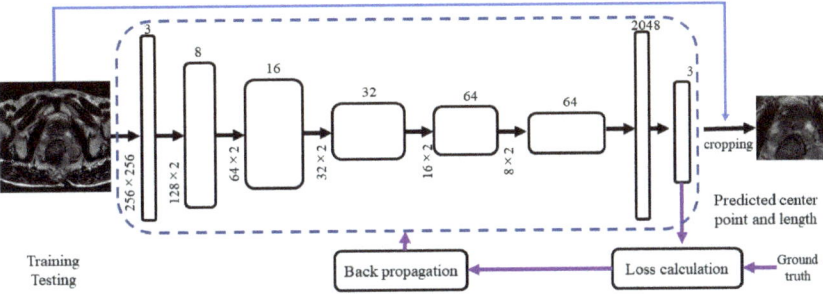

Figure 3. The figure shows the prostate detection and cropping procedure used in this paper. In the step of CNN-based prostate region detection, each rectangular box in the figure represents a feature map vector and shows the dimensional information of the feature map, the lower left corner of each feature map shows the length and width of the feature map, and the top shows the number of channels of the feature map. After this network, three output parameters can be obtained: the center coordinates (x, y) of the detected square region containing the prostate and the length of the square region L.

2.3. New Sequence-Based 3D-CNN

In the previous steps, we obtained the newly aligned DWI and T2 images. We arranged the aligned and cropped T2 and DWI prostate images and overlaid images in order to form a new 3D image sequence. In the next experiments, we resampled the new 3D image sequence of each patient 6 times (wince we used 3D convolution, the longer the z-axis of the input data was, the more z-axis features the model could learn, but considering that a longer input sequence for the model led to a significant increase in computation time and no significant improvement in the results, we chose to resample six times after the experiment); then, we input it into the 3D-CNN model to meet the training needs of the 3D-CNN model and obtained two outputs: (1) 3D class activation map, where the values of the pixels in the map represented the importance of having the model focus on this region; (2) high-dimensional semantic feature vectors, through which the 3D image sequence was classified.

There are three advantages to our use of this novel 3D-CNN input and training method: feature fusion, reinforcement features, and influence weight.

(1) Feature fusion: With the 3D convolution kernel process and the operation of the spatial convolution of the image sequence, the convolution kernel will convolve the single image adjacent to the z-axis in the sequence image, and the features of the single image adjacent to the z-axis will be calculated by the convolution kernel and extracted as high-dimensional vectors. This operation is good for fusing all of the adjacent image features and can replace the traditional method with a multiple-input multi-MRI-contrast image method. We formed the images with different MRI contrasts into a new 3D image sequence so that neighboring images of each image in the sequence

were images of various MRI contrasts. This method is a very cost-effective way to fuse image features with various MRI contrasts.
(2) Reinforcement features: In building a new 3D image sequence, we built the images with several MRI contrasts in a different order to create a new image sequence; thus, the adjacent image MRI contrasts were often diverse, and the cancerous tissue features would be different in images with various MRI contrasts. The operation of the 3D convolution kernel caused the model to remember the features of cancerous tissue in the images with different MRI contrasts, which could enhance the learning of cancerous features.
(3) Influence weight: In the learning of 3D convolution, the features of the image sequence were gradually high-dimensionalized, and the high-dimensional vector contained the full features of cancerous tissue; the linkage layer was expanded and the proportion of high-dimensional vectors containing cancerous tissue features to the total vectors increased, which could increase the accuracy of the prediction output. In the following, we provide detailed information on each step. In previous studies, the input of the 3D-CNN was usually a sequence of images of a patient with a particular MRI modality, but we fused images with different MRI contrasts into one sequence to be input into the network. The features of the image columns were extracted by the 3D-CNN, and the features of the z-axis were observable in the z-axis direction because each image of the new sequence had the most evident cancerous tissue. In Section 3, we use the best available 3D-CNN models for comparative experiments.

2.4. Implementations

All experiments in this study were conducted on a Windows computer using Python 3.6, with an Nvidia TITAN RTX graphics card and 24 GB of RAM, on an Intel(R) Core (TM) i7-9700K 3.60 GHz CPU. Pytorch [37] was used as the model backend to build the network architecture in all experiments. We used cross-entropy [38] as the loss function, trained for 2000 epochs with a batch size of 2, and the model converged at 500 epochs. We used Adam [39] as the model optimizer and set the learning rate to be automatically adjusted; the initial learning rate was 1×10^{-5}, the learning rate was multiplied by 0.1 every 50 epochs, and the input images were flipped at a random level with a probability of 0.5 during training. The data were normalized, and all data were randomly divided into training, validation, and test sets with a ratio of 50:30:20; the input size of the model was 128×128, and network model was set to the model that preserved the best results.

3. Experiments

3.1. Setup

We collected T2 and DWI images of the prostate, which were used to train the model and evaluate the performance of the model.

The prostate MRI data used in this paper consisted of 129 samples from Toho University Medical Center, Japan (dataset A) and were acquired with 3T MR scanners (SIEMENS Skyra; syngo MR E11), as well as 121 samples from the 2017 SPIE-AAPM-NCI PROSTATEx challenge dataset (dataset B). The PROSTATEx Challenge [40] ("SPIE-AAPM-NCI Prostate MR Classification Challenge") was held in conjunction with the 2017 SPIE Medical Imaging Symposium and focused on quantitative image analysis methods for diagnostic purposes and clinically meaningful prostate cancer classification. For each patient, the image with the most significant lesion area was selected.

The two datasets used—with data from different sites—were collected using different devices. We performed regularization preprocessing on these two datasets, as in the previous step. The method proposed in this paper was mainly used to predict high and low risk of early prostate cancer (according to the Gleason score, a score greater than or equal to 8 is considered clinically severe, and a score less than or equal to 7 is considered clinically insignificant). We used three main evaluation criteria to assess the performance of the model: the AUC (area under curve) value, sensitivity, and specificity, with the AUC being defined as the area under the ROC curve. Sensitivity (Se), called the true-positive fraction (TPF; or true-positive rate (TPR)), is the probability that a diagnostic test is correctly diagnosed as positive in a case group. Specificity (Sp), called the true-negative rate (TNF; or true-negative rate (TNR)), is the probability that the diagnostic test is correctly diagnosed as negative in the control group, and the false-negative rate (FNR; or false-negative fraction, FNF) is the probability that the diagnostic test is negative in the case group, which will lead to delayed disease and treatment. The false-positive fraction (FPF; or false positive rate (FPR)) is the probability that a diagnostic test is incorrectly diagnosed as positive in the control group. A false positive will result in incorrect treatment, and patients sometimes suffer from risky confirmatory tests.

$$\text{sensitivity} = \frac{TP}{TP + FN} \quad (2)$$

$$\text{specificity} = \frac{TN}{FP + TN} \quad (3)$$

In the above equation, TP, TN, FP, and FN represent the true positive, true negative, false positive, and false negative, respectively.

In the following sections, experiments are conducted to evaluate the performance of the proposed method in this paper. Table 1 shows the comparison experiments for the different 3D-CNN models, Table 2 shows the comparison experiments for the different newly ordered input sequences, and Table 3 shows the comparison experiments for the different modalities of the original image sequence; a comparison with the 3 latest methods is shown in Table 4.

Table 1. Comparison with 3D-CNN methodologies.

Methods	Sensitivity	Specificity	AUC	CI 95%	Parameters
C3D	0.83	0.79	0.81	0.80–0.83	78 M
3DSqueezeNet	0.73	0.68	0.70	0.72–0.78	2.15 M
3DMobileNet	0.74	0.67	0.69	0.73–0.75	8.22 M
3DShuffleNet	0.74	0.65	0.68	0.74–0.76	6.64 M
ResNext101	0.83	0.75	0.81	0.76–0.82	48.34 M
3DResnet101	0.88	0.88	0.83	0.84–0.85	83.29 M
Our method + 3DResNet50	0.88	0.84	0.85	0.85–0.87	44.24 M

Table 2. Comparison experiments with different sequence orders.

Methods	Sensitivity	Specificity	AUC	CI 95%	Parameters
Order 1	0.88	0.88	0.85	0.85–0.87	44.24 M
Order 2	0.84	0.84	0.82	0.80–0.83	-
Order 3	0.84	0.84	0.81	0.82–0.84	-
Order 4	0.88	0.84	0.84	0.79–0.84	-

Table 3. Comparison experiments of the original 3D sequence (input sizes were 384 × 384 and 128 × 128, respectively).

Methods	Sensitivity	Specificity	AUC	CI 95%	Parameters
T2(384)	0.63	0.59	0.68	0.66–0.688	-
T2(128)	0.71	0.63	0.72	0.71–0.74	-
DWI(384)	0.61	0.54	0.71	0.69–0.72	-
DWI(128)	0.65	0.54	0.74	0.73–0.76	-
Our method + 3DResnert50	0.88	0.88	0.85	0.85–0.87	44.24 M

Table 4. Comparison with the three cited methods used to classify the clinical severity of prostate cancer.

Methods	Sensitivity	Specificity	AUC	CI 95%	Parameters
Zhong et al., 2019 [18]	0.636	0.80	0.723	0.58–0.88	–
Ajdoj et al., 2020 [19]	0.74	0.70	0.78	–	–
Chen et al., 2017 [17]	0.78	0.83	0.83	–	–
Our method	0.88	0.88	0.85	0.85–0.87	44.24 M

3.2. Comparison with the Classic 3D CNN

In the first step of the experiment, we input the new 3D image sequences into different 3D-CNN models and uniformly used the pre-training weights of ucf-101 [41]. Table 1 shows the results of all of the 3D-CNN models when processing the new standard sequence images. All of the models were from [42]. From the comparisons, we found that, although the model parameters of ShuffNet were very limited, ResNet50 achieved the best AUC value in the test set. The sensitivity, specificity, and AUC values reached 0.88, 0.88, and 0.85, respectively.

3.3. Comparison of Different Input Orders

In the second step of the experiment, we input the images obtained in the previous steps into the model in different orders. In the previous step of the experiment (Section 3.2), the order of the single modal images in our new input image sequence was DWI, T2, and then overlaps. To find the most appropriate image alignment order for the input sequence, in this section, we divided the order in the new image sequence into four different orders:

(1) Order one: DWI, T2, and then overlap as a set of re-sampling six times;
(2) Order two: T2 re-sampling six times, DWI re-sampling six times, and then overlap re-sampling six times;
(3) Order three: DWI re-sampling six times, T2 re-sampling six times, and then overlap re-sampling six times;
(4) Order four: overlap re-sampling six times, T2 re-sampling six times, and then DWI re-sampling six times.

In the experiment in Section 3.2, 3DResNet50 achieved the best performance; we input different input sequences into the 3DResNet50 network, and in Table 2, we can see that the best results were produced by order 1.

3.4. Comparison Experiments with the Original 3D Sequence

In our study, we propose a new 3D-CNN sequence. In the experiment in this section, we compared this new sequence with the original image sequence (Table 3). We selected the integral unprocessed image sequence of each patient (T2 followed by DWI), and then we cropped the original 512 × 512 size to 384 × 384 and 128 × 128, respectively, for the input. The processed images were fed into the 3DResnet50 CNN, and Table 3 shows that the input of the original complete image sequence was not as good as the results of our proposed method.

3.5. Comparison with State-of-the-Art Methodologies

We also compared our proposed method with state-of-the-art methods, including the one proposed by Aldoj et al. [43] in 2020 for prostate cancer classification using multi-channel CNNs on multi-modal MRI images. Their method takes images of three modalities—ADC, DWI, and T2—as input, and inputs each modality into a different channel. There are 11 layers of 3D convolution with a convolution kernel of $3 \times 3 \times 3$, an ensemble step of $2 \times 2 \times 2$, and two fully connected layers. Because the method chooses data of three modes in the experiment, we only chose the results of two modes from Aldoj et al. [43] as input in order to balance the comparison of the experimental results. We can see that the sensitivity, specificity, and AUC values of our method were 0.14, 0.18, and 0.07 higher than those of the same two-modality image inputs, respectively. A recent study by Zhong et al. [44] used deep migration learning for prostate cancer classification based on multi-modal MRI images. It proposed feeding both T2 and ADC modality images into a deep migratory learning network for feature extraction and obtaining the prediction results after a fully connected layer. In the comparison experiments of Zhong et al. [44], they compared results using uni-modal and bi-modal image inputs. Here, for objectivity in the comparison experiments, we only selected the results of their comparison experiments with bi-modal inputs, and we found that the sensitivity, specificity, and AUC values of our model improved by 0.144, 0.08, and 0.127, respectively. Chen et al. [45] proposed an approach to classifying the clinical severity of prostate cancer using migration learning on the basis of multimodal MRI; the authors mainly used migration learning and pre-trained weights obtained after training on ImageNet, and they conducted their experiments using InceptionV3. The sensitivity, specificity, and AUC values of our method were 0.1, 0.05, and 0.002 higher than those of Chen et al. [45].

3.6. 3D-CNN Learning Process Visualization

There have been many previous studies [27,28] on deep learning model explanation and on deep learning visualization, among which the most well known is CAM. CAM shows the basis of its decision in the form of a heat map when a model is needed to explain the reason for its classification, such as when informing where there are focal points in the map. For a deep CNN, after multiple convolutions and pooling, the last convolutional layer contains the richest spatial and semantic information, and the next layers are the fully connected layer and softmax layer, which contain information that is difficult for humans to understand and display in a visual way. Therefore, in order to provide a reasonable explanation of the classification results of the convolutional neural network, it is necessary to make full use of the last convolutional layer, and CAM draws on the idea of the well-known paper on Network in Network [27], which uses GAP (global average pooling) to replace the fully connected layer. GAP can be considered as a special average pooling layer, except that its pool size is as large as the whole feature map, which is actually the average value of all pixels in each feature map. This greatly limits its use. If the model is already online or the training cost is very high, it is almost impossible to retrain it. The basic idea of Grad-cam is the same as that of CAM, which is to obtain the weights of each pair of feature maps and then find a weighted sum. CAM replaces the fully connected layers with GAP layers and retrains the weights, whereas Grad-cam takes a different approach and uses the global average of gradients to calculate the weights. Although Grad-cam and other similar methods are effective, they have limitations, such as the localization of multiple similar targets at the same time; even for a single object, Grad-cam cannot localize it completely. Based on Grad-cam, the authors of [28] proposed Grad-cam++, which improved the previous method, with the main contribution that ++ introduced a pixel-level weighting of the output gradient for a specific location. This method provides a measure of the importance of each pixel in the feature map, and more importantly, they derived closed-form solutions while obtaining exact higher-order representations, including softmax and exponential activation outputs. Our method requires one back-propagation, so the computational effort is consistent with the previous gradient-based method, but the results are more effective. It can be extended in the field of 3D deep learning visualization. In this paper, we used Grad-cam++ in a 3D image sequence, as shown in Figure 4; we found that the model accurately focused on the cancerous tissue by using the focus map and heat map, and it learned the feature details of the cancerous tissue.

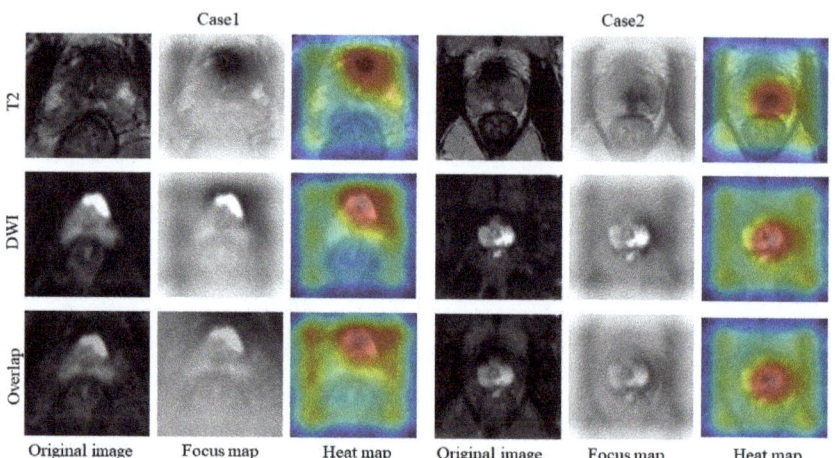

Figure 4. The 3D-CNN model was visualized for learning. The figure shows two cases; the first column of each case is the original image, the second column is the focus map obtained through calculation, and the third column is the heat map obtained through the 3D Grad-cam++ calculation.

Figure 4 shows the heat map obtained through 3D visualization, where the red area represents the area where the network model focused and learned features, and the area closest to the red indicates the area where the convolutional network focused more of its attention. From the figure, we can see that the areas on which the network model focused were the lesion areas.

4. Discussion

Few studies have used 3D-CNN to classify the clinical severity of prostate cancer. The main reason for this is that the cancerous tissue portion of a patient's whole prostate sequence often accounts for only a small part of the entire prostate image sequence. Due to the very small size of the cancerous tissue, although 3D-CNN can learn the features of the sequence images better than 2D-CNN, it is also difficult to learn the features of the cancerous tissue adequately with very small targets, and it is easy for the large number of useless features in the prostate cancer image sequence to affect the model's learning results. So, we proposed the method in this paper, which solves this problem perfectly, but it is difficult to determine an optimal sequence length when constructing a new image sequence; the original image sequence length is determined by the original sequence, but the newly constructed image sequence does not have a perfect graph column length. In this paper, we explored different alignment methods when constructing the sequence as much as possible, and in future experiments, the sequence length will be investigated in order to find an optimal sequence length. Although the method achieves great results in the direction of deep learning, it is not superior to the results of a simple semen test, so this method is one of the methods for assisting doctors in diagnosis. We carefully considered the issue of whether to use fully automatic segmentation of the prostate region when designing the method, and we also wish to automate the whole method as much as possible and to reduce the manual part as much as possible, so we will add this step to the CNN in future work to achieve full automation. However, in the current study, we also used some bounding boxes for manual animation, so the current method is still semi-automatic, and we will introduce automatic segmentation methods for medical images, such as U-net, into our method in future work.

5. Conclusions

In this paper, we proposed a novel method for constructing 3D-CNN sequences and used the newly constructed 3D image sequences as input for different 3D-CNN models in comparison experiments, compared the results after different fine-tuning based on the basic constructed method, and, finally, compared the results with those of other 3D-CNN methods. The results showed that our proposed method had the best AUC value of 0.85, and using the improved 3D model visualization method showed the focus of the model's learning.

Author Contributions: Conceptualization, B.L.,T.N. and P.X.; Methodology, B.L.; Software, T.N.; Validation, B.L. and Y.Y.; Resources, R.O.; Data curation, R.O. All authors have read and agreed to the published version of the manuscript.

Funding: This research received no external funding.

Institutional Review Board Statement: Not applicable.

Informed Consent Statement: Not applicable.

Data Availability Statement: Not applicable.

Conflicts of Interest: The authors declare no conflict of interest.

References

1. Mohler, J.; Bahnson, R.R.; Boston, B.; Busby, J.E.; D'Amico, A.; Eastham, J.A.; Enke, C.A.; George, D.; Horwitz, E.M.; Huben, R.P.; et al. Prostate cancer. *J. Natl. Compr. Cancer Netw.* **2010**, *8*, 162–200. [CrossRef] [PubMed]
2. Gillessen, S.; Attard, G.; Beer, T.M.; Beltran, H.; Bjartell, A.; Bossi, A.; Briganti, A.; Bristow, R.G.; Chi, K.N.; Clarke, N.; et al. Management of patients with advanced prostate cancer: Report of the advanced prostate cancer consensus conference 2019. *Eur. Urol.* **2020**, *77*, 508–547. [CrossRef] [PubMed]
3. Weinreb, J.C.; Barentsz, J.O.; Choyke, P.L.; Cornud, F.; Haider, M.A.; Macura, K.J.; Margolis, D.; Schnall, M.D.; Shtern, F.; Tempany, C.M.; et al. PI-RADS prostate imaging–reporting and data system: 2015, version 2. *Eur. Urol.* **2016**, *69*, 16–40. [CrossRef] [PubMed]
4. Schröder, F.H.; Hugosson, J.; Roobol, M.J.; Tammela, T.L.; Ciatto, S.; Nelen, V.; Kwiatkowski, M.; Lujan, M.; Lilja, H.; Zappa, M.; et al. Screening and prostate-cancer mortality in a randomized European study. *N. Engl. J. Med.* **2009**, *360*, 1320–1328. [CrossRef]
5. de Rooij, M.; Hamoen, E.H.; Fütterer, J.J.; Barentsz, J.O.; Rovers, M.M. Accuracy of multiparametric MRI for prostate cancer detection: A meta-analysis. *Am. J. Roentgenol.* **2014**, *202*, 343–351. [CrossRef] [PubMed]
6. Bai, X.; Jiang, Y.; Zhang, X.; Wang, M.; Tian, J.; Mu, L.; Du, Y. The Value of Prostate-Specific Antigen-Related Indexes and Imaging Screening in the Diagnosis of Prostate Cancer. *Cancer Manag. Res.* **2020**, *12*, 6821–6826. [CrossRef]
7. Fehr, D.; Veeraraghavan, H.; Wibmer, A.; Gondo, T.; Matsumoto, K.; Vargas, H.A.; Sala, E.; Hricak, H.; Deasy, J.O. Automatic classification of prostate cancer Gleason scores from multiparametric magnetic resonance images. *Proc. Natl. Acad. Sci. USA* **2015**, *112*, E6265–E6273. [CrossRef]
8. Turkbey, B.; Choyke, P.L. Multiparametric MRI and prostate cancer diagnosis and risk stratification. *Curr. Opin. Urol.* **2012**, *22*, 310. [CrossRef]
9. Peng, Y.; Jiang, Y.; Yang, C.; Brown, J.B.; Antic, T.; Sethi, I.; Schmid-Tannwald, C.; Giger, M.L.; Eggener, S.E.; Oto, A. Quantitative analysis of multiparametric prostate MR images: Differentiation between prostate cancer and normal tissue and correlation with Gleason score—a computer-aided diagnosis development study. *Radiology* **2013**, *267*, 787–796. [CrossRef]
10. Turkbey, B.; Xu, S.; Kruecker, J.; Locklin, J.; Pang, Y.; Bernardo, M.; Merino, M.J.; Wood, B.J.; Choyke, P.L.; Pinto, P.A. Documenting the location of prostate biopsies with image fusion. *BJU Int.* **2011**, *107*, 53. [CrossRef]
11. Valerio, M.; Donaldson, I.; Emberton, M.; Ehdaie, B.; Hadaschik, B.A.; Marks, L.S.; Mozer, P.; Rastinehad, A.R.; Ahmed, H.U. Detection of clinically significant prostate cancer using magnetic resonance imaging–ultrasound fusion targeted biopsy: A systematic review. *Eur. Urol.* **2015**, *68*, 8–19. [CrossRef] [PubMed]
12. Liu, P.; Wang, S.; Turkbey, B.; Grant, K.; Pinto, P.; Choyke, P.; Wood, B.J.; Summers, R.M. A prostate cancer computer-aided diagnosis system using multimodal magnetic resonance imaging and targeted biopsy labels. Medical Imaging 2013: Computer-Aided Diagnosis. In Proceedings of the International Society for Optics and Photonics, Lake Buena Vista, FL, USA, 26 February 2013; Volume 8670, p. 86701G.
13. Lemaitre, G. Computer-Aided Diagnosis for Prostate Cancer Using Multi-Parametric Magnetic Resonance Imaging. Ph.D. Thesis, Universitat de Girona, Escola Politècnica Superior, Girona, Spain, 2016.
14. Litjens, G.J.; Vos, P.C.; Barentsz, J.O.; Karssemeijer, N.; Huisman, H.J. Automatic computer aided detection of abnormalities in multi-parametric prostate MRI. Medical Imaging 2011: Computer-Aided Diagnosis. In Proceedings of the International Society for Optics and Photonics, Lake Buena Vista, FL, USA, 4 March 2011; Volume 7963, p. 79630T.

15. Litjens, G.J.; Barentsz, J.O.; Karssemeijer, N.; Huisman, H.J. Automated computer-aided detection of prostate cancer in MR images: From a whole-organ to a zone-based approach. In Proceedings of the Medical Imaging 2012: Computer-Aided Diagnosis, International Society for Optics and Photonics, San Diego, CA, USA, 23 February 2012; Volume 8315, p. 83150G.
16. Artan, Y.; Haider, M.A.; Langer, D.L.; Van der Kwast, T.H.; Evans, A.J.; Yang, Y.; Wernick, M.N.; Trachtenberg, J.; Yetik, I.S. Prostate cancer localization with multispectral MRI using cost-sensitive support vector machines and conditional random fields. *IEEE Trans. Image Process.* **2010**, *19*, 2444–2455. [CrossRef] [PubMed]
17. Niaf, E.; Rouvière, O.; Mège-Lechevallier, F.; Bratan, F.; Lartizien, C. Computer-aided diagnosis of prostate cancer in the peripheral zone using multiparametric MRI. *Phys. Med. Biol.* **2012**, *57*, 3833. [CrossRef] [PubMed]
18. Tiwari, P.; Kurhanewicz, J.; Madabhushi, A. Multi-kernel graph embedding for detection, Gleason grading of prostate cancer via MRI/MRS. *Med. Image Anal.* **2013**, *17*, 219–235. [CrossRef]
19. Wang, S.; Burtt, K.; Turkbey, B.; Choyke, P.; Summers, R.M. Computer aided-diagnosis of prostate cancer on multiparametric MRI: A technical review of current research. *BioMed Res. Int.* **2014**, *2014*, 789561. [CrossRef]
20. Rundo, L.; Han, C.; Zhang, J.; Hataya, R.; Nagano, Y.; Militello, C.; Ferretti, C.; Nobile, M.S.; Tangherloni, A.; Gilardi, M.C.; et al. CNN-based Prostate Zonal Segmentation on T2-weighted MR Images: A Cross-dataset Study. In *Neural Approaches to Dynamics of Signal Exchanges*; Esposito, A., Faundez-Zanuy, M., Morabito, F., Pasero, E., Eds.; Springe: Singapore, 2020; Volume 151, pp. 269–280. [CrossRef]
21. Rundo, L.; Han, C.; Nagano, Y.; Zhang, J.; Hataya, R.; Militello, C.; Tangherloni, A.; Nobile, M.S.; Ferretti, C.; Besozzi, D.; et al. USE-Net: Incorporating Squeeze-and-Excitation blocks into U-Net for prostate zonal segmentation of multi-institutional MRI datasets. *Neurocomputing* **2019**, *365*, 31–43. [CrossRef]
22. Chan, I.; Wells, W., III; Mulkern, R.V.; Haker, S.; Zhang, J.; Zou, K.H.; Maier, S.E.; Tempany, C.M. Detection of prostate cancer by integration of line-scan diffusion, T2-mapping and T2-weighted magnetic resonance imaging; a multichannel statistical classifier. *Med. Phys.* **2003**, *30*, 2390–2398. [CrossRef]
23. Langer, D.L.; Van der Kwast, T.H.; Evans, A.J.; Trachtenberg, J.; Wilson, B.C.; Haider, M.A. Prostate cancer detection with multi-parametric MRI: Logistic regression analysis of quantitative T2, diffusion-weighted imaging, and dynamic contrast-enhanced MRI. *J. Magn. Reson. Imaging Off. J. Int. Soc. Magn. Reson. Med.* **2009**, *30*, 327–334. [CrossRef]
24. Tiwari, P.; Viswanath, S.; Kurhanewicz, J.; Sridhar, A.; Madabhushi, A. Multimodal wavelet embedding representation for data combination (MaWERiC): Integrating magnetic resonance imaging and spectroscopy for prostate cancer detection. *NMR Biomed.* **2012**, *25*, 607–619. [CrossRef]
25. Castelvecchi, D. Can we open the black box of AI? *Nat. News* **2016**, *538*, 20. [CrossRef]
26. Zhou, B.; Khosla, A.; Lapedriza, A.; Oliva, A.; Torralba, A. Learning deep features for discriminative localization. In Proceedings of the IEEE Conference on Computer Vision and Pattern Recognition, Las Vegas, NV, USA, 27–30 June 2016; pp. 2921–2929.
27. Selvaraju, R.R.; Cogswell, M.; Das, A.; Vedantam, R.; Parikh, D.; Batra, D. Grad-cam: Visual explanations from deep networks via gradient-based localization. In Proceedings of the IEEE International Conference on Computer Vision, Venice, Italy, 22–29 October 2017; pp. 618–626.
28. Chattopadhay, A.; Sarkar, A.; Howlader, P.; Balasubramanian, V.N. Grad-cam++: Generalized gradient-based visual explanations for deep convolutional networks. In Proceedings of the 2018 IEEE Winter Conference on Applications of Computer Vision (WACV), Lake Tahoe, NV, USA, 12–15 March 2018; pp. 839–847.
29. Zitova, B.; Flusser, J. Image registration methods: A survey. *Image Vis. Comput.* **2003**, *21*, 977–1000. [CrossRef]
30. Hill, D.L.; Batchelor, P.G.; Holden, M.; Hawkes, D.J. Medical image registration. *Phys. Med. Biol.* **2001**, *46*, R1. [CrossRef] [PubMed]
31. Sankineni, S.; Osman, M.; Choyke, P.L. Functional MRI in prostate cancer detection. *BioMed Res. Int.* **2014**, *2014*, 590638. [CrossRef] [PubMed]
32. Gibbs, P.; Tozer, D.J.; Liney, G.P.; Turnbull, L.W. Comparison of quantitative T2 mapping and diffusion-weighted imaging in the normal and pathologic prostate. *Magn. Reson. Med. Off. J. Int. Soc. Magn. Reson. Med.* **2001**, *46*, 1054–1058. [CrossRef] [PubMed]
33. De Santi, B.; Salvi, M.; Giannini, V.; Meiburger, K.M.; Marzola, F.; Russo, F.; Bosco, M.; Molinariet, F. Comparison of Histogram-based Textural Features between Cancerous and Normal Prostatic Tissue in Multiparametric Magnetic Resonance Images. In Proceedings of the 2020 42nd Annual International Conference of the IEEE Engineering in Medicine & Biology Society (EMBC), Montreal, QC, Canada, 20–24 July 2020; pp. 1671–1674. [CrossRef]
34. Avants, B.B.; Tustison, N.J.; Song, G.; Cook, P.A.; Klein, A.; Gee, J.C. A reproducible evaluation of ANTs similarity metric performance in brain image registration. *Neuroimage* **2011**, *54*, 2033–2044. [CrossRef] [PubMed]
35. Girshick, R. Fast r-cnn. In Proceedings of the IEEE International Conference on Computer Vision, Santiago, Chile, 7–13 December 2015; pp. 1440–1448.
36. Yu, L.; Yang, X.; Chen, H.; Qin, J.; Heng, P.A. Volumetric ConvNets with mixed residual connections for automated prostate segmentation from 3D MR images. In Proceedings of the Thirty-First AAAI Conference on Artificial Intelligence, San Francisco, CA, USA, 4–9 February 2017.
37. Paszke, A.; Gross, S.; Massa, F.; Lerer, A.; Bradbury, J.; Chanan, G.; Killeen, T.; Lin, Z.; Gimelshein, N.; Antiga, L.; et al. Pytorch: An imperative style, high-performance deep learning library. *Adv. Neural Inf. Process. Syst.* **2019**, *32*, 8026–8037.
38. De Boer, P.T.; Kroese, D.P.; Mannor, S.; Rubinstein, R.Y. A tutorial on the cross-entropy method. *Ann. Oper. Res.* **2005**, *134*, 19–67. [CrossRef]

39. Kingma, D.P.; Ba, J. Adam: A method for stochastic optimization. *arXiv* **2014**, arXiv:1412.6980 2014.
40. Armato, S.G.; Huisman, H.; Drukker, K.; Hadjiiski, L.; Kirby, J.S.; Petrick, N.; Redmond, G.; Giger, M.L.; Cha, K.; Mamonov, A.; et al. PROSTATEx Challenges for computerized classification of prostate lesions from multiparametric magnetic resonance images. *J. Med. Imaging* **2018**, *5*, 044501. [CrossRef]
41. Karpathy, A.; Toderici, G.; Shetty, S.; Leung, T.; Sukthankar, R.; Fei-Fei, L. Large-scale video classification with convolutional neural networks. In Proceedings of the IEEE conference on Computer Vision and Pattern Recognition, Columbus, OH, USA, 23–28 June 2014; pp. 1725–1732.
42. Kopuklu, O.; Kose, N.; Gunduz, A.; Rigoll, G. Resource efficient 3d convolutional neural networks. In Proceedings of the IEEE/CVF International Conference on Computer Vision Workshops, Seoul, Korea, 27–28 October 2019; pp. 1910–1919.
43. Aldoj, N.; Lukas, S.; Dewey, M.; Penzkofer, T. Semi-automatic classification of prostate cancer on multi-parametric MR imaging using a multi-channel 3D convolutional neural network. *Eur. Radiol.* **2020**, *30*, 1243–1253. [CrossRef]
44. Zhong, X.; Cao, R.; Shakeri, S.; Scalzo, F.; Lee, Y.; Enzmann, D.R.; Wu, H.H.; Raman, S.S.; Sung, K. Deep transfer learning-based prostate cancer classification using 3 Tesla multi-parametric MRI. *Abdom. Radiol.* **2019**, *44*, 2030–2039. [CrossRef] [PubMed]
45. Chen, Q.; Xu, X.; Hu, S.; Li, X.; Zou, Q.; Li, Y. A transfer learning approach for classification of clinical significant prostate cancers from mpMRI scans. Medical Imaging 2017: Computer-Aided Diagnosis. In Proceedings of the International Society for Optics and Photonics, Orlando, FL, USA, 16 March 2017; Volume 10134, p. 101344F.

 *algorithms*

Article

Cancer Identification in Walker 256 Tumor Model Exploring Texture Properties Taken from Microphotograph of Rats Liver

Mateus F. T. Carvalho [1,†], Sergio A. Silva, Jr. [1,†], Carla Cristina O. Bernardo [2], Franklin César Flores [1], Juliana Vanessa C. M. Perles [2], Jacqueline Nelisis Zanoni [2] and Yandre M. G. Costa [1,*]

1 Departamento de Informática, Universidade Estadual de Maringá, Maringá 87020-900, Brazil; pg906708@uem.br (M.F.T.C.); ra115735@uem.br (S.A.S.J.); fcflores@din.uem.br (F.C.F.)
2 Departamento de Ciências Morfológicas, Universidade Estadual de Maringá, Maringá 87020-900, Brazil; pg401985@uem.br (C.C.O.B.); jvcmperles@uem.br (J.V.C.M.P.); jnzanoni@uem.br (J.N.Z.)
* Correspondence: yandre@din.uem.br
† These authors contributed equally to this work.

Abstract: Recent studies have been evaluating the presence of patterns associated with the occurrence of cancer in different types of tissue present in the individual affected by the disease. In this article, we describe preliminary results for the automatic detection of cancer (Walker 256 tumor) in laboratory animals using preclinical microphotograph images of the subject's liver tissue. In the proposed approach, two different types of descriptors were explored to capture texture properties from the images, and we also evaluated the complementarity between them. The first texture descriptor experimented is the widely known Local Phase Quantization (LPQ), which is a descriptor based on spectral information. The second one is built by the application of a granulometry given by a family of morphological filters. For classification, we have evaluated the algorithms Support Vector Machine (SVM), k-Nearest Neighbor (k-NN) and Logistic Regression. Experiments carried out on a carefully curated dataset developed by the Enteric Neural Plasticity Laboratory of the State University of Maringá showed that both texture descriptors provide good results in this scenario. The accuracy rates obtained using the SVM classifier were 96.67% for the texture operator based on granulometry and 91.16% for the LPQ operator. The dataset was made available also as a contribution of this work. In addition, it is important to remark that the best overall result was obtained by combining classifiers created using both descriptors in a late fusion strategy, achieving an accuracy of 99.16%. The results obtained show that it is possible to automatically perform the identification of cancer in laboratory animals by exploring texture properties found on the tissue taken from the liver. Moreover, we observed a high level of complementarity between the classifiers created using LPQ and granulometry properties in the application addressed here.

Keywords: texture; local phase quantization; granulometry; liver tissue

1. Introduction

Cancer is the second biggest cause of death worldwide, accounting for nearly 10 million deaths in 2020 [1]. This disease starts from the transformation of normal cells into tumor cells, in a multi-stage process that generally progresses from a pre-cancerous lesion to a malignant tumor. Different parts from the human body may be affected by this transformation. In this vein, several research studies have been developed aiming to investigate how these lesions happen in different types of tissue.

One of these investigations is under development in the Enteric Neural Plasticity Laboratory of the State University of Maringá. In that work, the researchers have been evaluating the transformations provoked by Walker 256 tumor in the cells contained in samples of tissue taken from the liver of laboratory rats in a preclinical scenario. By visually inspecting those images, they noticed that different patterns are present when samples taken from healthy and sick individuals are compared.

In this work, we describe results obtained in preliminary investigations developed aiming to accomplish the automatic identification of cancer using the aforementioned images. For this purpose, we decided to explore the textural properties of the images, inspired in another biomedical application previously investigated by our research group [2]. In that work, we evaluated the use of some widely known texture operators for the identification of chronic degenerative diseases from images taken from other types of tissue.

As far as we know, the automatic identification of cancer, using a spectral texture descriptor and granulometry-based properties of the tissue taken from the liver, is proposed for the first time in this work. Furthermore, we also investigate the complementarity between classifiers created on both scenarios (i.e., the LPQ texture operator [3], and a granulometry-based descriptor [4–6]). The experimental results demonstrate the existence of a high level of complementarity between both on the task evaluated here.

Taking it into account, we describe the following **Research Questions (RQ)** we intend to answer in this work:

- **RQ1**: What is the performance of LPQ to support cancer identification in a Walker 256 tumor model on microphotograph of rats liver?
- **RQ2**: What is the performance of granulometry-based descriptors (GBD) to support cancer identification in a Walker 256 tumor model on microphotographs of rat liver?
- **RQ3**: Is it possible to obtain better results for cancer identification in a Walker 256 tumor model by combining classifiers created using LPQ and GBD in this scenario?

The classification was performed using three of the most widely known shallow classifiers: k-NN, Logistic Regression, and SVM. The choice of shallow classifiers is justified by the size of the dataset, which is too small to feed deep learning models.

The remaining of this work is organized as follows: In Section 2, we describe some remarkable related works. Section 3 presents the main facts related to the dataset used in this work. In Section 4, we describe details about the feature extraction design adopted here. In Section 5, the methodology used for classification is showed in details. In Section 6, results and discussions are presented. Finally, we describe our concluding remarks.

2. Related Works

In a more general context, Matos et al. [7] recently described a review on the use of machine learning methods for histopathological image analysis. In that work, the authors easily found 2524 scientific works already published in the period between 2008 and 2020, using five widely known research portal engines (i.e., IEEExplore, ACM Digital Library, Science Direct, Web of Science and Scopus). In that work, the authors described the systematic review according to a taxonomy which takes into account some important aspects of machine learning methods: the use of segmentation as a preprocessing strategy; the use of handcrafted or non-handcrafted features; and the use of shallow or deep learning methods.

The choice for works from the literature related to this one is not such a trivial task, because this relationship may be seen from different perspectives, considering different arrangements. One of these possibilities is to make the stratification of the works in terms of the tissue/organ from which the images were obtained. In this vein, the work presented by Nativ et al. [8] is worth mentioning here. In that work, they proposed a particular image analysis technique to automatically identify the steatotic state of livers. The proposal was based on a carefully designed image analysis based on the segmentation of liver cellular and tissue structures. Following, some metrics were obtained from the segmented structures and used with a k-means unsupervised clustering algorithm. The authors claim that the proposed method overcame the performance of the strategies already presented at that moment.

Shi et al. [9] also performed automated liver fat quantification. For this purpose, they developed a pipeline in which high-relevant pixel-level features are firstly extracted from hematoxylin–eosin stained images. Following, the boundaries between nuclei, fat and other components are found clustering pixels using an unsupervised strategy. Finally, the fat regions are identified based on the use of morphological operations. The authors claim that the proposed approach presented a high accuracy and adaptability in fat droplets quantification.

Deeply analyzing the literature, we still found one more work closely related to this one. Thiran and Macq [10] performed morphological feature extraction for the Classification of Digital Images of Cancerous Tissues. The authors used a dataset composed of images from lungs and digestive tract obtained by biopsy. The proposal was based on the use of mathematical morphology to segment the nuclei of the cell, as the shape is an important attribute to make it. The sequence of operations used to perform this segmentation was the following: morphological opening, morphological reconstruction, and lastly, a threshold. Once the nuclei was segmented, the set of features was extracted using, once again, morphological operations to capture measures related to Nucleocytoplasmic Ratio, Anisonucleosis, Nuclear Deformity, and Hyperchromasia. Finally, they proposed a score obtained from these four values and used it to decide whether a given tissue is cancerous or not.

3. Dataset

The dataset used in this work was created by researchers of the Enteric Neural Plasticity Laboratory of the State University of Maringá. For this, male adult rats, of the Wistar (*Rattus norvegicus*) lineage were used. All the proceedings involving the animals were previously approved by the "Standing Committee on Ethics in Animals Experimentation" of the university.

The animals were randomly separated into a control group (C) and Walker tumor group (TW). Animals from the TW group were inoculated with Walker 256 tumor cells. The dataset is composed of 120 microphotographs taken from samples of rat liver tissue. The images are divided in two classes: control (C), containing 60 microphotographs taken from six healthy rats (10 from each rat) and Walker 256 tumor (TW), containing 60 microphotographs taken from six rats (ten from each rat) with the Walker 256 tumor.

The liver samples were made in a semi-serialized manner with 5 µm cuts; they were stained with haematoxylin and eosin. The images were obtained using the camera Moticam® 2500 5.0 Mega Pixel (Motic China Group Co, Shanghai, China) coupled to the microscope Motic BA 400 (Motic China Group Co., Shanghai, China). The images were collected with magnification of 40× and resolution of 1024 × 768 pixels, which corresponds to an area of 35,369.85 µm^2 per image. Figures 1 and 2 show samples from the classes C and TW, respectively. Some details about the images are summarized in Table 1, and additional information about the dataset can be found in [11]. The dataset used in this work was made freely available (https://github.com/Sersasj/Liver_Dataset, accessed on 1 April 2022) for research purposes in such a way that other researchers can benefit from it and properly compare the results obtained using different techniques with those obtained here.

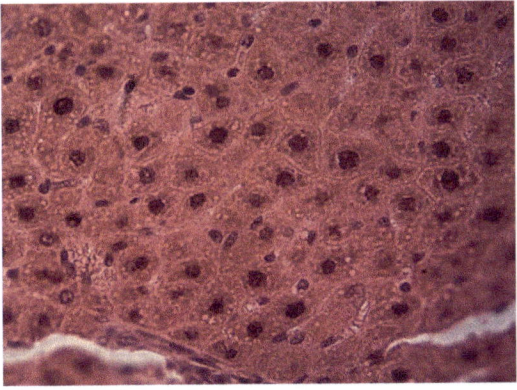

Figure 1. Liver microphotograph from the control group (C).

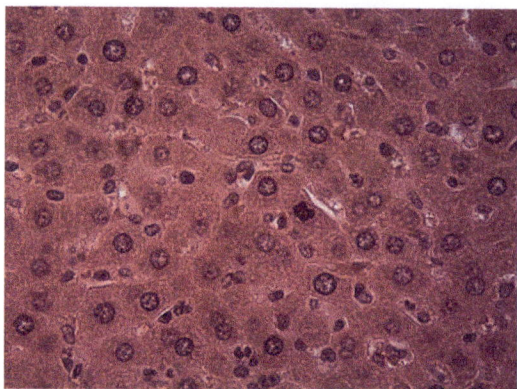

Figure 2. Liver microphotograph from the Walker 256 tumor group (TW).

Table 1. Dataset characteristics.

Class	Abbreviation	Image Dimension	Number of Samples
Walker 256 tumor	TW	1024 × 768	60
Control	C	1024 × 768	60

4. Feature Extraction

This section describes the descriptors used in this work: Local Phase Quantization (LPQ) and a granulometry-based descriptor. The rationale behind this choice is the following. Firstly, we chose LPQ because this operator is supposed to achieve a good performance when the images may be affected by blur, which is a noise that frequently occurs in this type of image due to the nature of the collection process, as we can see in the bottom right corner of Figure 1. Next, we decided to evaluate a granulometry-based descriptor [4,5], supposing that both could have a high level of complementarity.

4.1. Local Phase Quantization (LPQ)

Blurring in images can limit the analysis of texture information, and such degradation can happen for a number of reasons. Algorithms that enable image blur removal are computationally intensive and may introduce new artifacts, so algorithms that can analyze textures in a robust way are desired.

Ojansivu and Heikkila [3] proposed a texture descriptor insensitive to blur based on the quantized phase of the discrete Fourier transform, which is called Local Phase Quantization (LPQ). The information of the local phase of an image of size $N \times N$ is given by the Short-Term Fourier Transform in Equation (1), being Φ_{u_i} defined by the Equation (2), where $r = (m-1)/2$ and u_i is a 2D frequency vector

$$\hat{f}_{u_i}(x) = (f \times \Phi_{u_i})x, \tag{1}$$

$$\Phi_{u_i} = e^{-j2\pi u_i^T y} | y \in \mathbb{Z}^2 ||y||\infty \leq r. \tag{2}$$

Only four complex coefficients are considered in LPQ, which correspond to the 2D frequency $u_1 = [a, 0]^T$, $u_2 = [0, a]^T$, $u_3 = [a, a]^T$, $u_4 = [a, -a]^T$, where $a = 1/m$. The STFT (Equation (1)) is expressed using the vector described in Equation (3) with w_u being the STFT basis vector at a frequency u and $f(x)$, a vector of size m^2 containing the values of the image pixels in the $m \times m$ neighborhood of x.

$$\hat{f}_{u_i}(x) = w_{u_i}^T f(x) \tag{3}$$

Here, $F = [f(x_1), f(x_2)..., f(x_{n^2})]$ is denoted as a matrix $m^2 \times N^2$ containing the neighborhood of all image pixels and $w = [w_R, w_I]^T$, where $w_R = Re[w_{u_1}, w_{u_2}, w_{u_3}, w_{u_4}]$ and $w_I = Im[w_{u_1}, w_{u_2}, w_{u_3}, w_{u_4}]$. $Re[]$ and $Im[]$ represent, respectively, the real and imaginary parts of a complex number, and the $(8 \times N^2)$ transformation matrix is given by $\hat{F} = wF$.

Ojansivu and Heikkila [3] assume that the function $f(x)$ of an image is the result of the first-order Markov process, where the correlation coefficient between two pixels x_i and x_j is exponentially related to their L^2 distance. The vector f is defined by a covariance matrix of size $m^2 \times m^2$ according to the Equation (4), and the covariance matrix of the Fourier coefficients can be obtained by $D = wCw^T$. As long as D is not a diagonal matrix, the coefficients are correlated and may become not correlated through $E = V^T \hat{F}$, where V is an orthogonal matrix derivative from the singular value decomposition (SVD) of a matrix D, which is $D' = V^T DV$.

$$C_{i,j} = \sigma^{||x_i - x_j||} \tag{4}$$

The coefficients are quantized using Equation (5), in which e_{ij} are components of E. The coefficients are represented as integer values between 0 and 255 using the binary code obtained from Equation (6).

At last, a histogram of these integer values from all images positions is used to make a 256-dimensional feature vector used for classification. The pseudocode for LPQ is described in Algorithm 1.

$$q_{i,j} = \begin{cases} 1, & \text{if } e_{i,j} \geq 0, \\ 0, & \text{otherwise.} \end{cases} \tag{5}$$

$$b_j = \sum_{i=0}^{7} q_{i,j} 2^j \tag{6}$$

Algorithm 1: Pseudocode for LPQ based descriptors.

Input: *img*: Color image under the RGB color space model,
m: defines a sized $m \times m$ neighborhood size of the Short-Term Fourier Transform
Output: *H*: A 256-dimensional feature vector.
$img_r \leftarrow img$ red band
$img_g \leftarrow img$ green band
$img_b \leftarrow img$ blue band
$f \leftarrow img_r + img_g + img_b$
$a \leftarrow 1/m$
$u_1 \leftarrow [a, 0]^T$
$u_2 \leftarrow [0, a]^T$
$u_3 \leftarrow [a, a]^T$
$u_4 \leftarrow [a, -a]^T$ {compute the four coefficients u_i for the STFT}
Compute basis vectors w_{u_i}
$\hat{f}_{u_i}(x) \leftarrow w_{u_i}^T f(x)$ {compute the STFT}
Compute the covariance matrix C
$D \leftarrow wCw^T$ {compute the covariance matrix of the transform}
$E \leftarrow$ decorrelated matrix D   {$E = e_{ij}$}
$Q \leftarrow$ coefficients quantization (see Equation (5))
Quantized coefficients b_i are converted to an 8-bits values representation (see Equation (6))
$H \leftarrow$ {histogram of the quantized and converted coefficients}

4.2. Granulometry-Based Descriptors (GBD)

Mathematical Morphology (MM) is an algebraic theory that studies the decomposition of operators between complete lattices in terms of elementary operators (erosion and dilation) and operations (union, intersection and negation) [4,12]. It is a field of non-linear digital image processing tools, and it is widely applied to process and analyze topological and geometrical structures.

Two basic and important morphological operators are the *openings* and *closings* [4,5]. Openings are morphological filters with the following properties:
- *increasingness*: $f \leq g \Rightarrow \gamma(f) \leq \gamma(g)$.
- *idempotence*: $\gamma(\gamma(f)) = \gamma(f)$.
- *anti-extensivity*: $f \geq \gamma(f)$.

Closings operators are also morphological filters which are increasing, idempotent and *extensive* ($f \leq \varphi(f)$).

Considering images as a surface, an opening operator filters bright smaller peaks while maintaining the bigger ones. On the other hand, a closing operator sieves smaller darker valleys while preserving the bigger ones. Such removal depends on the type of the filter. For instance, structural openings remove peaks where a structuring element can not be fit [6]. More, the higher the size of the structuring element, the higher the amount of filtered structures.

This paper uses three types of openings:

Definition 1 (Structural opening). *Let f be an image. Let B be a structuring element [12]. The structural opening [4,5] is given by*

$$\gamma_B(f) = \delta_B(\varepsilon_B(f)), \tag{7}$$

where $\delta_B(f)$ and $\varepsilon_B(f)$ are, respectively, the dilation and erosion of f by a structuring element B [12].

Definition 2 (Opening by reconstruction). *Let f be an image. Let B be a structuring element. Let B_c be a structuring element that denotes connectivity [13]. The opening by reconstruction is given by*

$$\gamma_{B,B_c}^{\text{rec}}(f) = \delta_{B_c}^{\text{rec}}(\varepsilon_B(f), f), \tag{8}$$

where $\delta_{B_c}^{\text{rec}}(f,g)$ is the morphological reconstruction of g from f [5].

Definition 3 (Area opening). *Let f be an image. Let $\lambda \geq 0$. The graylevel area opening [14] of parameter λ is given by*

$$\gamma_\lambda^{\text{area}}(f) = \max\{h \leq f(x) : \text{area}(\gamma_x(T_h(f))) \geq \lambda\}, \tag{9}$$

where $T_h(f)$ is the threshold of f with parameter h [14]. In this paper, for simplicity, the graylevel area opening will be called area opening.

This paper also uses three types of closings:

Definition 4 (Structural closing). *Let f be an image. Let B be a structuring element. The structural closing [4,5,12] is given by*

$$\varphi_B(f) = \varepsilon_B(\delta_B(f)). \tag{10}$$

Definition 5 (Closing by reconstruction). *Let f be an image. Let B be a structuring element. Let B_c be a structuring element denoting connectivity. The closing by reconstruction [13] is given by*

$$\varphi_{B,B_c}^{\text{rec}}(f) = \varepsilon_{B_c}^{\text{rec}}(\delta_B(f), f), \tag{11}$$

where $\varepsilon_{B_c}^{\text{rec}}(f,g)$ is the morphological dual reconstruction of g from f [13].

Definition 6 (Area closing). *Let f be an image. Let $\lambda \geq 0$. The graylevel area closing [14] of parameter λ is given by*

$$\varphi_\lambda^{\text{area}}(f) = (\gamma_\lambda^{\text{area}}(f^c))^c, \tag{12}$$

where f^c is the negation of f [4]. Again, for simplicity, the graylevel area closing will be called area closing.

Figure 3 shows a detailed view of the pixels affected by application of two morphological filters, an opening by reconstruction and a closing by reconstruction. In each case, the affected pixels are highlighted in green.

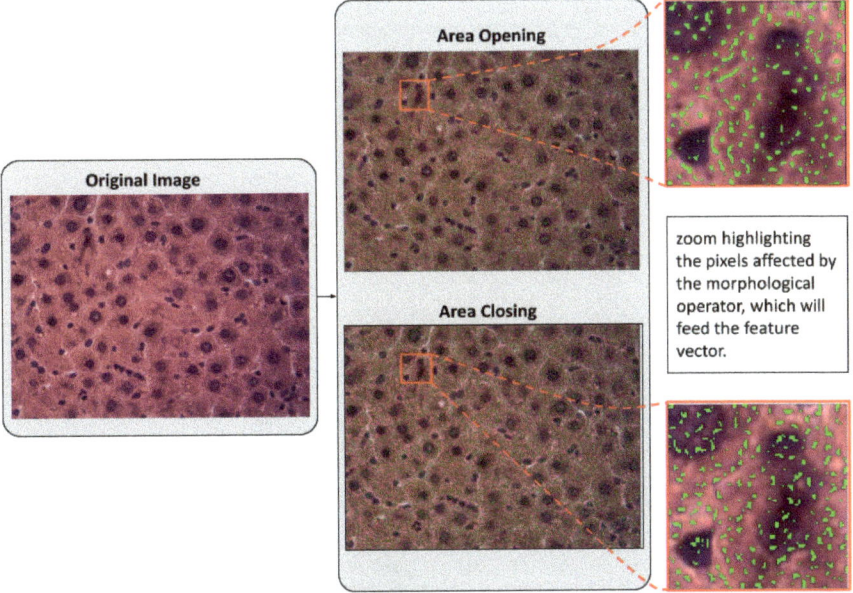

Figure 3. Pixels affected by application of a opening by reconstruction and of a closing by reconstruction, using a disk structuring element with radius one.

Definition 7 (Granulometry). *A granulometry [4,5] is a family of openings* $\Gamma = \{\gamma_\lambda : \lambda \geq 0\}$, *which has the following property:*

$$\forall \mu \geq 0, \ \gamma_\lambda(\gamma_\mu) = \gamma_\mu(\gamma_\lambda) = \gamma_{\max\{\lambda,\mu\}}. \tag{13}$$

Definition 8 (Anti-granulometry). *An anti-granulometry is given by a family of closings* $\Phi = \{\varphi_\lambda : \lambda \geq 0\}$, *such that*

$$\forall \mu \geq 0, \ \varphi_\lambda(\varphi_\mu) = \varphi_\mu(\varphi_\lambda) = \varphi_{\max\{\lambda,\mu\}}. \tag{14}$$

(In this paper, for simplicity, all granulometries and anti-granulometries will be called *granulometry*.)

Let $\Psi = \{\psi_\lambda : \lambda \geq 0\}$ be a granulometry. In the granulometric analysis, the amount of sieved structures by ψ_λ is computed for each increment of λ. Let $\Omega(\Psi)$ be the *size distribution* of Ψ such that $\forall \lambda \geq 0, \Omega(\Psi)(\lambda)$ is the amount of sieved structures by ψ_λ [5]. Note that since $\Omega(\Psi)(\lambda)$ increases as λ is incremented, $\Omega(\Psi)$ is an increasing function.

Definition 9 (Opening Top-Hat). *Let f be an image. The opening top-hat is given by*

$$th(\gamma)(f) = f - \gamma(f).$$

Definition 10 (Closing Top-Hat). *Let f be an image. The closing top-hat is given by*

$$th(\varphi)(f) = \varphi(f) - f.$$

Note that the opening top-hat and closing top-hat are residual operators, which gives the sieved structures (the residue) by application of their respective morphological filters.

Let $\Psi = \{\psi_\lambda : \lambda \geq 0\}$ be a granulometry. Let $\sum f = \sum_x f(x)$ be the sum of all intensities $f(x)$ from an image f. The size distribution of Ψ is given by, $\forall \lambda \geq 0$,

$$\Omega(\Psi)(\lambda) = \sum th(\psi_\lambda). \tag{15}$$

In this measurement, $\Omega(\Psi)(\lambda)$ gives the sum of the volumes of all structures sieved by ψ_λ.

Let $\beta(f)$ be the binarization function, which is given by

$$\beta(f)(x) = \begin{cases} 1 & \text{if } f(x) > 0 \\ 0 & \text{otherwise.} \end{cases}$$

Let $\Psi = \{\psi_\lambda : \lambda \geq 0\}$ be a granulometry. The *binary size distribution* $\Omega_\beta(\Psi)$ is given by $\forall \lambda \geq 0$,

$$\Omega_\beta(\Psi)(\lambda) = \sum \beta(th(\psi_\lambda)). \tag{16}$$

In this measurement, $\Omega_\beta(\Psi)(\lambda)$ gives the number of pixels of all structures sieved by ψ_λ.

Each one of the GBD assessed in this work is built as described in Algorithm 2.

Algorithm 2: Pseudocode for Granulometry-Based Descriptors.

Input: *img*: Color image under the RGB color space model,
binary: Boolean value: TRUE for binary granulometry; FALSE for gray level granulometry
Output: $\Psi = \{\psi_\lambda : 1 \leq \lambda \leq 50\}$: Feature vector with 50 elements.
$img_r \leftarrow img$ red band
$img_g \leftarrow img$ green band
$img_b \leftarrow img$ blue band
$f \leftarrow img_r + img_g + img_b$

if *binary* **then**
  for each $\lambda \in [1, \cdots, 50]$ **do**
    $\Omega(\Psi)(\lambda) \leftarrow \sum \beta(th(\psi_\lambda)(f))$
else
  for each $\lambda \in [1, \cdots, 50]$ **do**
    $\Omega_\beta(\Psi)(\lambda) \leftarrow \sum th(\psi_\lambda)(f)$

Table 2 summarizes the set of twelve GBD tested in this work. Figure 4 illustrates the construction of a size distribution $\Omega(\Gamma)$ from a granulometry given by a family of openings by reconstruction. For each λ, a disk structuring element B_λ of radius λ was used by the filter $\gamma^{rec}_{B_\lambda, B_c}$. The residue of such a filter is summed and taken as the λ-th component of the feature vector.

Figures 5 and 6 show two sets of binary size distributions computed for each image from the dataset introduced in Section 3. In this example, 120 binary size distributions were computed: the blue curves are related to control images; the red ones are related to the Walker 256 tumor images.

Table 2. Granulometry-based descriptors.

Descriptor	Morphological Filter	Size Distribution
SO	Structural Opening	$\Omega(\Gamma)$
BinSO	Structural Opening (binary)	$\Omega_\beta(\Gamma)$
RO	Opening by Reconstruction	$\Omega(\Gamma^{rec})$
BinRO	Opening by Reconstruction (binary)	$\Omega_\beta(\Gamma^{rec})$
AO	Area Opening	$\Omega(\Gamma^{area})$
BinAO	Area Opening (binary)	$\Omega_\beta(\Gamma^{area})$
SC	Structural Closing	$\Omega(\Phi)$
BinSC	Structural Closing (binary)	$\Omega_\beta(\Phi)$
RC	Closing by Reconstruction	$\Omega(\Phi^{rec})$
BinRC	Closing by Reconstruction (binary)	$\Omega_\beta(\Phi^{rec})$
AC	Area Closing	$\Omega(\Phi^{area})$
BinAC	Area Closing (binary)	$\Omega_\beta(\Phi^{area})$

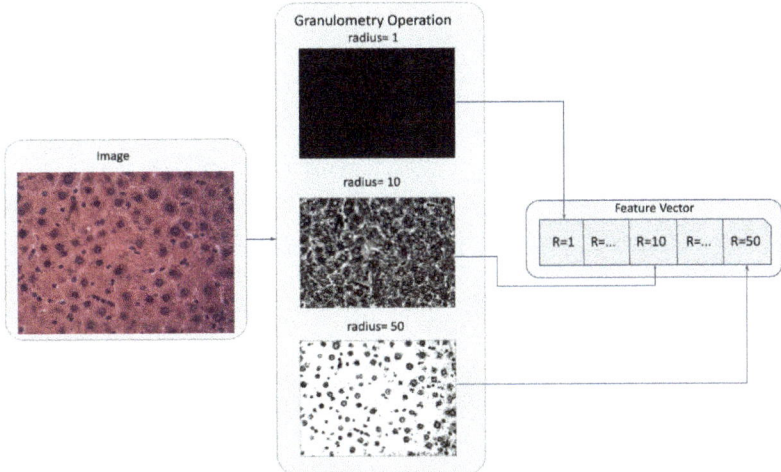

Figure 4. GBD generated by an opening by reconstruction. A disk-structuring element with radius λ was used for each λ.

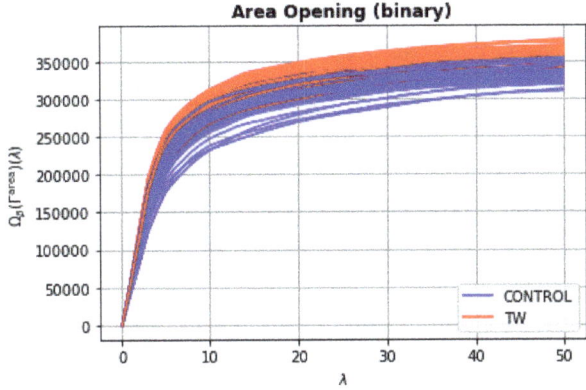

Figure 5. Binary size distributions from an area opening granulometry, $\lambda \in [1, \cdots, 50]$. One size distribution was computed for each image from the dataset introduced in Section 3.

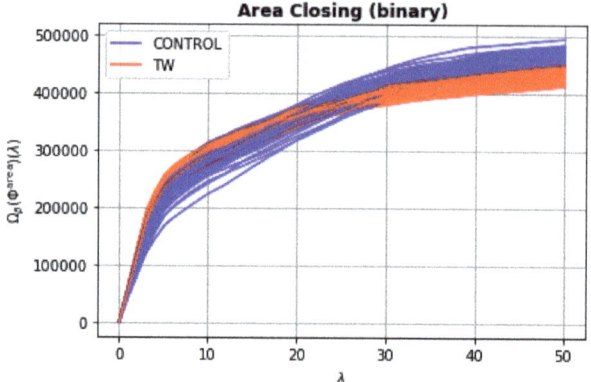

Figure 6. Binary size distributions from an area closing granulometry, $\lambda \in [1, \cdots, 50]$. One size distribution was computed for each image from the dataset introduced in Section 3.

5. Methodology Used For Classification

In this work, we have chosen three of the most popular classifiers algorithms frequently used in different classification scenarios. Figure 7 illustrates the general overview of the methodology used for classification.

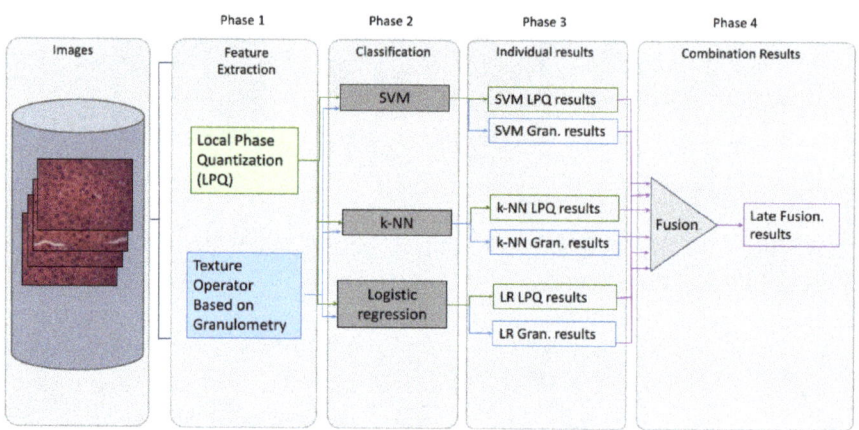

Figure 7. General overview of the methodology used for classification.

As we can see, in phase 1, the extraction of the handcrafted features is performed. The texture operators used are those already described in Section 4. Next, in phase 2, the classification is carried out using one of the three classifiers described in this section. In phase 3, the results are evaluated considering each possible combination *feature × classifiers* in isolation. Finally, in phase 4, the fusions combining the outputs of the classifiers with the best individual performances are evaluated, using late fusion strategies (i.e., max rule, sum rule and product rule) proposed by Kittler et al. [15]. Equations (17)–(19) describe the mathematical details behind the max, product and sum combinations rules, respectively. In these equations, x is the pattern to be classified, c is the number of classes involved in the problem, n is the number of classifiers involved in the combination, ω_k represents a class, with $k \in 1..c$, and $P(\omega_k|l_i(x))$ is the probability that x belongs to the class ω_k according to the classifier i.

$$\text{Max Rule }(x) = arg \max_{k=1}^{c} \max_{i=1}^{n} P(\omega_k|l_i(x)) \qquad (17)$$

$$\text{Product Rule } (x) = \arg\max_{k=1}^{c} \prod_{i=1}^{n} P(\omega_k | l_i(x)) \tag{18}$$

$$\text{Sum Rule } (x) = \arg\max_{k=1}^{c} \sum_{i=1}^{n} P(\omega_k | l_i(x)) \tag{19}$$

Three classifiers' algorithms were applied in this work: Support Vector Machines (SVM), K-Nearest Neighbor and Logistic Regression.

SVM: Support Vector Machine (SVM) was first proposed by Vladmir Vapnik [16]. The SVM algorithm is able to perform the classification by determining a hyperplane that best separates the classes in the training data [17]. In this work, we used the Gaussian kernel, and cost and gamma parameters were tuned using a grid search.

k-NN: k-NN is an instance-based algorithm widely used for classification. The K-Nearest Neighbor algorithm for binary classifications is considered simple when compared to other machine learning algorithms [18]. Despite its simplicity, k-NN is still one of the top 10 classification algorithms in machine learning [19]. This simplicity lies in the fact that it assumes all instances as points in the $\mathbb{R}^n$ dimensional space and uses a distance metric (e.g., the Euclidean distance is frequently used in this case) to decide whether the element belongs to class A or class B [18,20]. In the experiments, various numbers of neighbors were tested, and k = 5 was chosen as it performed better than the other odd values.

Logistic Regression: Logistic Regression is a special case of Regression [21]. Logistic Regression uses the following equation:

$$p(X) = \frac{e^{\beta_0 + \beta_1 X}}{1 + e^{\beta_0 + \beta_1 X}} = \frac{1}{1 + e^{-\beta_0 + \beta_1 X}},$$

in which β_0 and β_1 are associated with every independent variable and are calculated by the likelihood method based on the dataset. Reglog is a statistical technique that establishes a relationship between the variable of interest and the probability of the outcome occurring; this probability has the value of success (1) and failure (0) [21]. The values β_0 and β_1 assume the value that maximizes the probability of the observed sample [22].

The choice for shallow learning methods in this work is basically justified by the following aspects: (i) the number of samples available in the dataset is quite limited, which makes it not appropriate to be addressed using deep learning methods; (ii) the accuracy rates achieved using handcrafted features and shallow learning proved to be suitable to address the problem both in terms of accuracy and computational time.

6. Experimental Results and Discussion

In this section, we describe the results obtained using the LPQ descriptor, the GBD and the late fusion between them. As there were six animals per class (i.e., control and TW), we decided to organize the data making cross-validation such a way one subject per class was taken to compose the test set for each round of training.

Let us call the six control subjects C_1, C_2, C_3, C_4, C_5 and C_6 and the six subjects affected by Walker tumor TW_1, TW_2, TW_3, TW_4, TW_5 and TW_6. One control subject and one TW subject were separated to be tested on a model trained using all the remaining subjects. For example, in the first round, $\{C_1 \cup TW_1\}$ was tested on a model trained using $\{C_2 \cup C_3 \cup C_4 \cup C_5 \cup C_6 \cup TW_2 \cup TW_3 \cup TW_4 \cup TW_5 \cup TW_6\}$. On the second round, $\{C_2 \cup TW_2\}$ was used for the test, and so on, characterizing a six-fold cross-validation. This strategy was used to avoid the presence of samples taken from the same subject both on test and training sets simultaneously, which could introduce a bias on the classifier.

6.1. Results Obtained Using LPQ

Table 3 presents the accuracies found using SVM, k-NN and Logistic Regression classifiers, fed by the LPQ feature vector. Window sizes 3, 5, 7 and 9 were experimented. The best results were achieved using the SVM classifier with features vectors built using window sizes 5, 7 and 9.

Table 3. Classification accuracy using LPQ descriptor.

	SVM (%)	5-NN (%)	REG (%)
LPQ_3	76.67	65.83	66.67
LPQ_5	**91.67**	84.166	83.33
LPQ_7	**91.67**	80.83	74.16
LPQ_9	**91.67**	78.33	69.16

As we can see, an accuracy of 91.67% was achieved with LPQ_5, LPQ_7 and LPQ_9; with these results, we can now confirm our first research question (**RQ1**), that it is possible to perform cancer identification exploring a spectral-based texture descriptor on microphotographs of rat liver.

6.2. Results Obtained Using GBD

Tables 4 and 5 present the accuracies obtained using SVM, k-NN and Logistic Regression classifiers, trained with the feature vectors created using the GBD described in Section 6.2. The tables are divided according to the descriptor obtained by the closing and opening morphological operations. Table 4 represents, respectively, Area Closing (AC), Area Closing Binary (BinAC), Structural Closing (SC), Structural Closing Binary (BinSC), Reconstruction Closing (RC) and Reconstruction Closing Binary (BinRC). Table 5 represents, respectively, Area Opening (AO), Area Opening Binary (BinAO), Structural Opening (SO), Structural Opening Binary (BinSO), Reconstruction Opening (RO) and Reconstruction Opening Binary (BinRO).

Table 4. Classification accuracy using closing vectors.

	SVM (%)	5-NN (%)	REG (%)
AC	95.00	85.00	92.50
BinAC	**96.67**	95.83	88.33
SC	67.50	54.16	85.83
BinSC	71.66	75.83	92.50
RC	79.99	65.83	76.66
BinRC	82.50	70.83	75.83

Table 5. Classification accuracy using opening vectors.

	SVM (%)	5-NN (%)	REG (%)
AO	61.66	53.33	71.66
BinAO	**89.16**	88.33	86.66
SO	59.16	52.50	70.00
BinSO	70.00	70.83	87.50
RO	57.75	52.50	50.83
BinRO	73.33	69.16	67.50

The accuracies achieved with the vectors extracted using the Closing operation, as shown in Table 4, in almost all classifiers are superior to the accuracies achieved with the Opening vectors, as shown in Table 5. It is noticeable that the Area Closing Binary (BinAC) achieved the best results when compared to other morphological filters, reaching the 96.67% mark using SVM and 95.83% using k-NN ($k = 5$) classifier.

The Reconstruction Opening (RO) vector, as shown in Table 5, obtained the lowest accuracies in all experiments, 50.83%, with the Logistic Regression classifier.

The results obtained using vectors obtained by the granulometry operations were very divergent; AC, BinAC and BinSC performed even better than LPQ, and others such as SO and RO obtained very poor results. Concerning our **RQ2**, we can conclude it is possible to perform cancer identification exploring some granulometry filters described in Section 4, but not all of them.

6.3. Results Obtained Using Late Fusion strategies

Finally, aiming to achieve better results, the sum, max and product combination rules were employed as a late fusion strategy. In all cases, the sum rule obtained the best results. Due to this, we decided to describe in Table 6 only the results obtained with this rule. The results described were obtained combining the three classifiers chosen among those with the best performance in the experiments described previously.

Table 6. Accuracies obtained with late fusion combinations.

Classifier	Individual Results (%)	Combination Results (%)
LPQ_7–SVM	91.67	
BinAC–5-NN	95.83	**99.16**
BinSC–Reg	92.50	
LPQ_7–SVM	91.67	
AC–SVM	95.00	**99.16**
BinAC–5-NN	95.83	
LPQ_7–SVM	91.67	
AC–SVM	95.00	98.33
BinSC–SVM	82.50	

The best overall results obtained in this work, i.e., 99.16% of accuracy, were obtained in two different scenarios. The first one occurred in the combination between LPQ_7–SVM, BinAC–5-NN and BinSC–Reg. It is worth mentioning that in isolation, these classifiers had reached, respectively, 91.67%, 95.83% and 92.50%, as can be seen in the first section of Table 6.

The second scenario in which the best rate was obtained happened when the classifiers LPQ_7–SVM, AC–SVM and BinAC–5-NN were combined. In isolation, these classifiers had reached, respectively, 91.67%, 95.00% and 95.83%, as can be seen in the second section of Table 6.

An accuracy of 98.33% was reached by combining LPQ_7–SVM, AC–SVM and BinSC–SVM. In isolation, these classifiers had reached, respectively, 91.67%, 95.00% and 82.50%, as can be seen in the third section of Table 6.

6.4. Discussions

Aiming to check whether or not there is a statistical difference between the best results obtained using LPQ, Opening Vectors, Closing Vectors, and the best late fusion result, we performed the Friedman statistical test.

The Friedman test was made using the accuracies obtained by the Late Fusion (LPQ_7–SVM, BinAC–5-NN and BinSC–Reg), BinAC–SVM, BinAO–SVM and LPQ_7–SVM classifiers. The accuracies were computed over each folder, as described in the beginning of Section 6. The test presented a p-value of 0.0299; considering $\alpha = 0.05$, we can conclude that the performance of the classifiers are not all equivalent to each other.

Furthermore, the selected classifiers were ranked according to their accuracies, as can be seen in Table 7. As a result, the superior performance of the Late Fusion technique is attested.

In respect to **RQ3**, we can conclude that classifiers built with LPQ and GBD presented a good level of complementarity to each other. As a consequence of this complementarity, the late fusion obtained the best overall results reported in this work.

Table 7. Classifiers ranking.

Fold	Late Fusion	BinAC–SVM	BinAO–SVM	LPQ_7–SVM
f1	1	2.5	4	2.5
f2	1.5	1.5	3	4
f3	1.5	1.5	3.5	3.5
f4	1.5	1.5	3	4
f5	1.5	1.5	4	3
f6	1.5	4	1.5	3
Average	1.416	2.083	3.166	3.333

7. Concluding Remarks

We proposed a method for cancer identification exploring texture properties taken from microphotographs of rat liver. For this, we used the LPQ spectral texture operator, a widely used descriptor, especially when the images may be affected by blur, a noise that typically occurs in images such as those used in this work. We also experimented with GBD, and lastly, we investigated the complementarity between classifiers created in both scenarios by using late fusion strategies.

Experiments performed on a dataset created by researchers from Enteric Neural Plasticity Laboratory of the State University of Maringá confirm the efficiency of the proposed strategies in isolation. In addition, we noticed an important level of complementarity between the classifiers created using both descriptors experimented. The best result obtained using LPQ was 91.16% of accuracy. In this way, it is possible to state that cancer can be identified in the Walker 256 tumor model using the LPQ texture operator with reasonably good rates, answering **RQ1**. For GBD, the best result obtained was 96.67% of accuracy, which responds positively to **RQ2**. Finally, the best overall result was obtained combining classifiers created using both LPQ and GBD descriptors, achieving 99.16% of accuracy. Thus, we can state that **RQ3** was also positively answered.

Finally, we make a brief comment regarding the main limitation of this work. As happens in several works that deal with biomedical images, the main difficulty faced here refers to the limited size of the dataset, which makes it more difficult to create a more robust model and to make comparisons. Aiming to mitigate this issue, we performed the Friedman statistical test, and we confirmed that there is a meaningful difference between the results obtained by combining both strategies investigated here and the results obtained by each strategy in isolation.

As future work, we intend to expand our investigations using an additional dataset currently under development. This dataset is also being created by researchers from Enteric Neural Plasticity Laboratory of the State University of Maringá. In this new version of the dataset, two new classes will be included: treated control and treated Walker 256 tumor. Other tests using granulometry, such as pattern spectrum and others, are also planned to be made.

Author Contributions: Conceptualization, M.F.T.C., S.A.S.J., F.C.F., J.V.C.M.P., J.N.Z. and Y.M.G.C.; Data curation, C.C.O.B.; Funding acquisition, Y.M.G.C.; Investigation, M.F.T.C., S.A.S.J. and F.C.F.; Methodology, M.F.T.C., S.A.S.J., F.C.F. and Y.M.G.C.; Project administration, F.C.F. and Y.M.G.C.; Supervision, F.C.F. and Y.M.G.C.; Validation, M.F.T.C., S.A.S.J., C.C.O.B., F.C.F., J.V.C.M.P. and Y.M.G.C.; Visualization, J.N.Z.; Writing—original draft, M.F.T.C., S.A.S.J., F.C.F. and Y.M.G.C.; Writing—review and editing, M.F.T.C., S.A.S.J., F.C.F., J.V.C.M.P., J.N.Z. and Y.M.G.C. All authors have read and agreed to the published version of the manuscript.

Funding: This research has been partly supported by the Brazilian agencies National Council for Scientific and Technological Development (CNPq) and Coordination for the Improvement of Higher Education Personnel (CAPES).

Institutional Review Board Statement: Ethical review and approval were waived for this study due to the use of rats during the image acquisition phase of the dataset construction. The study follows the ethical principles under the terms set out in the Brazilian federal Law 11,794 (October 2008) and the Decree 66,689 (July 2009) established by the Brazilian Society of Science on Laboratory Animals (SBCAL). All the proceedings were submitted and approved by the Standing Committee on Ethics in Animals Experimentation of the State University of Maringá under Protocol number 8617130120.

Informed Consent Statement: Not applicable.

Data Availability Statement: The dataset used in this study will be made available in due course on GitHub at: https://github.com/Sersasj/Liver_Dataset (accessed on 1 April 2022).

Acknowledgments: We thank the support of the Enteric Neural Plasticity Laboratory and Intelligent Interactive Systems Laboratory of the State University of Maringá. We also thank the Brazilian agencies National Council for Scientific and Technological Development (CNPq), and Coordination for the Improvement of Higher Education Personnel (CAPES).

Conflicts of Interest: The authors declare no conflict of interest.

Abbreviations

The following abbreviations are used in this manuscript:

AC	Area Closing
AO	Area Opening
BinAC	Area Closing (binary)
BinAO	Area Opening (binary)
BinRC	Closing by Reconstruction (binary)
BinSC	Structural Closing (binary)
BinSO	Structural Opening (binary)
BinRO	Opening by Reconstruction (binary)
C	Control group
GBD	Granulometry-Based Descriptors
k-NN	k-Nearest Neighbor
LPQ	Local Phase Quantization
MM	Mathematical Morphology
RGB	Red, Green and Blue color space
RC	Closing by Reconstruction
RQ	Research Question
RO	Opening by Reconstruction
SC	Structural Closing
SE	Structuring Element
SO	Structural Opening
STFT	Shor-Time Fourier Transform
SVM	Support Vector Machine
TW	Walker 256 Tumor

References

1. Ferlay, J.; Ervik, M.; Lam, F.; Colombet, M.; Mery, L.; Piñeros, M.; Znaor, A.; Soerjomataram, I.; Bray, F. *Global Cancer Observatory: Cancer Today*; International Agency for Research on Cancer: Lyon, France, 2018; pp. 1–6.
2. Felipe, G.Z.; Zanoni, J.N.; Sehaber-Sierakowski, C.C.; Bossolani, G.D.; Souza, S.R.; Flores, F.C.; Oliveira, L.E.; Pereira, R.M.; Costa, Y.M. Automatic chronic degenerative diseases identification using enteric nervous system images. *Neural Comput. Appl.* **2021**, *33*, 15373–15395. [CrossRef]
3. Ojansivu, V.; Heikkilä, J. Blur insensitive texture classification using local phase quantization. In *International Conference on Image and Signal Processing*; Springer: Berlin/Heidelberg, Germany, 2008; pp. 236–243.
4. Najman, L.; Talbot, H. *Mathematical Morphology: From Theory to Applications*; John Wiley & Sons: Hoboken, NJ, USA, 2013.
5. Dougherty, E.R.; Lotufo, R.A. *Hands-On Morphological Image Processing*; SPIE Press: Bellingham, WA, USA, 2003; Volume 59.
6. Gonzalez, R.C.; Woods, R.E. *Digital Image Processing*; Prentice Hall: Upper Saddle River, NJ, USA, 2008.
7. de Matos, J.; Ataky, S.T.M.; de Souza Britto, A.; Soares de Oliveira, L.E.; Lameiras Koerich, A. Machine learning methods for histopathological image analysis: A review. *Electronics* **2021**, *10*, 562. [CrossRef]

8. Nativ, N.I.; Chen, A.I.; Yarmush, G.; Henry, S.D.; Lefkowitch, J.H.; Klein, K.M.; Maguire, T.J.; Schloss, R.; Guarrera, J.V.; Berthiaume, F.; et al. Automated image analysis method for detecting and quantifying macrovesicular steatosis in hematoxylin and eosin–stained histology images of human livers. *Liver Transplant.* **2014**, *20*, 228–236. [CrossRef] [PubMed]
9. Shi, P.; Chen, J.; Lin, J.; Zhang, L. High-throughput fat quantifications of hematoxylin-eosin stained liver histopathological images based on pixel-wise clustering. *Sci. China Inf. Sci.* **2017**, *60*, 092108. [CrossRef]
10. Thiran, J.P.; Macq, B. Morphological feature extraction for the classification of digital images of cancerous tissues. *IEEE Trans. Biomed. Eng.* **1996**, *43*, 1011–1020. [CrossRef] [PubMed]
11. Bernardo, C.C.O. Effect of supplementation with l-glutationa 1% on the liver of wistar rats implanted with walker's tumor 256. Master's Thesis, Maringá State University, Maringá, Brazil, 2021.
12. Haralick, R.M.; Sternberg, S.R.; Zhuang, X. Image analysis using mathematical morphology. In *IEEE Transactions on Pattern Analysis and Machine Intelligence*; IEEE: Piscataway, NJ, USA, 1987; pp. 532–550.
13. Vincent, L. Morphological grayscale reconstruction in image analysis: applications and efficient algorithms. *IEEE Trans. Image Process.* **1993**, *2*, 176–201. [CrossRef] [PubMed]
14. Vincent, L. Grayscale area openings and closings, their efficient implementation and applications. In Proceedings of the First Workshop on Mathematical Morphology and its Applications to Signal Processing, Barcelona, Spain, 10–14 May 1993; pp. 22–27.
15. Kittler, J.; Hatef, M.; Duin, R.P.; Matas, J. On combining classifiers. *IEEE Trans. Pattern Anal. Mach. Intell.* **1998**, *20*, 226–239. [CrossRef]
16. Vapnik Vladimir, N. *The Nature of Statistical Learning Theory*; Springer: Berlin/Heidelberg, Germany, 1995.
17. Kowalczyk, A. *Support Vector Machine Succinctly*; Syncfusion: Morrisville, NC, USA, 2017.
18. Shalev-Shwartz, S. *Understanding Machine Learning: From Theory to Algorithms*; Cambridge University Press: New York, NY, USA, 2014.
19. Zhang, S. Cost-sensitive KNN classification. *Neurocomputing* **2020**, *391*, 234–242. [CrossRef]
20. Mitchell, T.M. *Machine Learning*; MacGraw-Hill: New York, NY, USA, 1997.
21. Hosmer, D.W., Jr.; Lemeshow, S.; Sturdivant, R.X. *Applied Logistic Regression*; John Wiley & Sons: Hoboken, NJ, USA, 2013.
22. James, G.; Witten, D.; Hastie, T.; Tibshirani, R. *An Introduction to Statistical Learning: With Application in R*; Springer: Berlin/Heidelberg, Germany, 2021.

Article

Impact of Iterative Bilateral Filtering on the Noise Power Spectrum of Computed Tomography Images

Choirul Anam [1,*], Ariij Naufal [1], Heri Sutanto [1], Kusworo Adi [1] and Geoff Dougherty [2]

[1] Department of Physics, Faculty of Sciences and Mathematics, Diponegoro University, Semarang 50275, Indonesia
[2] Department of Applied Physics and Medical Imaging, California State University Channel Islands, Camarillo, CA 93012, USA
* Correspondence: anam@fisika.fsm.undip.ac.id

Abstract: A bilateral filter is a non-linear denoising algorithm that can reduce noise while preserving the edges. This study explores the characteristics of a bilateral filter in changing the noise and texture within computed tomography (CT) images in an iterative implementation. We collected images of a homogeneous Neusoft phantom scanned with tube currents of 77, 154, and 231 mAs. The images for each tube current were filtered five times with a configuration of sigma space (σ_d) = 2 pixels, sigma intensity (σ_r) = noise level, and a kernel of 5 × 5 pixels. To observe the noise texture in each filter iteration, the noise power spectrum (NPS) was obtained for the five slices of each dataset and averaged to generate a stable curve. The modulation-transfer function (MTF) was also measured from the original and the filtered images. Tests on an anthropomorphic phantom image were carried out to observe their impact on clinical scenarios. Noise measurements and visual observations of edge sharpness were performed on this image. Our results showed that the bilateral filter was effective in suppressing noise at high frequencies, which is confirmed by the sloping NPS curve for different tube currents. The peak frequency was shifted from about 0.2 to about 0.1 mm^{-1} for all tube currents, and the noise magnitude was reduced by more than 50% compared to the original images. The spatial resolution does not change with the number of iterations of the filter, which is confirmed by the constant values of MTF50 and MTF10. The test results on the anthropomorphic phantom image show a similar pattern, with noise reduced by up to 60% and object edges remaining sharp.

Keywords: bilateral filter; computed tomography; noise power spectrum

1. Introduction

Despite its popular applications in medical imaging, computed tomography (CT) provides a relatively high-radiation dose for patients that can increase the probability of malignancy [1,2] in leukemia and brain cancer [1,3]. Various efforts were made to overcome this problem by following the "as low as reasonably achievable" (ALARA) principle [4]. The two areas of study that are most frequently explored include reducing patient doses as effectively as possible [5–7] and improving image quality for diagnostic purposes [8,9].

Image quality can be determined by selecting appropriate input parameters before scanning, such as tube current, tube voltage, rotation time, pitch, reconstruction type, reconstruction filter, and so on [10–12], and it can be enhanced at the post-processing stage. Radiographers or medical physicists select the pre-scanning input parameters and can perform noise reduction to get an improved image during post-scanning (i.e., after scanning the patient or phantom). Filtering the image using a noise reduction algorithm can not only suppress image noise but also allows patients to be exposed to a lower dose. However, although these filters can suppress noise, they tend to produce blurriness in the images [13]. Many linear denoising algorithms have been developed, such as the Wiener [14] and Gaussian filters [15].

Non-linear filters, such as the bilateral filter, non-local mean filter, total variation filter, and wavelet filter [16], can be used to overcome the shortcomings of linear filters. The bilateral filter uses two weights in the process, namely distance weighting (σ_d) and intensity weighting (σ_r) [17]. Its behavior in filtering images based on these weights results in less-noisy images while preserving edges [18], making it one of the most widely used noise-reducing filters [19].

There have been many studies of the various aspects of the bilateral filter, including theoretical studies [20], determination of optimal parameters [21,22], modification [23,24], and acceleration of the process [25,26]. However, to our knowledge, there are no studies characterizing the bilateral filter in the context of iterative filtering. Since bilateral filters can be iterated [27,28], it is necessary to explore the impact of iteration on noise texture, because noise texture is an important parameter of image quality [29–31]. This study does not introduce a new perspective on the bilateral filter, but rather it investigated the effects of iteration on bilateral filtering of CT images and analyzed its impact on the noise texture. The study aims to provide a better understanding of the nature of bilateral filters and preferences for implementing them in CT images.

2. Materials and Methods

2.1. Phantom Images

We scanned a Neusoft CT phantom (Neusoft Medical System, Shenyang, China) with the parameters shown in Table 1. Variations in tube current were used to obtain images with various noise levels. Other parameters were set to standard values often used for quality control procedures. For filtering, 5 slices of the homogeneous water phantom body of each dataset were selected. Figure 1 shows sample images using various tube currents.

Table 1. Scan parameters.

Parameter	Value
Scanner	Neusoft NeuViz 16 Classic
Tube current (mAs)	77, 154, 231
Tube voltage (kVp)	120
Slice thickness (mm)	5
Scan option	Helical
Pitch	1.2
Convolution kernel	F20
Image reconstruction	Filtered-back projection

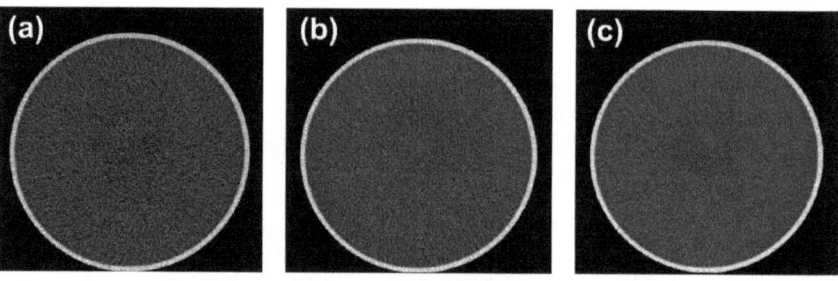

Figure 1. Sample images of a homogeneous water phantom scanned with tube currents of (**a**) 77, (**b**) 154, and (**c**) 231 mAs.

2.2. Bilateral Filter

The bilateral filter [16] uses non-linear image denoising. It was developed from the principle of spatial Gaussian convolution which is linear and only considers one weighting factor to apply smoothing to the image. Equation (1) shows the principle of Gaussian convolution.

$$g[i,j] = \frac{1}{W_s} \sum_m \sum_n f[m,n] G_{\sigma_d}[i-m, j-n] \tag{1}$$

where g is the result of convolution, W_s is the normalization factor, f is the initial pixel value, and G is Gaussian spatial convolution. Gaussian convolution weights each pixel within the kernel according to the weighting of the Gaussian distribution evenly, so that it is still in the linear smoothing category. The bilateral filter takes this principle and adds an intensity-weighted factor. Equation (2) shows the principle of the bilateral filter.

$$g[i,j] = \frac{1}{W_{sb}} \sum_m \sum_n f[m,n] G_{\sigma_d}[i-m, j-n] G_{\sigma_r}(f[m,n] - f[i,j]) \tag{2}$$

where G_{σ_d} is a Gaussian spatial convolution and G_{σ_r} is a Gaussian intensity. In the bilateral filter, the Gaussian spatial convolution is biased with its intensity weighting taken from the neighboring pixels inside the kernel. This consideration gives a non-linear nature that produces an image with reduced noise, while still preserving the edges [27,32].

2.3. Implementation of Bilateral Filter, Measurement of Noise Power Spectrum and Spatial Resolution

The noise power spectrum (NPS) describes the texture of noise in the frequency domain [29]. The 2D NPS is estimated as shown in Equation (3) [33].

$$NPS_{(u,v)} = \frac{d_x d_y}{N_x N_y} \cdot |\mathcal{F}[I(x,y) - P(x,y)]|^2 \tag{3}$$

where u and v are spatial frequency in the x and y direction, d_x and d_y are pixel size in mm, N_x and N_y are number of pixels in the x and y direction of the region of interest (ROI), $\mathcal{F}$ denotes the 2D Fourier transform, $I(x,y)$ is the pixel value in Hounsfield Units (HU), and $P(x,y)$ is the second order polynomial fit of $I(x,y)$.

The description of NPS is Summarized as the peak frequency (f_P) and the average frequency (f_A) shown in Equations (4) and (5) [34].

$$f_P = \mathrm{argmax}[NPS(f)] \tag{4}$$

$$f_A = \frac{\int f \cdot NPS(f)\, df}{\int NPS(f)\, df} \tag{5}$$

where f is the radial spatial frequency, and $NPS(f)$ is the radially averaged 1D NPS.

Before filtering an image, we measured NPS using ImQuest (Duke University, Durham, NC, USA) [35] with a total ROI of 5, a size of 64 pixels, and a sampling angle of 10. This was carried out to obtain a description of the noise in the original image before filtering. The ROIs for measuring NPS is shown in Figure 2.

The edge of the modulation transfer function (MTF) [36] was also measured automatically by IndoQCT [37] to get a more complete picture of the spatial resolution of the filtered image. The edge MTF was chosen as the spatial resolution parameter because the phantom used was a homogeneous phantom [36]. The steps to obtain the edge MTF are shown in Figure 3. A square ROI is placed on the edge of the phantom at the 12 o'clock position (Figure 3a) and then the pixels were averaged in the x-axis direction to obtain a curve called the edge spread function (ESF) (Figure 3b). Tail replacement is performed on this curve to obtain the corrected ESF shape (Figure 3c). The corrected ESF curve is then differentiated to produce a line spread function (LSF) curve (Figure 3d) which is then zeroed and normalized. The Fourier transform of the LSF curve gives the MTF curve (Figure 3e). Bilateral filtering, NPS and MTF measurements were performed sequentially on 5 selected images of a homogeneous phantom.

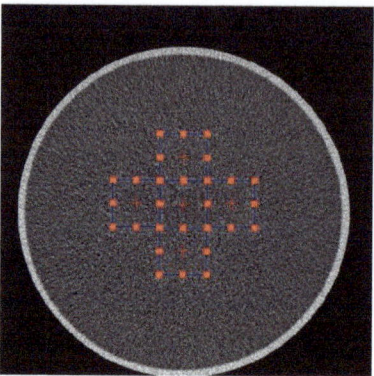

Figure 2. NPS measurement using 5 regions of interest (ROIs).

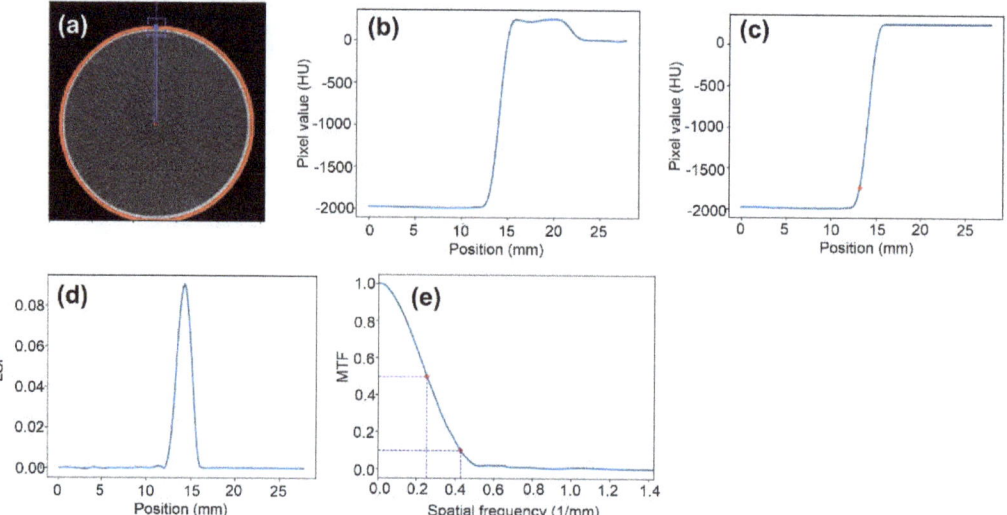

Figure 3. Edge MTF measurement. (**a**) ROI placement on the phantom, (**b**) ESF curve, (**c**) ESF curve after tail replacement, (**d**) LSF curve, and (**e**) MTF curve.

The bilateral filter was applied to these images with the configuration of sigma space (σ_d) = 2, sigma intensity (σ_r) = noise level, and kernel size 5 × 5 pixels. The noise (σ) was obtained using an automatic noise measurement algorithm [38] on the first image. After the images were filtered, the NPS and MTF measurement were performed using the same configuration as before. Filtering was performed repeatedly on the previously filtered image 5 times so that 6 NPS and 6 MTF curves were obtained including the original one. Both NPS and MTF measurement as well as the filtering processes were carried out on 5 slices of a homogeneous water phantom for each variation of tube current to obtain more stable and comprehensive results. Figure 4 shows an example of the filtered images.

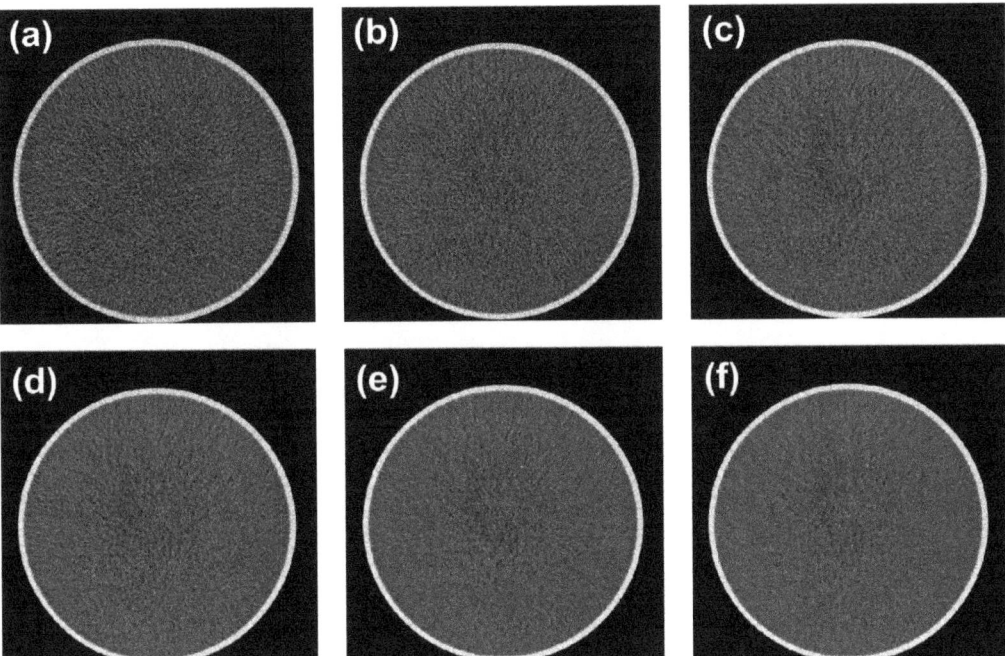

Figure 4. A homogeneous water phantom image on a tube current of 77 mAs filtered repeatedly. (**a**) Original image, filtered image iteratively in (**b**) 1, (**c**) 2, (**d**) 3, (**e**) 4, and (**f**) 5 times.

2.4. Implementation of Anthropomorphic Phantom Images

To observe the impact of bilateral filters in clinical scenarios, we obtained anthropomorphic images with scan parameters as shown in Table 2. As before, the bilateral filter was run for 5 iterations on the head anthropomorphic phantom image. The noise was measured using a circular ROI with a radius of 10 mm in the frontal lobe area (Figure 5a). In terms of spatial resolution, we used visual observations on the visible areas of soft tissue, bone, and air (Figure 5b). Comparisons using structural similarity (SSIM) were also carried out to get a more comprehensive description. SSIM was obtained by comparing the filtered image with the original image.

Table 2. Scan parameters on anthropomorphic phantoms.

Parameter	Value
Scanner	Toshiba Alexion
Tube current (mAs)	100
Tube voltage (kVp)	120
Slice thickness (mm)	7
Scan option	Helical
Pitch	1.5
Convolution kernel	FC13
Image reconstruction	Filtered-back projection

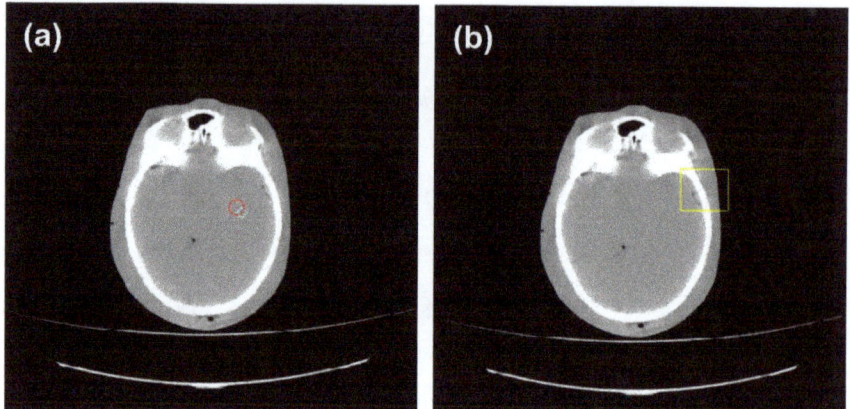

Figure 5. Anthropomorphic phantom image of the head. (**a**) ROI for measuring noise, (**b**) ROI for observing spatial resolution.

3. Results

3.1. Tube Current of 77 mAs

Figure 6 shows the 1D NPS at each filter iteration. The NPS at a frequency of about 0.2 mm^{-1} decreased significantly with the number of filter iterations. The peak frequency is shifted to a lower value, and the NPS at very high frequencies (>0.4 mm^{-1}) was almost completely suppressed by the 5th iteration. This shows the effectiveness of the bilateral filter in filtering noise at high frequencies.

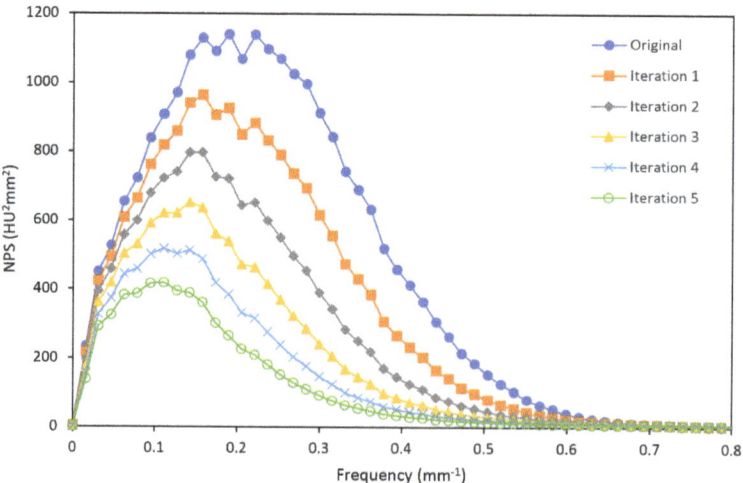

Figure 6. NPS on repeatedly filtered images at a tube current of 77 mAs.

Figure 7 shows the noise of the original image and the filtered image in five iterations with a tube current of 77 mAs. The noise magnitude decreased while the percentage of reduced noise increased with the number of filter iterations. The peak frequency and mean frequency shifted down gradually from 0.19 mm^{-1} to 0.11 mm^{-1} and from 0.24 mm^{-1} to 0.17 mm^{-1}, respectively. These results indicate a decrease in NPS at a certain frequency as a result of repeated filtering at low tube currents.

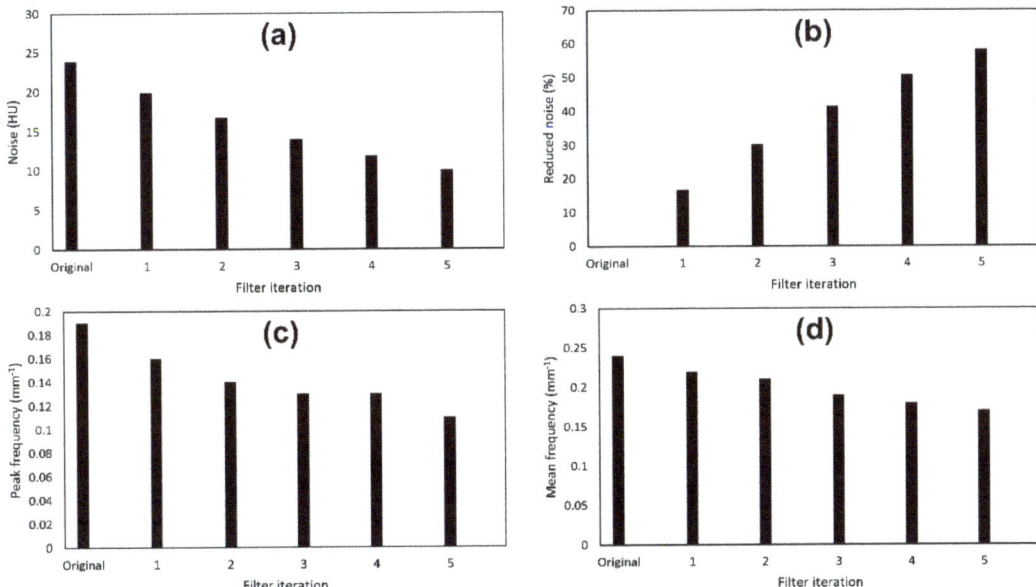

Figure 7. Noise measurement on homogeneous phantom with tube current of 77 mAs. (**a**) Noise, (**b**) Percentage of reduced noise, (**c**) Peak frequency, and (**d**) Mean frequency.

Figure 8 shows the spatial resolution of each filter iteration at a tube current of 77 mAs. Table 3 shows the MTF50 and MTF10 values. MTF curves that coincide after each filter iteration indicate that no degradation of the spatial resolution of the image due to iteration. This was also confirmed by the MTF50 and MTF10 values which did not change significantly. This shows the ability of bilateral filters to maintain the spatial resolution of the image.

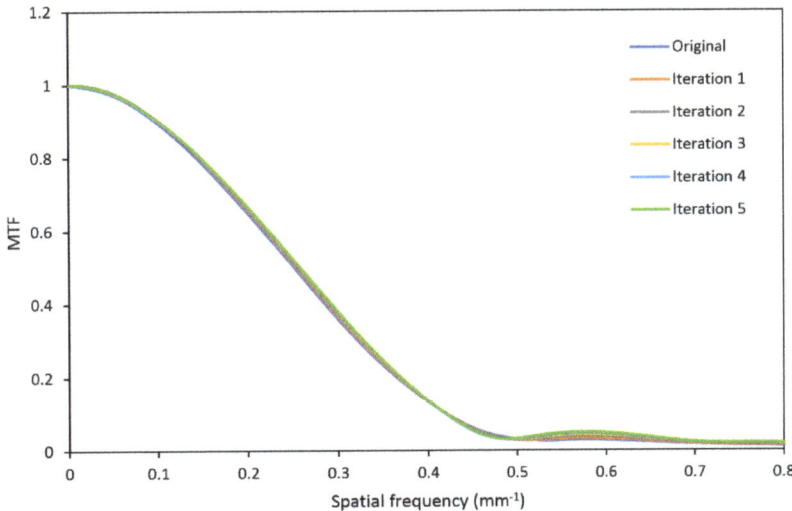

Figure 8. The MTF curve obtained from the edge of the image in 5 filter iterations at a tube current of 77 mAs.

Table 3. MTF50 and MTF10 value for every filter iteration at tube current of 77 mAs.

Filter Iteration	MTF50 (mm^{-1})	MTF10 (mm^{-1})
Original	0.25	0.42
1	0.25	0.42
2	0.26	0.42
3	0.26	0.42
4	0.26	0.42
5	0.26	0.42

3.2. Tube Current of 154 mAs

Figure 9 shows the impact of iterative filtration on an image using a tube current of 154 mAs. With increasing filter iterations, the noise at frequencies around >0.2 mm^{-1} decreases considerably, flattening the tail of the NPS curve

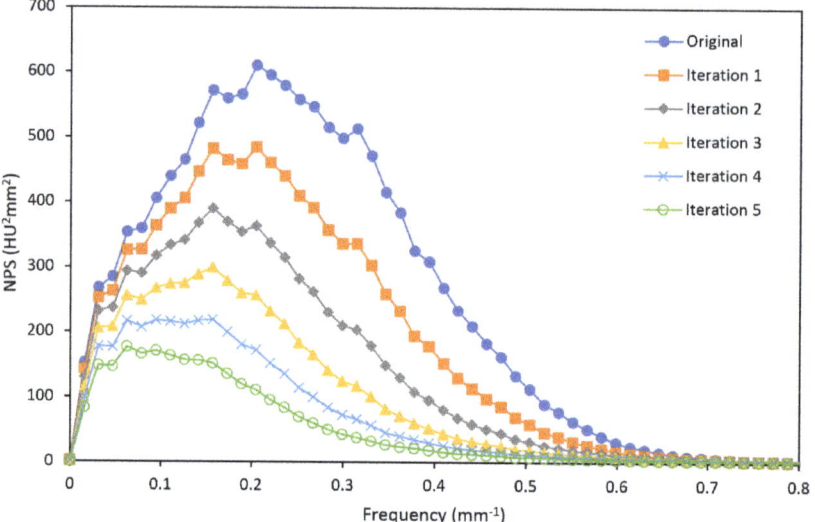

Figure 9. NPS on repeated filtered images at a tube current of 154 mAs.

Figure 10 shows the noise of the original image and the filtered image with up to five iterations at tube current 154 mAs. The noise was reduced by more than half of its original values. The peak frequency gradually shifted from 0.2 to 0.09 mm^{-1} after five iterations, and the mean frequency decreased from 0.25 to 0.18 mm^{-1}.

Figure 11 shows the spatial resolution of each filter iteration at a tube current of 154 mAs. Table 4 shows the MTF50 and MTF10 values. Similar to Figure 8, the MTF curves coincide with each other, indicating no change in spatial resolution for each filter iteration. The MTF values shown in Table 4 also do not show any change.

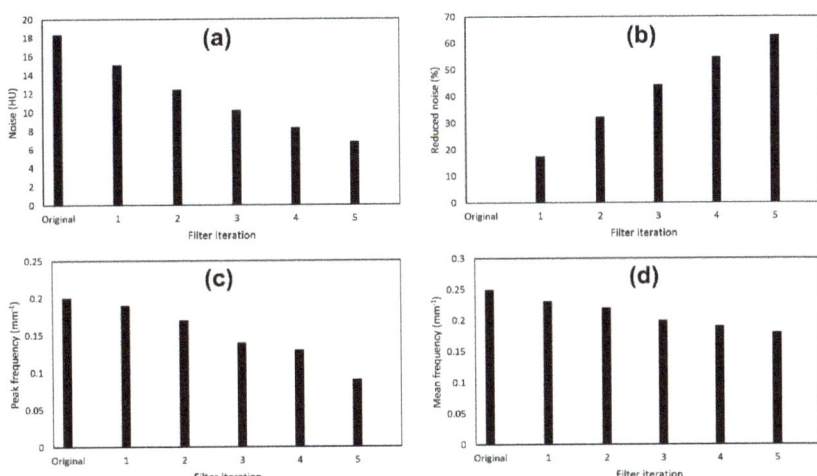

Figure 10. Noise measurement on homogeneous phantom with tube current of 154 mAs. (**a**) Noise, (**b**) Percentage of reduced noise, (**c**) Peak frequency, and (**d**) Mean frequency.

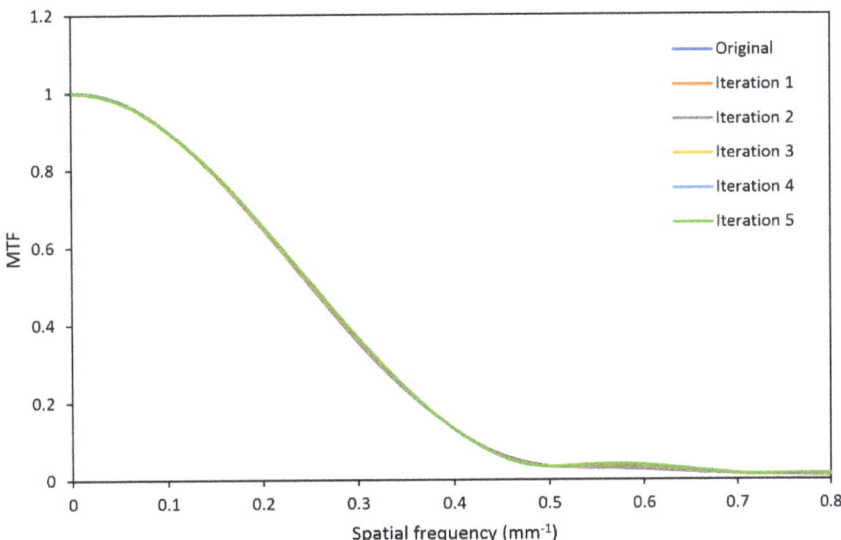

Figure 11. The MTF curve obtained from the edge of the image in 5 filter iterations at a tube current of 154 mAs.

Table 4. MTF50 and MTF10 value for every filter iteration at tube current of 154 mAs.

Filter Iteration	MTF50 (mm^{-1})	MTF10 (mm^{-1})
Original	0.25	0.42
1	0.25	0.42
2	0.25	0.42
3	0.25	0.42
4	0.25	0.42
5	0.25	0.42

3.3. Tube Current of 231 mAs

Figure 12 shows the impact of iterative filtration on an image using a tube current of 231 mAs. In the original image, the noise peaks at a frequency of about 0.2 mm^{-1}. By filtering it for many iterations, the noise at high frequencies gradually decreased, leaving more at a low frequency.

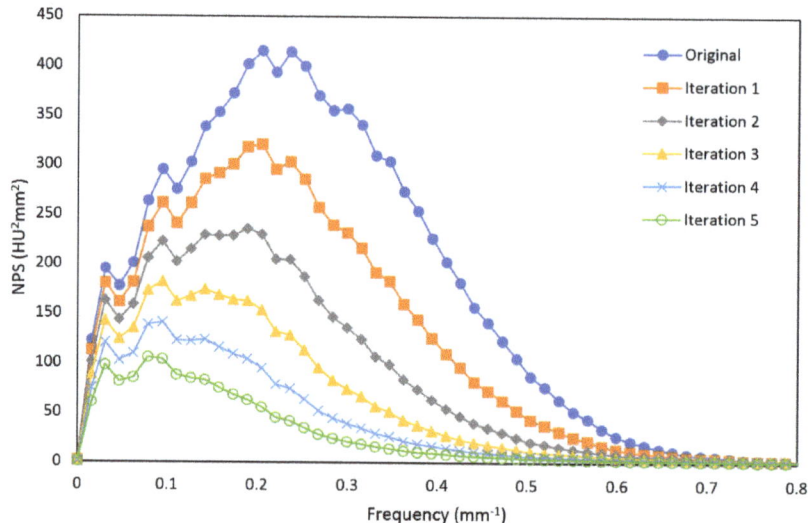

Figure 12. NPS on repeated filtered images at tube current of 231 mAs.

Figure 13 shows the NPS characteristics of the original image and the filtered image at up to five iterations for at tube current of 231 mAs. For five iterations of filtration, the noise magnitude decreased by more than 60%. The peak frequency dramatically shifted from 0.22 to 0.06 mm^{-1} and the average frequency gradually decreased from 0.26 to 0.17 mm^{-1}.

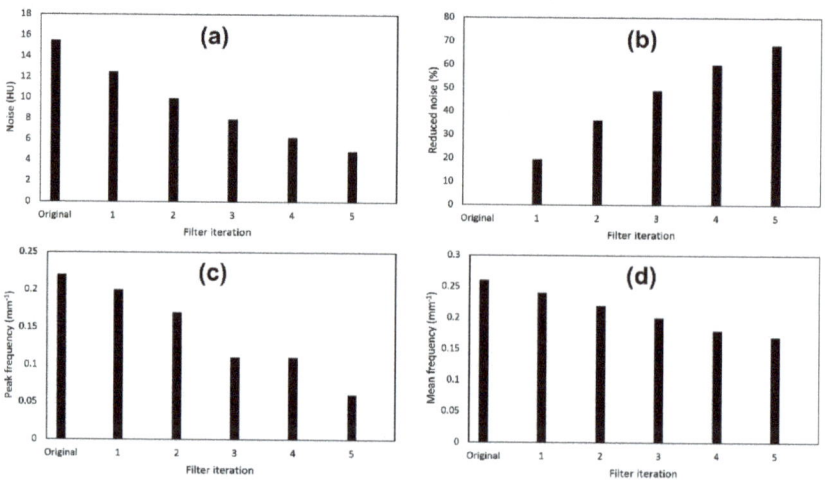

Figure 13. Noise measurement on homogeneous phantom with tube current of 231 mAs. (**a**) Noise, (**b**) Percentage of reduced noise, (**c**) Peak frequency, and (**d**) Mean frequency.

Figure 14 shows the spatial resolution of each filter iteration at a tube current of 154 mAs. Table 5 shows the MTF50 and MTF10 values for a tube current of 231 mAs. In Figure 14, the MTF curves coincide, indicating that iterative bilateral filtering leads to no change in spatial resolution. The MTF values shown in Table 5 also do not show any change for a tube current of 231 mAs, identical to a tube current of 154 mAs (Table 4).

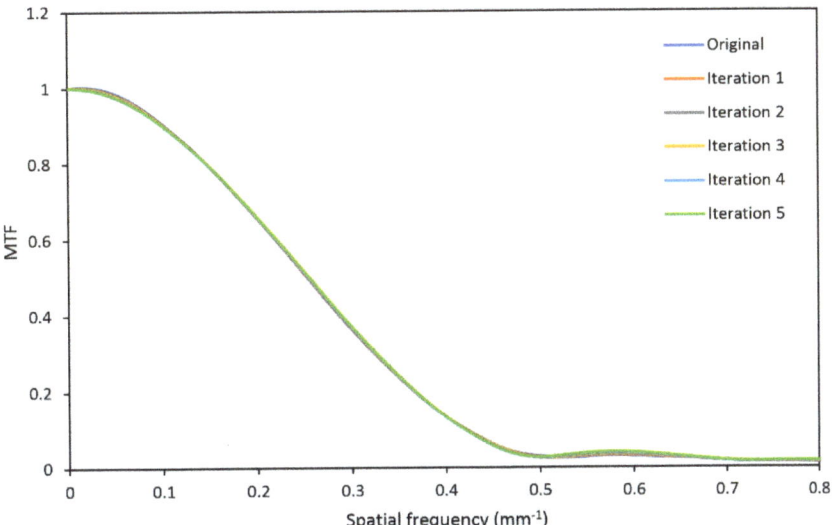

Figure 14. The MTF curve obtained from the edge of the image in 5 filter iterations at a tube current of 231 mAs.

Table 5. MTF50 and MTF10 value for every filter iteration at tube current of 231 mAs.

Filter Iteration	MTF50 (mm^{-1})	MTF10 (mm^{-1})
Original	0.25	0.42
1	0.25	0.42
2	0.25	0.42
3	0.25	0.42
4	0.25	0.42
5	0.25	0.42

3.4. Impact of Bilateral Filter on Anthropomorphic Images

Figure 15 shows noise measurements in the five iterations of the bilateral filter in the frontal lobe. It can be seen that, in the frontal lobe area, the bilateral filter can reduce noise by more than 60%, showing its effectiveness in reducing noise gradually as the filter iterations. The effects on spatial resolution can be seen in Figure 16. The bilateral filters did not significantly alter the structure at the edge between bone and soft tissue. There were no blurred edges or distortions at the edges between networks. Likewise, at the edge of the phantom with air, no significant changes were observed. This shows that the bilateral filter can maintain the edges of the object well, even though it is iterated many times. However, the soft tissue region looks more unnatural in the fifth iteration. These results are characterized using the SSIM presented in Table 6. SSIM decreases with filter iteration, but is never less than 0.5. This decrease is due to effective noise reduction and results in differences in the overall texture of the image.

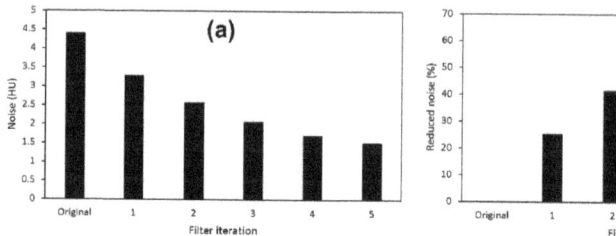

Figure 15. Measurement of noise in the head anthropomorphic phantom image. (**a**) Noise level, (**b**) percentage of reduced noise.

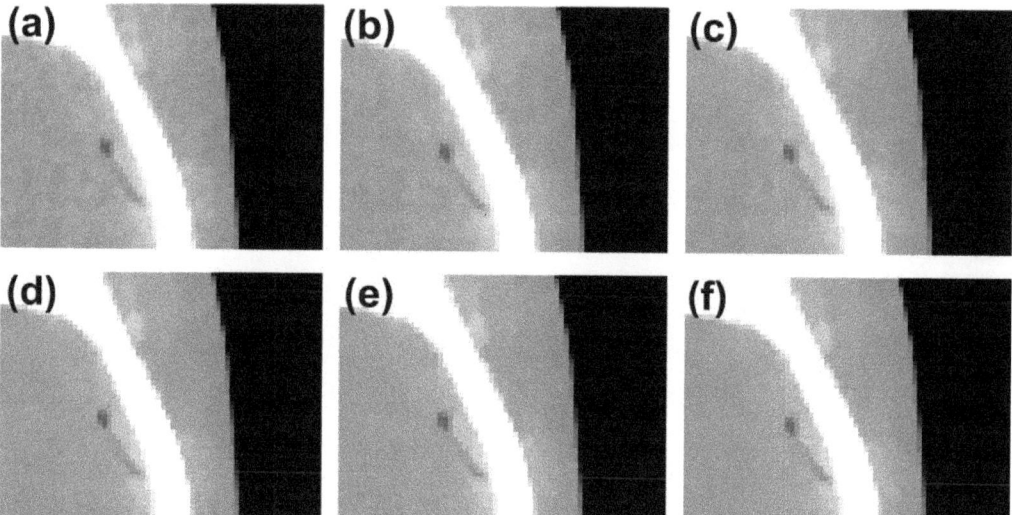

Figure 16. Anthropomorphic phantom images were filtered using a bilateral filter. (**a**) Original image, filtered image in (**b**) 1, (**c**) 2, (**d**) 3, (**e**) 4, and (**f**) 5 times iterations.

Table 6. Similarity index (SSIM) for each filter iteration.

Filter Iteration	SSIM
1	0.85
2	0.69
3	0.60
4	0.54
5	0.50

4. Discussion

This study aims to describe the characteristics of bilateral filters in filtering noise at various frequencies and their patterns in iterative filtering. We used the 1D NPS to characterize image noise. Previous studies that have been carried out have only explored the implementation of bilateral filters without iteration [21,32,39].

Bilateral filters increasingly suppress noise with each iteration. Figure 7, Figure 10, and Figure 13 show that with five iterations, the bilateral filter can suppress noise by more than 50%. This was observed in a homogeneous image with a homogeneous distribution of noise. Observations on areas with objects of various attenuations still need to be evaluated in the future. Anam et al. (2020) investigated several filter algorithms, including bilateral filters, using an in-house point phantom. Their results showed that bilateral filters can reduce noise by up to 18% for a single filter iteration, compared to the adaptive mean filter (AMF) which reduced noise by up to 29%, and the selective mean filter (SMF) which reduced it by up to 27%. The bilateral filter is not as aggressive as these other filters in reducing noise, but it maintains better spatial resolution [9].

Apart from the reduced noise magnitude, the texture also changes. The data showed interesting properties of bilateral filters in changing the noise texture. In the original images with tube currents of 77, 154, and 231 mAs, the NPS showed the peak frequency was about 0.2 mm^{-1}. When the images were filtered five times, the peak frequency shifted to lower values (Figures 6, 9 and 12). This phenomenon shows that the bilateral filter suppresses noise at high frequencies more aggressively than noise at low frequencies. By the fifth iteration, the NPS curve showed a flattening of its shape at frequencies above 0.2 mm^{-1}.

The loss of high-frequency noise caused the bilateral filters to suppress soft (i.e., smooth) textures. In an image with visible gradation, this behavior will give the appearance of a staircase effect, and make the image less realistic. There are several extensions and variants of the bilateral filter that have been developed to deal with this effect [13,40]. Notwithstanding, the bilateral filter shows very good results in reducing noise in general, especially in maintaining object edges when compared to other linear filters such as the mean filters and Gaussian filters. This was confirmed by the MTF50 and MTF10 obtained from the phantom edge which did not change significantly with filter iteration for all tube currents (Tables 3–5). This is an advantage of bilateral filters in clinical practice, where most filter algorithms tend to limit the spatial resolution to be able to suppress the noise. This was verified by testing the anthropomorphic phantom images. Behavior similar to that with the homogeneous phantom was observed, with noise decreasing with filter iteration (Figure 15). In the fifth iteration, noise is reduced by more than 60% (i.e., from 4.39 to 1.51 HU) in the frontal lobe area. In addition, the bilateral filter did not show aggressive behavior towards the edges of objects. In Figure 16, the edge between bone and soft tissue still looks sharp until the fifth iteration. There are no blurred edges or reverse effects. However, an unnatural appearance can be observed in the homogeneous areas of soft tissue. This causes the SSIM to decrease with increasing filter iterations. However, even with five iterations, the similarity does not fall below 0.5.

Knowledge of the noise texture becomes important in determining the most suitable strategy in the denoising procedure because each filter has different characteristics and must be adapted to the type of noise and the clinical purpose [41]. In the case of the bilateral filter, the configuration is more efficient if it is set according to the noise level. Small values of sigma intensity (σ_r) will make the edges of an object look sharper, while a higher value will make it behave more like a Gaussian filter which reduces more noise but blurs the edges [32]. A study by Peng (2010) [21] recommended $\sigma_r = 2.5\,\sigma$ for the best results on artificial images with Gaussian noise based on the peak signal-to-ratio (PSNR) value. In the case of medical images, further investigations need to be carried out to determine the optimal parameters for diagnostic purposes.

This study observes the iterative effect of bilateral filters on homogeneous and anthropomorphic phantom images and was not implemented on patient images. This study is the first step in investigating the effect of the bilateral filter on noise texture. Our findings are relevant only within the scope of the QA procedure. Investigations of patient images will be performed in future studies by an expert radiologist.

The paper only investigates the iterative bilateral filter in improving CT images; however, this approach can be implemented on other images such as images from mammography, magnetic resonance imaging (MRI), ultrasound (US), and other sources.

In addition to bilateral filters, state-of-the-art filters such as the non-local mean filter (NLM) [42] are also interesting to explore in terms of changing the image structure with increasing iterations. Since iterative reconstruction (IR) [43] and deep learning reconstruction (DLR) [44] produce non-linear properties in terms of noise and spatial resolution, it would be interesting to examine the impact of the NLM filter on IR and DLR images and to compare it with the bilateral filter.

5. Conclusions

The impact of bilateral filters in changing the noise texture and spatial resolution in CT images has been characterized. After five iterations, the bilateral filter shows its effectiveness in filtering noise at high frequencies as indicated by the flattening of the NPS curve on images produced with tube currents of 77, 154, and 231 mAs. The peak frequency shifts from about 0.2 to about 0.1 mm^{-1} for these tube currents and the noise magnitude was reduced by more than 50%. The spatial resolution does not change with increasing iterations of the filter, which is confirmed by the constant values of MTF50 and MTF10. The test results on an anthropomorphic phantom image show a similar pattern, with noise reduced by up to 60% and object edges remaining sharp. The impact of bilateral filters on clinical images and CT raw data still needs to be investigated in further studies.

Author Contributions: Conceptualization, C.A.; methodology, C.A. and H.S.; software, C.A., A.N. and K.A.; writing, C.A., A.N. and G.D. All authors have read and agreed to the published version of the manuscript.

Funding: This work was funded by the Riset Publikasi International Bereputasi Tinggi (RPIBT), Diponegoro University, No. 569-187/UN7.D2/PP/VII/2022.

Data Availability Statement: Not applicable.

Conflicts of Interest: The authors declare no conflict of interest.

References

1. Pearce, M.S.; Salotti, J.A.; Little, M.P.; McHugh, K.; Lee, C.; Kim, K.P.; Howe, N.L.; Ronckers, C.M.; Rajaraman, P.; Craft, A.W. Radiation exposure from CT scans in childhood and subsequent risk of leukaemia and brain tumours: A retrospective cohort study. *Lancet* **2012**, *380*, 499–505. [CrossRef]
2. Albert, J.M. Radiation risk from CT: Implications for cancer screening. *Am. J. Roentgenol.* **2013**, *201*, W81–W87. [CrossRef] [PubMed]
3. Chen, J.X.; Kachniarz, B.; Gilani, S.; Shin, J.J. Risk of malignancy associated with head and neck CT in children: A systematic review. *Otolaryngol.–Head Neck Surg.* **2014**, *151*, 554–566. [CrossRef] [PubMed]
4. Yeung, A.W.K. The "As Low As Reasonably Achievable" (ALARA) principle: A brief historical overview and a bibliometric analysis of the most cited publications. *Radioprotection* **2019**, *54*, 103–109. [CrossRef]
5. Ning, P.; Zhu, S.; Shi, D.; Guo, Y.; Sun, M. X-ray dose reduction in abdominal computed tomography using advanced iterative reconstruction algorithms. *PLoS ONE* **2014**, *9*, e92568. [CrossRef] [PubMed]
6. Barreto, I.; Verma, N.; Quails, N.; Olguin, C.; Correa, N.; Mohammed, T.L. Patient size matters: Effect of tube current modulation on size-specific dose estimates (SSDE) and image quality in low-dose lung cancer screening CT. *J. Appl. Clin. Med. Phys.* **2020**, *21*, 87–94. [CrossRef]
7. Whitebird, R.R.; Solberg, L.I.; Bergdall, A.R.; López-Solano, N.; Smith-Bindman, R. Barriers to CT Dose Optimization: The Challenge of Organizational Change. *Acad. Radiol.* **2021**, *28*, 387–392. [CrossRef]
8. Li, Z.; Yu, L.; Trzasko, J.D.; Lake, D.S.; Blezek, D.J.; Fletcher, J.G.; McCollough, C.H.; Manduca, A. Adaptive nonlocal means filtering based on local noise level for CT denoising. *Med. Phys.* **2014**, *41*, 011908. [CrossRef]
9. Anam, C.; Adi, K.; Sutanto, H.; Arifin, Z.; Budi, W.S.; Fujibuchi, T.; Dougherty, G. Noise reduction in CT images using a selective mean filter. *J. Biomed. Phys. Eng.* **2020**, *10*, 623–634. [CrossRef]
10. Cropp, R.J.; Seslija, P.; Tso, D.; Thakur, Y. Scanner and kVp dependence of measured CT numbers in the ACR CT phantom. *J. Appl. Clin. Med. Phys.* **2013**, *14*, 338–349. [CrossRef]
11. Einstein, S.A.; Rong, X.J.; Jensen, C.T.; Liu, X. Quantification and homogenization of image noise between two CT scanner models. *J. Appl. Clin. Med. Phys.* **2020**, *21*, 174–178. [CrossRef] [PubMed]
12. Takenaga, T.; Katsuragawa, S.; Goto, M.; Hatemura, M.; Uchiyama, Y.; Shiraishi, J. Modulation transfer function measurement of CT images by use of a circular edge method with a logistic curve-fitting technique. *Radiol. Phys. Technol.* **2015**, *8*, 53–59. [CrossRef] [PubMed]
13. Wang, J. Construction of local nonlinear filter without staircase effect in image restoration. *Appl. Anal.* **2011**, *90*, 1257–1273. [CrossRef]
14. Masoomi, M.A.; Al-Shammeri, I.; Kalafallah, K.; Elrahman, H.M.; Ragab, O.; Ahmed, E.; Al-Shammeri, J.; Arafat, S. Wiener filter improves diagnostic accuracy of CAD SPECT images-comparison to angiography and CT angiography. *Medicine* **2019**, *98*, e14207. [CrossRef] [PubMed]
15. Vasilache, S.; Ward, K.; Cockrell, C.; Ha, J.; Najarian, K. Unified wavelet and Gaussian filtering for segmentation of CT images; application in segmentation of bone in pelvic CT images. *BMC Med. Inform. Decis. Mak.* **2009**, *9* (Suppl. 1), S8. [CrossRef]

16. Patil, P.D.; Kumbhar, A.D. Bilateral Filter for Image Denoising. In Proceedings of the 2015 International Conference on Green Computing and Internet of Things (ICGCIoT), Greater Noida, India, 8–10 October 2015; pp. 299–302.
17. Zhang, M.; Gunturk, B.K. Multiresolution bilateral filtering for image denoising. *IEEE Trans. Image Process.* **2008**, *17*, 2324–2333. [CrossRef]
18. Zhang, B.; Allebach, J.P. Adaptive bilateral filter for sharpness enhancement and noise removal. *IEEE Trans. Image Process.* **2008**, *17*, 664–678. [CrossRef]
19. Joseph, J.; Periyasami, R. An image driven bilateral filter with adaptive range and spatial parameters for denoising Magnetic Resonance Images. *Comput. Electr. Eng.* **2018**, *6*, 782–795. [CrossRef]
20. Zheng, Y.; Fu, H.; Au, O.K.-C.; Tai, C.-L. Bilateral Normal Filtering for Mesh Denoising. *IEEE Trans. Vis. Comput. Graph.* **2011**, *17*, 1521–1530. [CrossRef]
21. Peng, H.; Rao, R. Bilateral kernel parameter optimization by risk minimization. In Proceedings of the IEEE International Conference on Image Processing, Hong Kong, China, 26–29 September 2010; pp. 3293–3296.
22. Akar, S.A. Determination of optimal parameters for bilateral filter in brain MR image denoising. *Appl. Soft Comput.* **2016**, *43*, 87–96. [CrossRef]
23. Ghosh, S.; Nair, P.; Chaundhury, K.N. Optimized Fourier Bilateral Filtering. *IEEE Signal Process. Lett.* **2018**, *25*, 1555–1559. [CrossRef]
24. Xu, H.; Zhang, Z.; Gao, Y.; Liu, H.; Xie, F.; Li, J. Adaptive Bilateral Texture Filter for Image Smoothing. *Front. Neurorobot.* **2022**, *16*, 729624. [CrossRef] [PubMed]
25. Bronstein, M.M. Lazy Sliding Window Implementation of the Bilateral Filter on Parallel Architectures. *IEEE Trans. Image Process.* **2011**, *20*, 1751–1756. [CrossRef]
26. Galiano, G.; Velasco, J. On a Fast Bilateral Filtering Formulation Using Functional Rearrangements. *J. Math. Imaging Vis.* **2015**, *53*, 346–363. [CrossRef]
27. Paris, S.; Kornprobst, P.; Tumblin, J.; Durand, F. Bilateral Filtering: Theory and Applications. *Found. Trends Comput. Graph. Vis.* **2009**, *4*, 1–73. [CrossRef]
28. Anh, D.N. Iterative Bilateral Filter and Non-Local Mean. *Int. J. Comput. Appl.* **2014**, *106*, 33–38.
29. Zeng, R.; Gavrielides, M.A.; Petrick, N.; Sahiner, B.; Li, Q.; Myers, K.J. Estimating local noise power spectrum from a few FBP-reconstructed CT scans. *Med. Phys.* **2016**, *43*, 568–582. [CrossRef]
30. Li, G.; Liu, X.; Dodge, C.T.; Jensen, C.T.; Rong, X.J. A noise power spectrum study of a new model-based iterative reconstruction system: Veo 3.0. *J. Appl. Clin. Med. Phys.* **2016**, *17*, 428–439. [CrossRef]
31. Dolly, S.; Chen, H.C.; Anastasio, M.; Mutic, S.; Li, H. Practical considerations for noise power spectra estimation for clinical CT scanners. *J. Appl. Clin. Med. Phys.* **2016**, *17*, 392–407. [CrossRef]
32. Park, J.; Han, J.; Lee, B. Performance of bilateral filtering on Gaussian noise. *J. Electron. Imag.* **2014**, *23*, 043024. [CrossRef]
33. Solomon, J.B.; Christianson, O.; Samei, E. Quantitative comparison of noise texture across CT scanners from different manufacturers. *Med. Phys.* **2012**, *39*, 6048–6055. [CrossRef] [PubMed]
34. Samei, E.; Bakalyar, D.; Boedeker, K.L.; Brady, S.; Fan, J.; Leng, S.; Myers, K.J.; Popescu, L.M.; Ramirez Giraldo, J.C.; Ranallo, F.; et al. Performance evaluation of computed tomography systems: Summary of AAPM Task Group 233. *Med. Phys.* **2019**, *46*, e735–e756. [CrossRef]
35. ImQuest. Available online: https://deckard.duhs.duke.edu/~{}samei/tg233.html (accessed on 10 July 2022).
36. Anam, C.; Budi, W.S.; Fujibuchi, T.; Haryanto, F.; Dougherty, G. Validation of the tail replacement method in MTF calculations using the homogeneous and non-homogeneous edges of a phantom. *J. Phys. Conf. Ser.* **2019**, *1248*, 012001. [CrossRef]
37. Anam, C.; Naufal, A.; Fujibuchi, T.; Matsubara, K.; Dougherty, G. Automated development of the contrast-detail curve based on statistical low-contrast detectability in CT images. *J. Appl. Clin. Med. Phys.* **2022**, *9*, e13719. [CrossRef]
38. Anam, C.; Arif, I.; Haryanto, F.; Lestari, F.P.; Widita, R.; Budi, W.S.; Sutanto, H.; Adi, K.; Fujibuchi, T.; Dougherty, G. An improved method of automated noise measurement system in CT images. *J. Biomed. Phys. Eng.* **2021**, *11*, 163–174. [PubMed]
39. Mendrik, A.M.; Vonken, E.J.; van Ginneken, B.; de Jong, H.W.; Riordan, A.; van Seeters, T.; Smit, E.J.; Viergever, M.A.; Prokop, M. TIPS bilateral noise reduction in 4D CT perfusion scans produces high-quality cerebral blood flow maps. *Phys. Med. Biol.* **2011**, *56*, 3857–3872. [CrossRef] [PubMed]
40. Buades, A.; Coll, B.; Morel, J.M. The staircasing effect in neighborhood filters and its solution. *IEEE Trans. Image Process.* **2006**, *15*, 1499–1505. [CrossRef] [PubMed]
41. Al-Hinnawi, A.R.; Daear, M.; Huwaijah, S. Assessment of bilateral filter on 1/2-dose chest-pelvis CT views. *Radiol. Phys. Technol.* **2013**, *6*, 385–398. [CrossRef] [PubMed]
42. Buades, A.; Coll, B.; Morel, J.M. A non-local algorithm for image denoising. In Proceedings of the IEEE Computer Society Conference on Computer Vision and Pattern Recognition (CVPR'05), San Diego, CA, USA, 20–25 June 2005; Volume 2, pp. 60–65.
43. Stiller, W. Basics of iterative reconstruction methods in computed tomography: A vendor-independent overview. *Eur. J. Radiol.* **2018**, *109*, 147–154. [CrossRef]
44. McLeavy, C.M.; Chunara, M.H.; Gravell, R.J.; Rauf, A.; Cushnie, A.; Talbot, C.S.; Hawkins, R.M. The future of CT: Deep learning reconstruction. *Clin. Radiol.* **2021**, *76*, 407–415. [CrossRef]

 algorithms

Article

Biomedical Image Classification via Dynamically Early Stopped Artificial Neural Network

Giorgia Franchini [1,*,†], Micaela Verucchi [1,2,†], Ambra Catozzi [1,3,†], Federica Porta [1,†] and Marco Prato [1]

1. Department of Physics, Informatics and Mathematics, University of Modena and Reggio Emilia, 41125 Modena, Italy
2. HiPeRT Srl, 41125 Modena, Italy
3. Department of Mathematical, Physical and Computer Sciences, University of Parma, 43124 Parma, Italy
* Correspondence: giorgia.franchini@unimore.it
† These authors contributed equally to this work.

Abstract: It is well known that biomedical imaging analysis plays a crucial role in the healthcare sector and produces a huge quantity of data. These data can be exploited to study diseases and their evolution in a deeper way or to predict their onsets. In particular, image classification represents one of the main problems in the biomedical imaging context. Due to the data complexity, biomedical image classification can be carried out by trainable mathematical models, such as artificial neural networks. When employing a neural network, one of the main challenges is to determine the optimal duration of the training phase to achieve the best performance. This paper introduces a new adaptive early stopping technique to set the optimal training time based on dynamic selection strategies to fix the learning rate and the mini-batch size of the stochastic gradient method exploited as the optimizer. The numerical experiments, carried out on different artificial neural networks for image classification, show that the developed adaptive early stopping procedure leads to the same literature performance while finalizing the training in fewer epochs. The numerical examples have been performed on the CIFAR100 dataset and on two distinct MedMNIST2D datasets which are the large-scale lightweight benchmark for biomedical image classification.

Keywords: image classification; biomedical imaging; early stopping; artificial neural network; GreenAI; health care; machine learning in healthcare

Citation: Franchini, G.; Verucchi, M.; Catozzi, A.; Porta, F.; Prato, M. Biomedical Image Classification via Dynamically Early Stopped Artificial Neural Network. *Algorithms* 2022, 15, 386. https://doi.org/10.3390/a15100386

Academic Editors: Lucia Maddalena and Laura Antonelli

Received: 28 August 2022
Accepted: 17 October 2022
Published: 20 October 2022

Publisher's Note: MDPI stays neutral with regard to jurisdictional claims in published maps and institutional affiliations.

Copyright: © 2022 by the authors. Licensee MDPI, Basel, Switzerland. This article is an open access article distributed under the terms and conditions of the Creative Commons Attribution (CC BY) license (https:// creativecommons.org/licenses/by/ 4.0/).

1. Introduction

In recent years, the healthcare field has experienced a massive growth in the acquisition of digital biomedical images due to a pervasive increase in ordinary and preventive medical exams. In view of this amount of medical data, new methods based on machine learning (ML) and deep learning (DL) have therefore become necessary. The application of ML and DL techniques to the biomedical imaging field can promote the development of new diagnostics and treatments, making it a challenging area of investigation. In particular, image classification represents one of the main problems in the biomedical imaging context. Its aim is to arrange medical images into different classes to help physicians in disease diagnosis. ML and DL methods are employed to predict the class membership of the unknown data instance, based on the class membership of the training set data, which is known. If the learning procedure performs a good classification, a proper automatic diagnosis of a disease can be achieved, starting only from the medical image.

From a mathematical point of view, given a training set of n instances, a learning approach to the image classification involves the solution of a minimization problem of the form

$$\min_{x \in \mathbb{R}^d} F(x) \equiv \frac{1}{n} \sum_{i=1}^{n} f_i(x) \tag{1}$$

where F is the so-called loss function and it computes the difference between the actual ground-truth and predicted values, n is the cardinality of the training set and d is the number of features. Each $f_i : \mathbb{R}^d \to \mathbb{R}$ denotes the loss function related to the i-th instance of the training set. Because n can be a very large number, it is prohibitively expensive to compute all the terms of the objective function $F(x)$ or its gradient. Moreover, the whole dataset may be too large to be completely stored in memory. Finally, in the online learning setting, where the dataset is not available from the beginning in its completeness but is acquired during the learning process, it is impossible to work with $F(x)$. In all these cases, the minimization problem is faced by exploiting stochastic approximations of the gradient that lead to the use of stochastic gradient (SG) methods [1]. Given at each iteration k a sample S_k of size $n_k \ll n$ randomly and uniformly chosen from $\mathcal{N} = \{1, \ldots, n\}$, the SG algorithm to solve problem (1) can be written as

$$x_{k+1} = x_k - \eta_k g(x_k) \tag{2}$$

where η_k is a positive parameter called the *learning rate* (LR) and the stochastic direction $g(x_k)$ is computed as

$$g(x_k) := \frac{1}{n_k} \sum_{i \in S_k} \nabla f_i(x_k).$$

The sample S_k is the *mini-batch* at the k-th iteration and its cardinality n_k is the mini-batch size (MBS). In order to accelerate the convergence rate of the SG method, a *momentum* term [2] can be added to the iteration (2). In more detail, chosen $\beta \in [0,1)$ and setting $m_0 = 0$, the momentum version of the SG scheme has the following form:

$$\begin{cases} m_{k+1} = \beta m_k + g(x_k) \\ x_{k+1} = x_k - \eta_k m_{k+1} \end{cases} \tag{3}$$

where η_k is the positive LR.

In general, to design efficient and accurate ML or DL methodologies, it is needed to properly set the hyperparameters connected to the algorithm chosen for the training phase, particularly the LR and the MBS. We define the hyperparameters of a learning method as those parameters which are not trained during the learning process but are set a priori as the input data. In the literature, there are different philosophies to approach the problem of setting the hyperparameters. One of these is related to the Neural Architecture Search (NAS) area [3], which explores the best configurations related to the optimization hyperparameters before the beginning of the training. However, there also exist techniques that directly address the search during the training phase, including static rules, i.e., rules that do not depend on the training phase, and dynamic rules, which only operate under certain conditions connected to the training phase itself. Regarding the LR and the MBS, the class of dynamic rules is preferable. Indeed, a variable LR strategy allows starting the iterative process with higher LR values than those employed close to the local minimum. As for the MBS, a standard approach is to dynamically increase it along the iterations, without however reaching the whole dataset in order to comply with the architectural constraints and control the possible data redundancy. There also exist techniques for decreasing the LR while the MBS is increasing.

Together with suitable choices of both the LR and the MBS, the training phase can be optimized by means of an early stopping technique. Given a validation set (VS), namely a subset of examples held back from training the model, standard early stopping procedures are based on the so-called patience parameter criterion. In more detail, if, after a number of epochs equal to the value of the patience, the loss function computed on the VS has not been reduced, the training is stopped even if the maximum number of epochs is not reached.

The aim of this paper is twofold. First, we combine the previously described strategies to reduce the training time. Indeed, we suggest a dynamic combined technique to select the LR and the MBS by modifying classical early stopping procedures. In particular, if a decrease in the loss function on the validation set is not achieved after the patience time, the patience value itself can be reduced, the learning rate is decreased and/or the mini-batch size is increased and the training is allowed to continue until the values of the learning rate and the mini-batch are acceptable from a practical point of view. Secondly, we test the SG algorithm with momentum, equipped with a such developed rule for the selection of the LR and MBS hyperparameters, in training an artificial neural network (ANN) for biomedical image classification problems. We remark that the dynamical early stopping procedure we describe in this paper can be adopted for general image classification problems. Moreover, it is worth highlighting that the suggested approach does not belong to the class of NAS hyperparameters procedures. Indeed, unlike the proposed scheme, NAS techniques aim to set good hyperparameters values at the beginning of the training phase and to keep them fixed until convergence. On the other hand, the hyperparameters selection rule developed in this work is adaptive because the hyperparameters connected to the optimizer can be conveniently changed during the training phase. This can have benefits in terms of both the performance and computational and energy savings from a GreenAI (Artificial Intelligence) perspective.

The paper is organized as follows. In Section 2, we present a brief survey about the state-of-the-art approaches to fix both the LR and the MBS hyperparameters. Section 3 is devoted to describing a novel technique to dynamically adjust the LR and/or the MBS, using the VS. Section 4 reports the results of the numerical experiments on standard and biomedical image classification problems, aimed to evaluate the effectiveness of the proposed approach. In Section 5, in addition to the conclusions, the current directions of research that we are pursuing to expand and complete the work carried out are illustrated.

2. Related Works

The aim of this section is to recall the standard techniques to select the LR and the MBS in stochastic gradient methods typically employed for ML and DL methodologies.

2.1. Standard LR Selection Rules

Properly setting the LR in stochastic gradient algorithms is an important issue and there exist many attempts in the literature to address it. Indeed, inappropriate values for the LR can lead to two different scenarios: a too small fixed value often implies a very slow learning process, while a too high fixed value can make the method divergent. In general, choosing a fixed LR along the iterative process is not suitable, also because the convergence of standard first-order stochastic schemes is ensured if the LR is properly bounded by the Lipschitz constant of the gradient of the objective function [1]. Unfortunately, this constant is often not known.

As for a variable LR rule, several works in the literature show that, from a practical point of view, modifying the LR during the learning process can bring benefits for both ML and DL applications [4,5]. In order to guarantee convergence, the SG schemes require the LR to be chosen as a value of a diminishing sequence, i.e., $\alpha_k = \mathcal{O}(\frac{1}{k})$. However, this choice would practically lead to a too rapid reduction in the LR by giving rise to the interruption of the learning process in a few iterates. For this reason, in practice, the so-called LR annealing can be adopted: with this strategy, the LR is decreased along the iterations but with a much slower speed. The basic idea of the LR annealing is to diminish the LR after some iterations from the beginning of the learning process, in an automatic and non-adaptive way. This technique is widely used in the most recent ANN for segmentation and other tasks [6–8]. For example, in [7], the authors use the LR annealing technique, with a YOLO architecture, for the detection and the localization of lung nodules from low-dose CT scans. Even in biomedical contexts, where the dataset size is often limited, LR annealing techniques have been shown to be effective. In [9], the authors demonstrate that the suggested LR annealing strategy improves the image classifiers performance, in terms of both the accuracy and training time, on a set of dermatological diagnostic images with an unbalanced nature.

2.2. Standard MBS Selection Rules

In [10], Masters and Luschi point out that modern DL training is typically based on mini-batch SG optimization. While the use of large mini-batches increases the available computational parallelism, small-batch training has been shown to provide a better generalization performance and allows a significantly smaller memory footprint, which might also be exploited to improve machine throughput. For this reason, the authors stress that, for the learning process, it is crucial to choose a proper MBS selection technique that allows the method to achieve a high accuracy while reducing the time spent on the learning phase as much as possible.

In the context of standard ML, several authors suggest a linear growth of the MBS to allow the process of reaching the entire dataset, while others (see, e.g., [11]) propose a hybrid approach. The hybrid approach consists of starting the iterative process with an SG method (by exploiting its property of decreasing the objective function especially in the first iterations) and then moving onto a deterministic scheme (by taking advantage of its stability and avoiding an oscillating behavior around the minimum point). Obviously, these techniques cannot be applied to every setting, but only to offline learning frameworks and/or datasets of limited size.

For the DL approaches, the MBS is often selected as powers of 2 (commonly 32, 64 and 128) with the aim of facilitating the use of internal memories of accelerators, such as a Graphics Processing Unit (GPU) and Field-Programmable Gate Array (FPGA). However, besides static MBS selection strategies, simply driven by heuristics or hardware constraints, there exist other adaptive ones driven by the learning process itself [12,13]. For example, in [12], the authors design a practical SG method capable of learning the optimal batch size adaptively throughout its iterations for strongly convex and smooth functions. On the other hand, in [13], the authors propose a method to dynamically use the VS to set the MBS. The impact of a suitable MBS selection procedure on the effectiveness of DL schemes has been also analyzed in the field of medical applications. In [14], the authors studied the effect of the MBS on the performance of CNNs employed to classify histopathology images. They empirically found that when the LR values are high, a large MBS performs better than with a small LR. Moreover, lowering the learning rate and decreasing the batch size allow the network to train better, especially in the case of fine-tuning. About the high correlation between the LR and the MBS selection rules, there exist different works [15,16] in the literature. For this reason, effective strategies to set these hyperparameters should consider their mutual interaction.

The techniques described above could assist other types of application, such as those reported in [17–19], in addition to those already mentioned.

3. A New Dynamic Early Stopping Technique

The previous section has shown that the LR and the MBS need to be properly selected in order to have robust and efficient learning methodologies and that many efforts have been made in the literature in this regard. In this section, we propose a novel adaptive strategy to fix both these hyperparameters by exploiting and modifying the standard early stopping procedure. The resulting approach can be seen as a new dynamic early stopping strategy able to combine the advantages of both the early stopping and the dynamic strategies to define the LR and the MBS.

In all the methodologies involving learning from examples, it is important to avoid the phenomenon of overfitting. To this end, it is effective to adopt the early stopping technique [20] which interrupts the learning process by allowing to possibly use a number of epochs lower than the prefixed maximum, also from a GreenAI perspective [21]. The early stopping technique is based on the idea of periodically evaluating, during the minimization process, the error that the network commits on the auxiliary VS by evaluating the performance obtained on the VS itself. In general, in the first iterations, the error on the VS decreases with the objective function, while it can increase if the error which occurs on the training set (TS) (the training set is a set of examples used to fit the parameters of the model, e.g., the weights of an ANN) becomes "sufficiently small". In particular, the training process ends when the error on the VS starts to increase, because this might correspond to the point in which the network begins to overfit the information provided by the TS and loses its ability to generalize to data other than those of the TS. In order to practically implement the early stopping procedure, it is typical to define a patience parameter, i.e., the number of epochs to wait before early stopping the training process if no progress on the VS is achieved. Fixing the value of the patience is not obvious: it really depends on the dataset and the network. The suggested early stopping strategy aims to also overcome this difficulty.

3.1. The Proposal

In this section, we detail the new early stopping technique we are proposing. The main steps of this technique can be summarized as follows.

- We borrow the basic idea of the standard early stopping in order to avoid overfitting the information related to the TS.
- We introduce a patience parameter which can be adaptively modified along the training process.
- We dynamically adjust both the LR and the MBS hyperparameters along the iterations, according to the progress on the VS.

The complete scheme is described in Algorithm 1. The main features are reported below.

3.1.1. Lines 4–9—Update of the Iterates for One Epoch

The iterates are updated by means of a stochastic gradient algorithm (Algorithm 1 line 8) for an entire epoch. In particular, a stochastic estimate of the gradient of the objective function is computed by means of the current mini-batch S_i of cardinality n_k chosen randomly and uniformly from $\mathcal{N}$ (lines 6–7). Examples of the stochastic gradient estimations are provided in (2) and (3).

3.1.2. Line 10—Evaluation of the Model

The model is evaluated on the VS, namely the accuracy is computed on the VS and saved in the variable $AccVal_k$.

3.1.3. Lines 11–15—Check for Accuracy Improvement

The current accuracy computed on the VS is compared to the one computed at the previous epoch and saved in the variable $BestAcc$.

3.1.4. Lines 17–29—Dynamic Early Stopping

If the accuracy on the VS is not improved, a counter is increased (line 17). Subsequently (line 18), the value of the counter is compared to the prefixed value p of the patience. In standard early stopping strategies, if the counter is greater than the value of p, then the training phase is stopped. On the contrary, in the suggested dynamic early stopping technique, the training phase is not immediately stopped, but it is allowed to continue with different hyperparameters. In particular, the LR is decreased by a factor $c_1 \in (0,1)$ (line 20) and/or the MBS is increased by a proper rule (line 22) depending on $c_2 \in [1, M]$ and $dim \in \{0, \cdots, M\}$, where M is a constant related to hardware or memory limitations, for example, it can be the maximum number of samples which can be stored in the GPU. Finally (line 23), the value of the patience is divided by a factor $\gamma > 1$. Thanks to a smaller LR and/or a mini-batch of a larger size, the optimizer employed in the training phase should stabilize and provide new iterates closer to the minimum point. However, if the LR becomes too small and the MBS reaches the hardware limitations, then the ending of the training process is forced. In particular, if the patience is reduced more than a prefixed value $\bar{p}$, then the training is stopped (lines 27–29).

To summarize, different from the standard early stopping, the proposed one avoids a sharp ending of the training process and the difficult tuning of a fixed value of the patience.

Moreover, it allows to really exploit the nature of the dynamic selection rules for the LR and MBS, thus ensuring a more efficient learning phase. Finally, we remark that the possibility to refine the values for the LR and the MBS along the iterative process allows to make their initial setting less crucial than in the static approaches where the hyperparameters are kept fixed during the training.

Algorithm 1: A stochastic gradient method with dynamical early stopping

---

1 Choose *maxepochs*, x_0, η_0, $\mathcal{S}_0 \subset \mathcal{N}$ of cardinality n_0, $c_1 \in (0,1)$, $c_2 \in [1, M]$, $dim \in \{0, \ldots, M\}$, $\gamma \geq 1$, $p, \overline{p} \in \mathbb{N}$
2 Initialize $BestAcc = 0$, $p_{red} = 0$
3 **for** $k = 0, \ldots,$ *maxepochs* **do**
4   **while** $i \leq \frac{n}{n_k}$ **do**
5       $i = i + 1$
6   Select a mini-batch $\mathcal{S}_i$ randomly and uniformly from $\mathcal{N}$ of cardinality n_k
7   Compute a stochastic direction d_i on the mini-batch $\mathcal{S}_i$
8   Compute $x_{i+1} = x_i - \eta_i \cdot d_i$
9   **end**
10   Save the parameters of the final model: $x_k = x_{i+1}$ and evaluate the model on the VS: $AccVal_k$
11   **if** $AccVal_k > BestAcc$ **then**
12      $counter = 0$
13      $p_{red} = 0$
14      $BestAcc = AccVal_k$
15   Save the parameters of the best model: $x_{best} = x_k$
16   **else**
17      $counter = counter + 1$
18   **if** $counter > p$ **then**
19         $counter = 0$
20   Learning rate decreasing: $\eta_{k+1} = c_1 \eta_k$
21   and/or
22   Mini-batch size increasing: $n_{k+1} = c_2 n_k + dim$ or
            $n_{k+1} = \max\{dim, c_2 n_k\}$
23         $p = \frac{p}{\gamma}$
24         $p_{red} = p_{red} + 1$
25   **end**
26   **end**
27   **if** $p_{red} > \overline{p}$ **then**
28   **return**
29   **end**
30 **end**

4. Numerical Experiments

In this section, we investigate the effectiveness of the developed early stopping procedure combined with the SG method with momentum on image classification problems. More in detail, we consider Algorithm 1 where the stochastic direction (line 7) and the update of the iterates (line 8) are performed by means of the scheme defined in (3) with $\beta = 0.9$. The loss function in (1) is the cross entropy; hence, $f_i(x) = -t_i \log(s_i(x))$ where $s_i(x)$ is the probability of the Softmax function of the class i and t_i is the true label. We consider both a standard database for image classification tasks as the CIFAR-100 [22] and two different biomedical databases of 2D images obtained by computed tomography tools [23–27].

4.1. Image Classification on CIFAR-100 Dataset

We present the results for three different CNNs for 100-classes classification on the CIFAR-100 dataset: ResNet18 [28], VGG16 [29] and MobileNet [30]. The numerical experiments have been performed on an Intel i9-9900KF coupled with an NVIDIA RTX 2080Ti. The code has been developed starting from an established framework to train several CNNs on the CIFAR-100 dataset (https://github.com/weiaicunzai/pytorch-cifar100, accessed on 1 October 2022) and has been made public for the sake of reproducibility (https://github.com/mive93/pytorch-cifar100, accessed on 1 October 2022). In the considered framework, the CIFAR-100 dataset was divided into training and test sets. We used 10% of the training set to create the validation set. The optimizer employed for the reference training of the CNNs is the SG with momentum; it uses a starting LR of 0.1 and schedules its annealing at epochs [60, 120, 160], multiplying it by 0.2 in those so-called milestones.

The performance of the optimization method employed for the CNNs reference training has been compared with the performance of two different versions of Algorithm 1 (with an SG with momentum at lines 7–8). In particular, we consider the possibility of either reducing the LR while the MBS is such that $n_{k+1} = n_0$ or decreasing the LR and increasing the MBS. Both versions of Algorithm 1 have been implemented by setting $maxepochs = 200$, $\eta_0 = 0.1$, $n_0 = 2$, $c_1 = 0.2$, $n_{k+1} = \max\{max_{memory} = 1000, c_2 * n_k\}$, where $max_{memory} \in \mathbb{N}$ is the maximum number of samples that can be stored in the GPU, and $c_2 = 2$. Moreover, in order to understand how the patience values affect the performance, we consider three different values for p—8, 15 and 20—and two different values for γ—2 and 4. Finally, $\bar{p}$ has been fixed either equal to 6 if both the LR is reduced and the MBS is increased or equal to 3 if only the LR is decreased but the MBS is not changed along the iterations. In the results, the name of the different considered algorithms for the training reports:

- LR if only the LR is changed along the iterative process or LRBS if both the hyperparameters are variable;
- p followed by its value;
- γ followed by its value.

For example, LRBS_p20_γ2 points out that the selection rules for the LR and the MBS are both dynamic and the values for p and γ are 20 and 2, respectively.

All the tests have been performed five times, and the average accuracy on the test set and the number of epochs are reported, knowing that the standard deviation on the accuracy is at most equal to 0.0145. As usual, the best result obtained with the check on the VS is verified on the test set.

Figure 1 shows the results of all the experiments carried out on the MobileNet CNN. In this case, the reference training achieves an accuracy of 65.39% in 200 epochs. From the chart, it can be seen that all the trainings that follow the methodology proposed in this paper achieve similar results in terms of accuracy while needing less than half the epochs of the original one. Moreover, some configurations outperform the original, such as, e.g., the LRBS version with patience equal to 15 or 20. Table 1 reports all the results for the three CNNs for the LRBS configurations. From the last two columns of Table 1, it is possible to conclude that the accuracy results obtained by the proposed method are in line with those of the original version, sometimes slightly lower and sometimes higher. What is truly remarkable is the number of epochs required to obtain such a performance, which is at least halved compared to the original method.

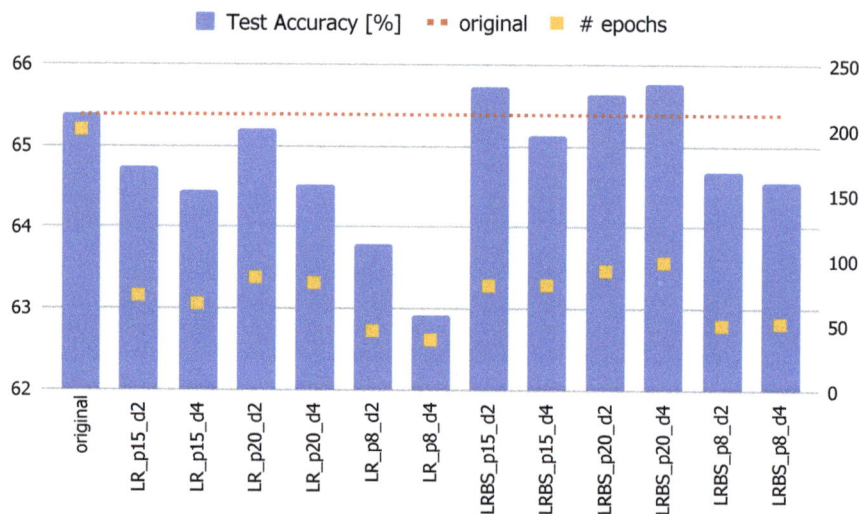

Figure 1. Performance of the various training for MobileNet on CIFAR-100. The blue bars represent the accuracy on the test set (left axis), the yellow squares report the number of epochs needed (right axis) and the red dotted line is the accuracy provided by the reference training.

Table 1. Results obtained on the three CNN models on the CIFAR-100 dataset.

CNN Model	Configuration	p	p Decay	Test Accuracy (%)	# Epochs
MobileNet	Original	-	-	65.39	200.00
MobileNet	LRBS	15	2	65.73	80.60
MobileNet	LRBS	15	4	65.14	81.00
MobileNet	LRBS	20	2	65.63	91.80
MobileNet	LRBS	20	4	65.76	98.20
ResNet18	Original	-	-	74.86	200.00
ResNet18	LRBS	15	2	73.96	73.00
ResNet18	LRBS	15	4	74.03	67.40
ResNet18	LRBS	20	2	74.30	90.20
ResNet18	LRBS	20	4	74.16	85.00
VGG16	Original	-	-	71.24	200.00
VGG16	LRBS	15	2	70.37	90.40
VGG16	LRBS	15	4	69.63	72.40
VGG16	LRBS	20	2	70.54	88.40
VGG16	LRBS	20	4	70.55	101.20

4.2. Biomedical Image Classification

The second part of the numerical experiments involved two types of bidimensional biomedical image datasets for multi-class classification: MedMNIST2D OrganSMNIST (https://medmnist.com/, accessed on 1 October 2022) and MedMNIST OCTMNIST (https://medmnist.com/, accessed on 1 October 2022) [26,27]. The former is composed of 25,221 abdominal CT images (the first panel of Figure 2) with labels from 0 to 10, each one corresponding to an organ or a bone of the abdomen. Each image is 28 × 28 pixels and the original dataset is split up into training, validation and test sets whose dimensions correspond to 70%, 9% and 21% of the total number of samples, respectively. The second one is made up of 109309 optical coherence tomography (OCT) images for retinal diseases (the second panel of Figure 2) and there are four labels of which three correspond to different diseases and one is related to normal health conditions. Each image is 28 × 28 pixels and the original dataset is divided similarly to the previous case.

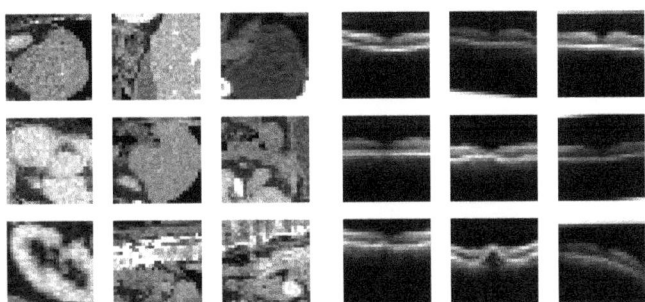

Figure 2. Some examples from MedMNIST2D OrganSMNIST (**left half**) and OCTMNIST (**right half**).

These two applications have been processed on MSI Sword 15 A11UC-630XIT with a GPU NVIDIA GeForce RTX 3050 Laptop, CPU i7-11800H, 8 GB of RAM, Windows 11 and Python 3.10.2. We opportunely modified the official code (https://github.com/MedMNIST/MedMNIST, accessed on 1 October 2022) which implements various artificial neural networks, from the data splitting point of view. In particular, we divided the dataset into the following disjointed subsets: the 70% of the total examples gives the TS, the 9% is employed for the VS and the remaining 21% of the data forms the test set. Our code is publicly available (https://github.com/AmbraCatozzi/ResNet18_Biomedical.git, accessed on 1 October 2022) for the sake of reproducibility.

For all the experiments, we compared the performance of the ResNet18 model trained by means of:

- The SG optimizer (3) with $\beta = 0.9$ (hereafter denoted by Original);
- The same optimizer but equipped with a classical early stopping technique (hereafter denoted by ES);
- Algorithm 1 (hereafter denoted by LRBS).

The hyperparameters setting for all the three optimization techniques are discussed in the following section.

4.2.1. Hyperparameters Setting

Because the performance of a stochastic gradient method is strictly related to the configuration of its hyperparameters, this section aims to fix the best hyperparameters setting for the algorithms employed to train the ResNet18. This preliminary study is carried out on the MedMNIST2D OrganSMNIST dataset and the best found hyperparameters configurations will be used for all the other experiments.

Setting p for the ES Method

First of all, we compare the performance of the ES method for different values of the patience p. In particular, given $\eta_0 = 10^{-3}$ and $n_0 = 128$, we report in Table 2 the values of the accuracy reached by ES with p equal to 5, 20 and 30. In the same table, the results corresponding to the Original optimizer are also reported (for the same setting of η_0 and n_0).

Table 2. Results on MedMNIST2D OrganSMNIST dataset in a maximum of 50 epochs. σ is the standard deviation and each result is the mean of five trials.

Configuration	Test Accuracy (%)	σ (%)	# Epochs
Original	88.14	0.20	50
ES ($p = 5$)	88.22	0.03	3.4
ES ($p = 20$)	88.51	0.53	21
ES ($p = 30$)	87.84	0.51	27.6

The value of p, which ensures the best accuracy on the test set, is 20. In the following, p is always set to this value for the ES method.

Setting η_0 and n_0 for the Original and the ES Methods

In order to properly tune the LR and the MBS for both the Original and the ES schemes, we performed several experiments with different settings, illustrated in Table 3.

Table 3. Hyperparameters analysis on MedMNIST2D OrganSMNIST dataset in a maximum of 50 epochs. σ is the standard deviation and each result is the mean of five trials.

Hyperparameters	Configuration	Test Accuracy (%)	σ (%)	# Epochs
$\eta_0 = 10^{-2}, n_0 = dim = 64$	Original	92.80	0.22	50
	ES	92.68	0.36	23.2
$\eta_0 = 10^{-2}, n_0 = dim = 128$	Original	92.49	0.31	50
	ES	92.58	0.33	16.2
$\eta_0 = 10^{-2}, n_0 = dim = 256$	Original	91.54	0.53	50
	ES	91.51	0.42	13.6
$\eta_0 = 10^{-3}, n_0 = dim = 64$	Original	91.05	0.82	50
	ES	91.08	0.72	19.8
$\eta_0 = 10^{-3}, n_0 = dim = 128$	Original	88.61	0.60	50
	ES	88.62	0.59	18.8
$\eta_0 = 10^{-3}, n_0 = dim = 256$	Original	86.89	0.41	50
	ES	86.86	0.37	24.6
$\eta_0 = 10^{-4}, n_0 = dim = 64$	Original	86.06	0.48	50
	ES	86.19	0.50	17.8
$\eta_0 = 10^{-4}, n_0 = dim = 128$	Original	84.84	0.89	50
	ES	85.48	0.28	38.4
$\eta_0 = 10^{-4}, n_0 = dim = 256$	Original	83.16	0.52	50
	ES	84.55	0.67	38

From the results of Table 3, the best hyperparameters setting for both the Original and the ES approaches is $\eta_0 = 10^{-2}$ and $n_0 = 64$. We remark that to find this setting was very demanding in terms of computational costs.

Robustness of the LRBS Method against Hyperparameters

The proposed method aims to get rid of the dependence on its intrinsic hyperparameters while maintaining a high performance. In this section, we investigate the response of the LRBS method to the variation in the values of the hyperparameters used in Algorithm 1. In particular, we consider different values for: c_1, c_2, dim and γ. It is worth highlighting that we do not need to also properly tune the values for the patience, the LR and the MBS as performed for the Original and the ES schemes. Indeed, the LRBS algorithm automatically adjusts the values of these hyperparameters along the epochs. For this reason, we just consider $p = 20$, $\eta_0 = 10^{-2}$ and $n_0 = 64$: we select a quite large value for both the patience and the initial LR and a quite small value for the initial MBS by allowing the procedure to adapt them (by increasing the former ones and decreasing the latter one). To confirm this thesis, in the next section (see Table 7), we show that the LRBS algorithm is much less sensitive to the selection of the hyperparameters than the other two methods in training the ResNet18 for the MedMNIST2D OrganSMNIST dataset. In Table 4, we present the values of the accuracy for different configurations. We run each experiment five times with different seeds and we report the means and standard deviations in the table.

Table 4. Mean and std. of the values of the accuracy obtained on MedMNIST2D OrganSMNIST dataset by the LRBS approach in a maximum of 50 epochs and different values of the hyperparameters. The initial mini-batch size is $n_0 = 64$ and the initial learning rate is $\eta_0 = 10^{-2}$.

	$\gamma = 2$		$\gamma = 4$	
	$c_1 = 1/4$	$c_1 = 1/2$	$c_1 = 1/4$	$c_1 = 1/2$
$c_2 = 2$, $dim = 0$	92.46% ± 0.43	92.88% ± 0.3	92.46% ± 0.34	93.33% ± 0.24
$c_2 = 1$, $dim = 64$	93.11% ± 0.35	93.18% ± 0.39	92.78% ± 0.37	92.93% ± 0.37

Table 4 allows to conclude that the LRBS method is very stable with respect to the reasonable choices of the hyperparameters involved; particularly, both the mean and variance over the 5 trials are very good in all cases.

A Comparison with the AdaM Optimizer

Finally, for the sake of completeness, we show that to employ the AdaM optimizer [31], instead of the SG one with momentum, leads to analogous results. Table 5 reports the values of the accuracy reached by the considered approaches equipped by AdaM with $\eta_0 = 10^{-3}$ and $n_0 = dim = 64$. The value of p is 20 for both the ES and LRBS. The LRBS method improves the accuracy obtained with the Original ResNet18 by one percentage point, with the lowest number of epochs.

Table 5. Results on MedMNIST2D OrganSMNIST dataset in a maximum number of 50 epochs. The AdaM optimizer is employed with $\eta_0 = 10^{-3}$ and $n_0 = dim = 64$.

Configuration	Test Accuracy (%)	σ (%)	# Epochs
Original	91.43	1.03	50
Early Stopping	92.52	0.57	19
LRBS	92.40	0.24	17.8

4.2.2. Numerical Results

In this section, we perform three different experiments. We firstly summarize the hyperparameters setting for the three compared approaches in view of the considerations made in the previous section. For the Original, ES and LRBS, we fixed $\eta_0 = 10^{-2}$ and $n_0 = 64$. The value of p is 20 for both the ES and LRBS. Moreover, the other hyperparameters defining the LRBS are set as $c_1 = 0.5$, $c_2 = 1$, $dim = 64$, $\gamma = 2$, $p = 20$ and $\bar{p} = 6$. In the following paragraphs, we present the results obtained by fixing the maximum number of epochs, $maxepochs$, to both 50 and 100.

Results for OrganSMNIST in a Maximum Number of 50 Epochs

In Table 6, we show the numerical results for the abdominal CT dataset: each column reports the mean accuracy on the test set, the standard deviation and the mean number of epochs obtained in five runs for the OrganSMNIST. The proposed method outperforms both the ResNet18 model and the early stopped one in terms of accuracy with the same number of epochs needed by the classical early stopping implementation.

Table 6. Results on MedMNIST2D OrganSMNIST dataset in maximum 50 epochs.

Configuration	Test Accuracy (%)	σ (%)	# Epochs
Original	92.80	0.22	50
ES	92.68	0.36	23.2
LRBS	92.81	0.37	23.2

We also observed that if we left fixed the value for the MBS but we increase the initial learning rate by either one or two orders of magnitude, the LRBS method outperforms both the standard model and the early stopped version (see Table 7) by confirming the less dependence on the hyperparameters setting of the LRBS approach.

Table 7. Results on MedMNIST2D OrganSMNIST dataset in a maximum of 50 epochs.

Learning Rate	Configuration	Test Accuracy (%)	σ (%)	# Epochs
$\eta_0 = 10^{-1}$	Original	93.02	0.20	50
	ES	93.12	0.17	23.2
	LRBS	93.21	0.30	11.8
$\eta_0 = 1$	Original	89.57	0.73	50
	ES	90.73	0.84	31.4
	LRBS	91.68	0.42	21.4

Results for OCTMNIST Dataset in a Maximum Number of 50 Epochs

The results related to the MedMNIST2D OCTMNIST dataset are illustrated in the same vein, but the means are calculated on the best five values of each configuration chosen from 20 runs; the numerical outcomes are presented in Table 8. It can be seen that the proposed method slightly improves the accuracy, but it reaches this value in half of the time with respect to the standard early stopping procedure.

Table 8. Results on MedMNIST2D OCTMNIST dataset in maximum 50 epochs.

Configuration	Test Accuracy (%)	σ (%)	# Epochs
Original	93.72	0.17	50
ES	93.80	0.12	21.8
LRBS	93.89	0.13	11.2

Results for OCTMNIST in a Maximum Number of 100 Epochs

To highlight the effectiveness of Algorithm 1, another experiment has been conducted. We trained the same models presented in the previous section for a maximum number of 100 epochs by considering the dataset OCTMNIST (see Table 9).

Table 9. Results on MedMNIST2D OCTMNIST dataset in maximum 100 epochs.

Configuration	Test Accuracy (%)	σ (%)	# Epochs
Original	93.65	0.14	100
ES	93.69	0.16	10.4
LRBS	93.68	0.15	17.2

As in the previous experiments, comparable values for the accuracy can be obtained by all the considered strategies; however, the number of epochs related to the early stopped models is less than the 20% of the total number of epochs. However, we remark that the LRBS does not suffer from the computational expensive phase of the hyperparameters tuning.

5. Conclusions and Future Works

In this paper, we propose a dynamic early stopping technique for the training of a neural network, based on variable selection strategies to fix both the learning rate and the mini-batch size in SG methods. The suggested scheme is able to avoid the overfitting phenomena and reduce the training phase. The numerical experiments carried out on biomedical image classification problems show the benefits of employing the proposed dynamic early stopping procedure: performances comparable to those of the reference network can be achieved in a significantly lower number of epochs. Moreover, the suggested approach avoids the computational expensive setting of the best hyperparameters values needed by standard training techniques.

Author Contributions: All authors contributed equally to the study conception and design. Data curation, M.V.; software, A.C.; supervision, M.P.; validation, F.P.; writing—original draft, G.F. All authors have read and agreed to the published version of the manuscript.

Funding: This research received no external funding.

Institutional Review Board Statement: Not applicable.

Informed Consent Statement: Not applicable.

Data Availability Statement: https://github.com/weiaicunzai/pytorch-cifar100 (accessed on 1 October 2022), https://github.com/mive93/pytorch-cifar100 (accessed on 1 October 2022).

Acknowledgments: This work was also supported by the Gruppo Nazionale per il Calcolo Scientifico (GNCS-INdAM). The publication was created with the co-financing of the European Union-FSE-REACT-EU, PON Research and Innovation 2014-2020 DM1062/2021. The publication is co-financed by the project Unimore FAR Mission Oriented "Artificial Intelligence-based Mathematical Models and Methods for low dose CT imaging".

Conflicts of Interest: The authors declare no conflict of interest.

Abbreviations

The following abbreviations are used in this manuscript:

AI	Artificial Intelligence
ML	Machine Learning
DL	Deep Learning
SG	Stochastic Gradient
MBS	Mini-Batch Size
NAS	Neural Architecture Search
LR	Learning Rate
VS	Validation Set
ANN	Artificial Neural Network
GPU	Graphics Processing Unit
FPGA	Field-Programmable Gate Array
CNN	Convolutional Neural Network
TS	Training Set

References

1. Bottou, L.; Curtis, F.; Nocedal, J. Optimization Methods for Large-Scale Machine Learning. *SIAM Rev.* **2018**, *60*, 223–311. [CrossRef]
2. Loizou, N.; Richtárik, P. Momentum and Stochastic Momentum for Stochastic Gradient, Newton, Proximal Point and Subspace Descent Methods. *Comput. Optim. Appl.* **2020**, *77*, 653–710. [CrossRef]
3. Franchini, G.; Ruggiero, V.; Porta, F.; Zanni, L. Neural architecture search via standard machine learning methodologies. *Math. Eng.* **2022**, *5*, 1–21 . [CrossRef]
4. Nakkiran, P. Learning Rate Annealing Can Provably Help Generalization, Even for Convex Problems. In Proceedings of the OPT2020: 12th Annual Workshop on Optimization for Machine Learning, Bangkok, Thailand, 18–20 November 2020; p. 35.

5. Li, Y.; Wei, C.; Ma, T. Towards Explaining the Regularization Effect of Initial Large Learning Rate in Training Neural Networks. In Proceedings of the 33rd International Conference on Neural Information Processing Systems, Vancouver, BC, Canada, 8–14 November 2019; Curran Associates Inc.: Red Hook, NY, USA, 2019; p. 1047.
6. Bochkovskiy, A.; Wang, C.; Liao, H.M. YOLOv4: Optimal Speed and Accuracy of Object Detection. *arXiv* **2020**, arXiv:abs/2004.10934.
7. Ramachandran, S.; George, J.; Skaria, S.; Varun, V. Using YOLO based deep learning network for real time detection and localization of lung nodules from low dose CT scans. In Proceedings of the Medical Imaging 2018: Computer-Aided Diagnosis, Houston, TX, USA, 12–15 February 2018; Volume 10575, p. 105751I. [CrossRef]
8. Takase, T.; Oyama, S.; Kurihara, M. Effective neural network training with adaptive learning rate based on training loss. *Neural Netw.* **2018**, *101*, 68–78. [CrossRef]
9. Mishra, S.; Yamasaki, T.; Imaizumi, H. Improving image classifiers for small datasets by learning rate adaptations. In Proceedings of the 16th International Conference on Machine Vision Applications (MVA), Tokyo, Japan, 27–31 May 2019. [CrossRef]
10. Masters, D.; Luschi, C. Revisiting Small Batch Training for Deep Neural Networks. *arXiv* **2018**, arXiv:1804.07612.
11. Friedlander, M.; Schmidt, M. Hybrid Deterministic-Stochastic Methods for Data Fitting. *SIAM J. Sci. Comput.* **2012**, *34*, A1380–A1405. [CrossRef]
12. Alfarra, M.; Hanzely, S.; Albasyoni, A.; Ghanem, B.; Richtarik, P. Adaptive Learning of the Optimal Mini-Batch Size of SGD. In Proceedings of the OPT2020: 12th Annual Workshop on Optimization for Machine Learning, Bangkok, Thailand, 18–20 November 2020; p. 10.
13. Franchini, G.; Burgio, P.; Zanni, L. Artificial Neural Networks: The Missing Link Between Curiosity and Accuracy. In Proceedings of the Intelligent Systems Design and Applications, Vellore, India, 12–15 December 2020; Abraham, A., Cherukuri, A., Melin, P., Gandhi, N., Eds.; Springer International Publishing: Cham, Switzerland, 2020; pp. 1025–1034.
14. Kandel, I.; Castelli, M. The effect of batch size on the generalizability of the convolutional neural networks on a histopathology dataset. *ICT Express* **2020**, *6*, 312–315. [CrossRef]
15. Smith, S.; Kindermans, P.J.; Le, Q. Don't Decay the Learning Rate, Increase the Batch Size. In Proceedings of the 6th International Conference on Learning Representations, Vancouver, BC, Canada, 30 April–3 May 2018.
16. Franchini, G.; Ruggiero, V.; Zanni, L. Steplength and Mini-batch Size Selection in Stochastic Gradient Methods. In Proceedings of the Machine Learning, Optimization, and Data Science, Siena, Italy, 19–23 July 2020; Nicosia, G., Ojha, V., La Malfa, E., Jansen, G., Sciacca, V., Pardalos, P., Giuffrida, G., Umeton, R., Eds.; Springer International Publishing: Berlin/Heidelberg, Germany, 2020; pp. 259–263.
17. Chen, C.; Zhang, Y.; Wang, Z.; Wan, S.; Pei, Q. Distributed computation offloading method based on deep reinforcement learning in ICV. *Appl. Soft Comput.* **2021**, *103*, 107108. [CrossRef]
18. Wu, Y.; Yue, Y.; Tan, X.; Wang, W.; Lu, T. End-to-end chromosome Karyotyping with data augmentation using GAN. In Proceedings of the 2018 25th IEEE International Conference on Image Processing (ICIP), Athens, Greece, 7–10 October 2018; pp. 2456–2460.
19. Sun, L.; Feng, S.; Liu, J.; Lyu, G.; Lang, C. Global-local label correlation for partial multi-label learning. *IEEE Trans. Multimed.* **2021**, *24*, 581–593. [CrossRef]
20. Prechelt, L. Early Stopping—But When? In *Neural Networks: Tricks of the Trade*, 2nd ed.; Montavon, G., Orr, G.B., Müller, K.R., Eds.; Springer: Berlin/Heidelberg, Germany, 2012; pp. 53–67.
21. Schwartz, R.; Dodge, J.; Smith, N.; Etzioni, O. Green AI. *Commun. ACM* **2020**, *63*, 54–63. [CrossRef]
22. Krizhevsky, A.; Hinton, G. *Learning Multiple Layers of Features from Tiny Images*; Technical Report TR-2009; University of Toronto: Toronto, ON, Canada, 2009.
23. Yang, J.; Shi, R.; Wei, D.; Liu, Z.; Zhao, L.; Ke, B.; Pfister, H.; Ni, B. MedMNIST v2: A Large-Scale Lightweight Benchmark for 2D and 3D Biomedical Image Classification. *arXiv* **2021**, arXiv:2110.14795.
24. Kermany, D.; Goldbaum, M. Identifying Medical Diagnoses and Treatable Diseases by Image-Based Deep Learning. *Cell* **2018**, *172*, 1122–1131. [CrossRef]
25. Yang, J.; Shi, R.; Ni, B. MedMNIST Classification Decathlon: A Lightweight AutoML Benchmark for Medical Image Analysis. In Proceedings of the IEEE 18th International Symposium on Biomedical Imaging (ISBI), Nice, France, 13–16 April 2021; pp. 191–195.
26. Bilic, P.; Christ, P.F.; Vorontsov, E.; Chlebus, G.; Chen, H.; Dou, Q.; Menze, B.H. The Liver Tumor Segmentation Benchmark (LiTS). *arXiv* **2019**, arXiv:1901.04056.
27. Xu, X.; Zhou, F.; Liu, B.; Fu, D.; Bai, X. Efficient Multiple Organ Localization in CT Image Using 3D Region Proposal Network. *IEEE Trans. Med. Imaging* **2019**, *38*, 1885–1898. [CrossRef] [PubMed]
28. He, K.; Zhang, X.; Ren, S.; Sun, J. Deep residual learning for image recognition. In Proceedings of the IEEE Conference on Computer Vision and Pattern Recognition, Las Vegas, NV, USA, 27–30 June 2016; pp. 770–778.
29. Simonyan, K.; Zisserman, A. Very deep convolutional networks for large-scale image recognition. *arXiv* **2014**, arXiv:1409.1556.
30. Howard, A.G.; Zhu, M.; Chen, B.; Kalenichenko, D.; Wang, W.; Weyand, T.; Andreetto, M.; Adam, H. MobileNets: Efficient convolutional neural networks for mobile vision applications. *arXiv* **2017**, arXiv:1704.04861.
31. Kingma, D.; Ba, J. Adam: A Method for Stochastic Optimization. *arXiv* **2017**, arXiv:1412.6980.

Article

A Hybrid Direct Search and Model-Based Derivative-Free Optimization Method with Dynamic Decision Processing and Application in Solid-Tank Design

Zhongda Huang [1], Andy Ogilvy [2], Steve Collins [2], Warren Hare [1,*], Michelle Hilts [1,3] and Andrew Jirasek [2]

[1] Department Mathematics, University of British Columbia—Okanagan, Kelowna, BC V1V 1V7, Canada
[2] Department Physics, University of British Columbia—Okanagan, Kelowna, BC V1V 1V7, Canada
[3] Medical Physics, BC Cancer, Kelowna, BC V1Y 5L3, Canada
* Correspondence: warren.hare@ubc.ca

Abstract: A derivative-free optimization (DFO) method is an optimization method that does not make use of derivative information in order to find the optimal solution. It is advantageous for solving real-world problems in which the only information available about the objective function is the output for a specific input. In this paper, we develop the framework for a DFO method called the DQL method. It is designed to be a versatile hybrid method capable of performing direct search, quadratic-model search, and line search all in the same method. We develop and test a series of different strategies within this framework. The benchmark results indicate that each of these strategies has distinct advantages and that there is no clear winner in the overall performance among efficiency and robustness. We develop the SMART DQL method by allowing the method to determine the optimal search strategies in various circumstances. The SMART DQL method is applied to a problem of solid-tank design for 3D radiation dosimetry provided by the UBCO (University of British Columbia—Okanagan) 3D Radiation Dosimetry Research Group. Given the limited evaluation budget, the SMART DQL method produces high-quality solutions.

Keywords: derivative-free optimization; black-box optimization; local optimization; direct search method; model-based method; 3D radiation dosimetry

1. Introduction

An optimization problem

$$\min\{f(x) : x \in \Omega\} \tag{1}$$

is considered a black-box optimization (BBO) problem if the objective function f is provided by a black box. That is, for a given input, the function returns an output, but provides no information on how the output was generated. As such, no higher-order information (gradients, Hessians, etc.) are available. Developing methods to solve BBO problems is a highly valued field of research, as the methods are used in a wide range of applications [1–8] (amongst many more).

In many BBO problems, heuristic techniques are used [1–3]. In this paper, we focus on provably convergent algorithms. The study of provably convergent algorithms that do not explicitly use high-order information in their execution is often referred to as derivative-free optimization (DFO). We refer readers to [9,10] for a general overview of DFO and to [11,12] for recent surveys of applications of DFO.

DFO is often separated into two disjoint strategies: direct search methods and model-based methods [10]. Direct search methods involve looking for evaluation candidate(s) directly in the search domain [9,10]. Conversely, model-based methods involve building a surrogate model from the evaluated points to find the next evaluation candidate [9,10].

As DFO research has advanced, researchers have proposed that these two strategies should be merged to create hybrid algorithms that applied both techniques [9,10,13–15]. However, very few algorithms have been published that hybridize theses two methods.

In this research, we seek to develop a framework that allows for direct search and model-based methods to be united into a single algorithm. We further seek to develop dynamic approaches to select and adjust how the direct search and model-based methods are used. In doing so, we aim to apply both a mathematical analysis that guarantees convergence (under reasonable assumptions) and numerical testing to determine techniques that work well in practice.

1.1. Overview of DQL and Smart DQL Method

Some efforts have been made to hybridize direct search and model-based methods. For example, the SID-PSM method involves combining a search step of minimizing the approximated quadratic model over a trust region with the direct search [13,14]. The RQLIF method, which we discuss next, provides a more versatile approach [15].

To understand the RQLIF method, we note that there are two common ways to find the next evaluation candidate during a model-based method [10]. First, methods can find the candidate at the minima of the surrogate model within some trust region or constraints. These are referred to as model-based trust-region (MBTR) methods. Second, methods can use the model to predict the descent direction and perform a line-search on the direction. These are referred to as model-based descent (MBD) methods.

At each iteration, the RQLIF method searches for an improvement using three distinct strategies without relying on gradient or higher-order derivative information. These steps are referred to as the direct step, quadratic step, and linear step. These three steps correspond to three distinct search strategies from the direct search method, MBTR methods, and MBD methods.

Inspired by the structure of the RQLIF method, we propose the DQL method framework. The purpose of this framework is to allow a flexible hybrid method that permits a direct search, quadratic-model search, and line-search all in the same method. Our objective is to design a framework that allows the development of a variety of search strategies and to determine the strategies that perform best. The DQL method is a local method for solving unconstrained BBO problems. We ensure its local convergence by implementing a two-stage procedure. The first stage focuses on finding an improvement in an efficient manner. It accepts an improvement whenever the candidate yields a better solution. We call this stage the exploration stage. The second stage focuses on the convergence to a local optimum; we call this stage the convergence stage.

In Section 2, we introduce the DQL method's framework and the search strategies. In Section 3, we conduct the convergence analysis. Provided that the objective function has a compact level set $L(x_0)$ and the gradient of the objective function is Lipschitz continuous in an open set containing $L(x_0)$, the convergence analysis indicates that there exists a convergent subsequence of iterations with a gradient of zero at its limit. This demonstrates that when the evaluation budget is large enough, the method will converge to a stationary point.

Using the framework of the DQL method, we obtain a series of combinations of quadratic and linear step strategies. In order to select the best combination among them, in Section 3, we perform a numerical benchmark across all the possible combinations. The quadratic step strategies are capable of improve the overall performance of the method. However, the linear steps show a mixed performance and there is no clear winner on efficiency or robustness. This inspires the idea that by employing an appropriate strategy in certain circumstances, we may be able to achieve an overall improvement in performance.

This idea of allowing the method to make decisions on search strategies in various circumstances leads to the Smart DQL method, which we discuss in Section 4. By analyzing the search results from various strategies, we develop decision processes that select the appropriate strategies for the search steps during the optimization. This allows the method to dynamically decide the appropriate strategies for the given information. In Section 4, we perform numerical tests on the SMART DQL method and discover that the SMART DQL method outperforms the DQL methods in terms of both robustness and performance.

In Section 5, we apply the SMART DQL method to the problem of design of solid tanks for optical computed tomography scanning of 3D radiation dosimeters described in [16]. The original paper employs a grid-search technique combined with a manual refinement to solve the problem. This process involves considerable human interaction. Conversely, we find that the SMART DQL method is capable of producing a high-quality solution without human interaction.

1.2. Definitions

Throughout this paper, we assume $f : \mathbb{R}^n \to \mathbb{R}$. Let x_{best}^k denote the best solution found by the method at iteration k and f_{best}^k denote the corresponding function value.

We present the definitions that are used to approximate gradient and Hessian by the DQL method as follows. We begin with the Moore–Penrose pseudoinverse.

Definition 1 (Moore–Penrose pseudoinverse). *Let $A \in \mathbb{R}^{n \times m}$. The Moore–Penrose pseudoinverse of A, denoted by $A^\dagger$, is the unique matrix in $\mathbb{R}^{m \times n}$ that satisfies the following four equations:*

$$AA^\dagger A = A, \tag{2}$$

$$A^\dagger A A^\dagger = A, \tag{3}$$

$$(AA^\dagger)^\top = AA^\dagger, \tag{4}$$

$$(A^\dagger A)^\top = A^\dagger A. \tag{5}$$

The generalized centred simplex gradient and generalized simplex Hessian are studied in [17,18], respectively.

Definition 2 (Generalized centred simplex gradient [17]). *Let $f : \mathbb{R}^n \to \mathbb{R}$, $x_0 \in \mathbb{R}^n$ be the point of interest, and $D = \begin{bmatrix} d^1 & d^2 & \cdots & d^k \end{bmatrix} \in \mathbb{R}^{n \times k}$. The generalized centred simplex gradient of f at x_0 over D is denoted by $\nabla_c f(x_0; D)$ and defined by,*

$$\nabla_c f(x_0; D) = (D^\top)^\dagger \delta_f^c(x_0; D) \in \mathbb{R}^n, \tag{6}$$

where

$$\delta_f^c(x_0; D) = \frac{1}{2} \left[f(x_0 + d^1) - f(x_0 - d^1), \cdots, f(x_0 + d^k) - f(x_0 - d^k) \right]^\top. \tag{7}$$

Definition 3 (Generalized simplex Hessian). *Let $f : \mathbb{R}^n \to \mathbb{R}$ and x_0 be the point of interest. Let $S = \begin{bmatrix} s^1 & s^2 & \cdots & s^m \end{bmatrix} \in \mathbb{R}^{n \times m}$ and $\{D^i : D^i \in \mathbb{R}^{n \times k}, i = 0, 1, 2, \cdots, m\}$ be the set of direction matrices used to approximate the gradients at $x_0, x_0 + s^1, \cdots, x_0 + s^m$, respectively. The generalized simplex Hessian of f at x_0 over S and $\{D^i\}$ is denoted by $\nabla_s^2 f(x_0; S, \{D^i\})$ and defined by*

$$\nabla_s^2 f(x_0; S, \{D^i\}) = (S^\top)^\dagger \delta_{\nabla_c f}(x_0; S, \{D^i\}), \tag{8}$$

where

$$\delta_{\nabla_c f}(x_0; S, \{D^i\}) = \begin{bmatrix} (\nabla_c f(x_0 + s^1; D^1) - \nabla_c f(x_0; D^0))^\top \\ (\nabla_c f(x_0 + s^2; D^2) - \nabla_c f(x_0; D^0))^\top \\ \vdots \\ (\nabla_c f(x_0 + s^m; D^m) - \nabla_c f(x_0; D^0))^\top \end{bmatrix} \in \mathbb{R}^{m \times n}. \tag{9}$$

In Section 3, in order to prove convergence of our method, we make use of the cosine measure as defined in [9].

Definition 4 (Cosine measure). *Let $D = \begin{bmatrix} d^1 & d^2, \cdots, d^m \end{bmatrix} \in \mathbb{R}^{n \times m}$ form a positive basis. We say D forms a positive basis if $\{x : x = \sum_{i=1}^{m} \lambda d^i, \lambda \geq 0\} = \mathbb{R}^n$ but no proper subset of D has the same property. The cosine measure of D is defined by,*

$$cm(D) = \min_{\omega \in \mathbb{R}^n} \left\{ \max_{d \in D} \left\{ \frac{\omega^\top d}{\|\omega\| \|d\|} \right\} : \|\omega\| = 1 \right\}. \tag{10}$$

2. DQL Method

In this section, we introduce the framework of the DQL method. At each iteration, the method starts from an initial search point x_0^k and a search step length δ^k. Note that at the first iteration, the initial search point and the search step length are given by the inputs x_0 and δ_0, so $x_0^1 = x_0$ and $\delta^1 = \delta_0$. The initial search point and the search step length are used to initiate three distinct search steps: the direct step, the quadratic step, and the linear step. A variable x_{best}^k is used to track the current best solution at iteration k. If an improvement is found in the search step length at iteration k, the method updates x_{best}^k. Three Boolean values are used to track the results from each search step: DIRECT_FLAG, QUADRATIC_FLAG, and LINEAR_FLAG. If a search step succeeds at finding an improvement, it sets the corresponding FLAG to TRUE; otherwise, the corresponding FLAG is set to FALSE. These search steps are then followed by the update step. In the update step, the search step length is updated according to the search results and the method uses the current best solution as the starting search point of the next iteration.

As mentioned, the DQL method utilizes two different stages: the exploration stage and the convergence stage. In the exploration stage, the method enables all the search steps, and it accepts the improvement whenever the evaluation candidate yields a lower value than the current best solution. If the iteration counter k reaches the given MAX_SEARCH, then the method proceeds with the convergence stage, the method disables the quadratic and the linear step and the solution acceptance implements a sufficient decrease rule.

This framework allows various search strategies to be implemented. We provide some basic strategies for performing the search steps. The analysis of the convergence and the performance of these search steps are discussed in the next section.

2.1. Solution Acceptance Rule

In the DQL method, each search step returns a set of candidate(s). Then, these candidate(s) are evaluated and compared to the current best solution x_{best}^k. If the best candidate is accepted by the solution acceptance rule, then x_{best}^k is updated. There are two solution acceptance rules that are used in the DQL method. The first rule is used in the exploration stage and updates x_{best}^k whenever an improvement is found. The second rule is used in the convergence stage and updates x_{best}^k only when the candidate makes sufficient decrease. Specifically, in the convergence stage of the DQL method, a candidate $x_{\text{current}} \in \text{CANDIDATE\_SET}$ is accepted as x_{best}^k only if

$$f(x_{\text{current}}) < f(x_{\text{best}}^k) - (\delta^k)^2, \tag{11}$$

where δ^k is the current search step length. We show that this sufficient decrease rule is crucial for the convergence of the DQL method in the next section. The algorithm of the solution acceptance is denoted as

IMPROVEMENT_CHECK(CANDIDATE_SET, x_{BEST}^k, δ^k)

and is shown in Algorithm 1.

Algorithm 1 IMPROVEMENT_CHECK(CANDIDATE_SET, x_{BEST}^k, δ^k)

1: Evaluate CANDIDATE_SET
2: $x_{\text{current}} \leftarrow \arg\min\{\text{function evaluations of CANDIDATE\_SET}\}$
3: **if** $k \leq$ MAX_SEARCH **then**
4:     **if** $f(x_{\text{current}}) < f(x_{\text{best}}^k)$ **then**
5:         $x_{\text{best}}^k \leftarrow x_{\text{current}}$
6:     **end if**
7: **else**
8:     **if** $f(x_{\text{current}}) < f(x_{\text{best}}^k) - (\delta^k)^2$ **then**
9:         $x_{\text{best}}^k \leftarrow x_{\text{current}}$
10:     **end if**
11: **end if**

2.2. Direct Step

2.2.1. Framework of the Direct Step

In the direct step, the method searches from the starting search point x_0^k in the positive and negative coordinate directions or a rotation thereof. We denote the set of search directions at iteration k as $\bar{D}^k$. The positive and negative coordinate directions can be written as the columns of an $n \times 2n$ matrix $\begin{bmatrix} I_n & -I_n \end{bmatrix}$. The method applies an $n \times n$ rotation matrix $D^k = \begin{bmatrix} d_1^k & d_2^k & \cdots & d_n^k \end{bmatrix} \in \mathbb{R}^{n \times n}$, so $\bar{D}^k$ can be written as $\begin{bmatrix} D^k & -D^k \end{bmatrix}$.

We first need to determine how we want to rotate the search directions. We have two possible situations. First, if the method predicts a direction for which improvement is likely to be found, then we call this direction a *desired* direction. Notice that, since we search on both positive direction and negative direction, we also search the direction where an improvement is unlikely to be found. Conversely, if the method predicts a direction that is highly unlikely to provide improvement, then we call the corresponding direction an *undesired* direction. Denoting the predicted direction by r^k, we have the following 2 possibilities.

- If r^k is a *desired* direction, then we construct D^k such that it rotates one of the search directions to align with r^k.
- If r^k is an *undesired* direction, then we construct D^k such that it rotates the vector $\begin{bmatrix} 1 & \cdots & 1 \end{bmatrix}$ to align with r^k. In this way, the coordinate directions are rotated to point away from r^k as much as possible.

Figure 1 shows how the method rotates the search direction matrix $\bar{D}^k$ towards a desired direction or away from an undesired direction for an $\mathbb{R}^2$ problem.

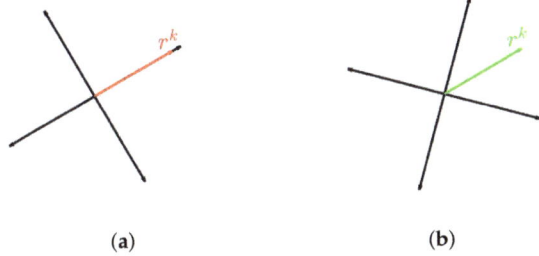

(a)   (b)

Figure 1. An example of rotating search direction $\bar{D}^k$ (black) for (**a**) a desired direction (red) and (**b**) an undesired direction (green). (**a**) Align $\bar{D}^k$ towards the desired direction r^k. (**b**) Align $\bar{D}^k$ away from the undesired direction r^k.

For an n-dimensional rotation ($n > 3$), the rotation is described as rotating by an angle of α on an $n - 1$ dimension hyperplane that is spanned by a pair of orthogonal unit vectors u and $v \in \mathbb{R}^n$. According to Masson, such a rotation matrix D can be defined as follows [19],

$$L(\alpha, u, v) = I_n + (vu^\top - uv^\top)\sin\alpha + (uu^\top + vv^\top)(\cos\alpha - 1). \qquad (12)$$

For a desired direction r^k, the rotation matrix D^k can be found by rotating the coordinate directions on the hyperplane spanned by one coordinate direction, e.g., e_1, and r^k by the angle between e_1 and r^k. Notice that if e_1 and r^k are linearly dependent, then r^k lies on the coordinate direction e_1, so D^k is the identity matrix. In conclusion, if r^k is a desired direction, the search directions D^k is calculated as follows,

$$D^k = L(\arccos(r^{k\top} e_1), r^k, e_1). \qquad (13)$$

For an undesired direction r^k, the method needs to keep the search directions as far from r^k as possible. In order to do so, it first constructs a normalized one-vector $\hat{\mathbf{1}}$, which is calculated as follows,

$$\hat{\mathbf{1}} = \frac{\sum_{i=1}^n e_i}{\left\|\sum_{i=1}^n e_i\right\|} = \frac{\sum_{i=1}^n e_i}{\sqrt{n}}. \qquad (14)$$

Then, the method aligns $\hat{\mathbf{1}}$ with the undesired direction r^k. The rotation matrix D^k for an undesired direction r^k is calculated as follows,

$$D^k = L(\arccos(r^{k\top}\hat{\mathbf{1}}), r^k, \hat{\mathbf{1}}). \qquad (15)$$

After the search directions $\bar{D}^k$ are built, the search candidates from the direct step at iteration k can be determined as

$$\mathbb{D}^k = \{x_0^k + \delta^k d^k : d^k \in \bar{D}^k\}. \qquad (16)$$

We then check if any of the candidates yield improvement by
IMPROVEMENT_CHECK($\mathbb{D}^k, x_{BEST}^k, \delta^k$).
If an improvement is found, then the DIRECT_FLAG is set to be TRUE. Otherwise, the DIRECT_FLAG is set to be FALSE.

The pseudocode of the direct step in the DQL method is shown in Algorithm 2. The direct step is always initiated at every iteration, and it produces $\left|\mathbb{D}^k\right| = 2n$ candidates, so it requires $2n$ function evaluations to perform. Since these candidates are independent from each other, the function evaluations proceed in parallel. Although this step is computationally expensive, it is necessary to prove convergence of our method as shown in Theorem 4. The freedom of choosing the rotation direction is essential to the development of the SMART DQL method. This allows us to develop a variety of rotation strategies that are discussed in the next section.

Algorithm 2 DIRECT_STEP(x_0^k, δ^k)

1: Determine the rotation direction $r^k \in \mathbb{R}^n$
2: **if** r^k is a desired direction **then**
3:     Align D^k towards r^k
4: **else**
5:     Align D^k away from r^k
6: **end if**
7: The direct search candidates $\mathbb{D}^k = \{x_0^k + \delta^k d^k : d^k \in \bar{D}^k\}$
8: IMPROVEMENT_CHECK($\mathbb{D}^k, x_0^k, \delta^k$)
9: Update DIRECT_FLAG accordingly

Direct Step Strategy

The first direct step strategy is inspired by the direct step in the RQLIF method [15]. The rotation directions alternate between two options:

- A coordinate direction being the desired direction;
- A random direction being the desired direction.

At odd iterations, the method searches on the positive and negative coordinate directions. At even iterations, the method searches on the random rotations of the coordinate directions. We denote this strategy as direct step strategy 1. In Section 4, when developing the SMART DQL method, we introduce new rotation strategies.

2.3. Quadratic Step

2.3.1. Framework of Quadratic Step

If the direct step fails to find an improvement, then the method proceeds to the quadratic step. Note that after a failed direct step, the best point remains at x_0^k. In the quadratic step, the method first selects the points that have been previously evaluated within some radius $q^k \geq \beta \delta^k$ of the point of centre x_0^k for some $\beta \geq 1$. These points are used to construct a quadratic model of the objective function. The radius condition $q^k \geq \beta \delta^k$ ensures that all the points from the direct search are taken into account. The method extracts the quadratic information from these calculated points using a least-squares quadratic model or Hessian approximation. The pseudocode of the quadratic step is shown in Algorithm 3. Note that in the third line of Algorithm 3, the methods of extracting and utilizing the quadratic information varies for different strategies. The idea of the quadratic step is to use these previously evaluated points $\{x_i\}$ to predict a candidate by using quadratic approximations.

Algorithm 3 QUADRATIC_STEP($x_0^k, \beta, \delta^k, \{x_i\}$)

1: $q^k \leftarrow \beta \delta^k$
2: Determine the set of evaluated points within the trust region $Q^k = \{x_i : \|x_i - x_0^k\| \leq q^k\}$
3: Determine the quadratic search candidates $\mathbb{Q}^k$ using the quadratic information from Q^k
4: IMPROVEMENT_CHECK($\mathbb{Q}^k, x_0^k, \delta^k$)
5: Update QUADRATIC_FLAG accordingly

Quadratic Step Strategies

Our first option for the quadratic step begins by constructing a least-squares quadratic model. We use the QUADPROG and TRUST functions from MATLAB [20] to find the least-squares quadratic model and its optimum within the trust region. We label this quadratic step strategy as quadratic step strategy 1.

Our second option for the quadratic step is to take one iteration of an approximated Newton's method. Approximation techniques are introduced to obtain the required gradient and Hessian. Notice that at the end of the direct step, the centred simplex gradient approximation is performed, so we take

$$\nabla f(x_0^k) \approx \nabla_c f(x_0^k; \delta^k D^k). \tag{17}$$

To approximate the Hessian at x_0^k, we need all the points within radius q^k that have a gradient approximation. Since the gradient approximations are performed in previous unsuccessful direct steps, we can reuse those approximation. First, the points that have gradient approximation and are within the radius q^k are determined. We denote these by x_h^j ($j = 1, 2, \cdots, m$). The corresponding search directions and search step lengths are denoted by D_h^j and δ_h^j ($j = 1, 2, \cdots, m$). We take D_h^0 and δ_h^0 as the search direction and search step length in the direct step of the current iterate. We obtain

$$S = [x_h^1 - x_0^k \quad x_h^1 - x_0^k \quad \cdots \quad x_h^m - x_0^k]. \tag{18}$$

The Hessian at x_0^k can be approximated as,

$$\nabla^2 f(x_0^k) \approx \nabla_s^2 f(x_0^k; S, \{\delta_h^j D_h^j\}) = (S^\top)^\dagger \delta_{\nabla_c f}(x_0^k; S, \{\delta_h^j D_h^j\}), \tag{19}$$

where $\delta_{\nabla_c f}(x_0^k; S, \{\delta_h^j D_h^j\})$ is defined in Definition 3.

If the approximated Hessian is positive definite, then the search candidate is determined via

$$x_Q = x_0^k - (\nabla_s^2 f(x_0^k; S, \{\delta_h^j D_h^j\}))^{-1} \nabla_c f(x_0^k; \delta^k D^k). \tag{20}$$

If the approximate Hessian is not positive definite, we can perform a trust-region search by building a quadratic model with the approximate gradient and Hessian at x_0^k.

We label this quadratic step strategy as quadratic step strategy 2.

Discussion on Quadratic Step Strategies

Both quadratic step strategies try to build a quadratic model and extract the optima from the quadratic model. However, there are some major differences between the two strategies.

- The points chosen to construct the model are different. In the quadratic step strategy 1, any evaluated points that are within the trust region are chosen. In the quadratic step strategy 2, the chosen points have an additional requirement that they should also have a gradient approximation.
- In the quadratic step strategy 1, x_Q lies within the trust region. In the quadratic step strategy 2, if the approximated Hessian is positive definite, then x_Q may lie outside of the trust region.

We demonstrate in the numerical benchmarking that these differences lead to distinct behaviours and performances.

2.4. Linear Step

2.4.1. Framework of Linear Step

If the quadratic step fails to find an improvement, then the method performs the linear step. The idea of the linear step is to find evaluation candidate(s) in a desired direction $d \in \mathbb{R}^n$ at some step length(s) $\alpha^j \in \mathbb{R}^n$. The search candidates can be obtained as

$$x_l^j = x_0^k + \alpha^j d, \tag{21}$$

and we denote the set of all candidates as $\mathbb{L}^k$. The idea of the linear step is to perform a quick search in the direction that is likely to be a descent direction. The pseudocode of the linear step in the DQL method is shown in Algorithm 4. Note that in order to perform Line 2 of Algorithm 4, there are two components we need to determine: the desired direction and the step length(s). We discuss this in the next section.

Algorithm 4 LINEAR_STEP (x_0^k, δ^k)

1: Determine the search direction $d \in \mathbb{R}^n$
2: Determine the step lengths $\{\alpha^j \in \mathbb{R}\}$
3: The linear search candidates $\mathbb{L}^k = \{x_0^k + \alpha^j d^j\}$
4: IMPROVEMENT_CHECK($\mathbb{L}^k$, x_0^k, δ^k)
5: Update LINEAR_FLAG;

The linear step is an efficient and quick method to quickly search for an improvement. Not only does it not require as many function calls as the direct step, but it also does not require as much computational power to determine the candidate as the quadratic step. However, it is not as robust as the direct step or as precise as the quadratic step. If a linear step fails, then it indicates that we are either converging to a solution, or the method to determine the desired direction is not performing well for the current problem. In either case, the result from the linear step can provide some crucial information for future iterations, which is discussed in Section 4.

Linear Step Strategies

We propose two methods to find the linear search directions. The first method is to use the centred-simplex gradient from the direct step. In particular, $d = -\nabla_c f(x_0^k; \delta^k D^k)$ is the approximated steepest descent direction.

The second method is to use the last descent direction as the desired direction. If the method was able to find an improvement in this direction, then it is likely that an improvement can be found again in this direction. This direction can be calculated as $d = x_0^k - x_0^s$, where the index s is the most recent successful iteration before x_0^k.

To determine the step length, the simplest way is to use δ_k as the search step length, that is $\mathbb{L}^k = \{x_0^k + \delta^k d\}$. The other method is to consider (approximately) solving the following problem

$$\min_{\alpha}\{F(\alpha) : \alpha \geq 0\}, \tag{22}$$

where $F(\alpha) = f(x_0^k + \alpha d)$. To solve this problem, we utilize the safeguarded bracketing line search method [21]. Combining the two ways of determining the search directions and the two ways of determining the search step, we obtain four linear search strategies, as shown in Table 1.

Table 1. Linear Search Strategies

Label	Search Direction d	Search Step α
Strategy 1	$-\nabla_c f(x_0^k; \delta^k D^k)$	$\{\delta^k\}$
Strategy 2	$-\nabla_c f(x_0^k; \delta^k D^k)$	$\{0, 1/2\delta^k, \delta^k\} \cup A_{\text{BRACKET\_SEARCH}}$
Strategy 3	$x_{\text{best}}^k - x_{\text{best}}^s$	$\{\delta^k\}$
Strategy 4	$x_{\text{best}}^k - x_{\text{best}}^s$	$\{-\delta^k, 0, \delta^k\} \cup A_{\text{BRACKET\_SEARCH}}$

2.5. Update Step

Depending on the search results from the direct, quadratic and linear steps, the method updates the search step length for the next iterate δ^{k+1} in different ways. If an improvement is found in the direct step, then the search step length is increased for the next iteration. If an improvement is not found in the direct step, then the method proceeds with the quadratic step. If an improvement is found in the quadratic step, then the search step length remains the same. If no improvement is found in either quadratic or direct steps, then the method initiates the linear step. If an improvement is still not found, then the search step length is decreased. Otherwise, if an improvement is found in the linear step, then the search step length remains the same. Algorithm 5 shows the pseudocode for the update step of the DQL method. Notice that an update parameter γ needs to be selected to perform the DQL method.

2.6. Pseudocode for DQL Method

The input of the DQL method requires the objective function f, the initial point x_0, the initial search step length δ^0, and the update parameter γ. In addition, a maximum iteration threshold for the exploration stage, MAX_SEARCH is required for the convergence of the method. The method implements a sufficient decrease rule for the search candidates and stops searching in the quadratic and direct step after the maximum iteration threshold MAX_SEARCH. The necessity of this threshold is discussed in the next section.

The stopping condition(s) need to be designed for specific applications. For example, the method can be stopped when it reaches a certain maximum number of iterations, maximum number of function calls, or maximum run-time. In addition, a threshold for the search step length and the norm of the approximate gradient can be set to stop the method. The pseudocode for the DQL method is shown in Algorithm 6.

Algorithm 5 PARAMETER_UPDATE (δ^k, $0 < \gamma < 1$, DIRECT_FLAG, QUADRATIC_FLAG, LINEAR_FLAG)

1: **if** DIRECT_FLAG == TRUE **then**
2:    set $\delta^{k+1} = \gamma^{-1} \delta^k$
3: **else**
4:    **if** QUADRATIC_FLAG == FALSE **AND**
5:    LINEAR_FLAG == FALSE **THEN**
6:      SET $\delta^{k+1} = \gamma \delta^k$
7:    **ELSE**
8:      SET $\delta^{k+1} = \delta^k$
9:    END IF
10: END IF
11: SET $k \leftarrow k + 1$

Algorithm 6 DQL(f, x_0, δ_0, $0 < \gamma < 1$, $\beta > 1$, MAX_SEARCH)

1: Initiate $k \leftarrow 1$, $\delta^1 \leftarrow \delta_0$, STOP_FLAG $\leftarrow$ FALSE
2: **while** STOP_FLAG == FALSE **do**
3:    Initiate DIRECT/QUADRATIC/LINEAR_FLAGS $\leftarrow$ FALSE;
4:    Initiate $x_0^k \leftarrow x_{best}^{k-1}$ ($x_0^1 \leftarrow x_0$)
5:    DIRECT_STEP(x_0^k, δ^k)
6:    **if** an improvement is found in the direct step **then**
7:      DIRECT_FLAG $\leftarrow$ TRUE
8:    **else**
9:      DIRECT_FLAG $\leftarrow$ FALSE
10:    end if
11:    **if** stopping conditions are met **then**
12:      STOP_FLAG $\leftarrow$ TRUE
13:      Program terminates
14:    end if
15:    **if** $k \leq$ MAX_SEARCH **then**
16:      **if** DIRECT_FLAG == FALSE **then**
17:         QUADRATIC_STEP(x_0^k, β, δ^k, $\{x_i\}$)
18:         **if** an improvement is found in the quadratic step **then**
19:            QUADRATIC_FLAG $\leftarrow$ TRUE
20:         **else**
21:            QUADRATIC_FLAG $\leftarrow$ FALSE
22:            LINEAR_STEP(x_0^k, δ^k)
23:            **if** an improvement is found in the direct step **then**
24:               LINEAR_FLAG $\leftarrow$ TRUE
25:            **else**
26:               LINEAR_FLAG $\leftarrow$ FALSE
27:            end if
28:         end if
29:      end if
30:    end if
31:    PARAMETER_UPDATE(δ^k, γ, DIRECT_FLAG, ...
32:    QUADRATIC_FLAG, LINEAR_FLAG)
33: **end while**

3. Analysis of the DQL Method

3.1. Convergence Analysis

In this section, we show that the DQL method converges to a critical point at the limit of the iteration and its direct step is crucial for the convergence. To analyze the convergence of the DQL method, we introduce another well-studied method, the directional direct search method ([9] p. 115).

3.1.1. Directional Direct Search Method

There are three steps in a directional direct search method. First, in the search step, it tries to find an improvement by evaluating at a finite number of points. If it fails, then in the poll step, it chooses a positive basis $\bar{D}^k$ from a set D and tries to find an improvement among $\mathbb{D}^k = \left\{x_0^k + \delta^k d : d \in \bar{D}^k\right\}$. Last, the algorithm updates the search step length depending on the result of the poll step. The pseudocode for the directional direct search method can be found in ([9] p. 120).

Notice that the linear and the quadratic step of the DQL method can be treated as the search step of the directional direct search method. In addition, the update step from the DQL method only decreases the search step length in an unsuccessful iteration, which is identical to the update step from the directional direct search method. The direct step from the DQL method can be seen as the poll step from the directional direct search method, with the set D being an infinite set that consists of all the rotations of the coordinate directions. As such, the DQL method fits under the framework of the directional direct search method.

3.1.2. Convergence of the Directional Direct Search Method

The convergence theorem of the directional direct search method is cited from ([9] p. 122). The convergence of the directional direct search method uses the following assumptions.

Assumption 1. *The level set $L(x_0) = \{x \in \mathbb{R}^n : f(x) \leq f(x_0)\}$ is compact.*

Assumption 2. *If there exists an $\alpha > 0$ such that $\alpha_k > \alpha$, for all k, then the algorithm visits only a finite number of points.*

Assumption 3. *Let $\xi_1, \xi_2 > 0$ be some fixed positive constants. The positive bases D_k used in the algorithm are chosen from the set*

$$D = \left\{\bar{D} \text{ positive basis} : cm(\bar{D}) > \xi_1, \|\bar{d}\| \leq \xi_2, \bar{d} \in \bar{D}\right\}. \tag{23}$$

Assumption 4. *The gradient ∇f is Lipschitz continuous in an open set containing $L(x_0)$ (with Lipschitz constant $v > 0$).*

Notice that Assumption 2 holds if the directional direct search method uses a finite set of positive bases. However, as we desired the ability to use an infinite set of positive basis, we implemented a sufficient decrease rule to ensure Assumption 2 held.

Theorem 1. *Suppose the directional direct search method only accepts new iterates if $f(x^{k+1}) < f(x^k) - (\delta^k)^2$ holds. Let Assumption 1 hold. If there exists an $\alpha > 0$ such that $\delta^k > \alpha$, for all k, then the DQL method visits only a finite number of points, i.e., Assumption 2 holds.*

Proof. See Theorem 7.11 of [9]. □

We have the following convergence theorem.

Theorem 2. *Let Assumptions 1–4 hold. Then,*

$$\liminf_{k\to+\infty}\|\nabla f(x_k)\| = 0, \qquad (24)$$

and the sequence of iterates $\{x_k\}$ has a limit point $x_\star$ for which

$$\nabla f(x_\star) = 0. \qquad (25)$$

Proof. See Theorem 7.3 of [9]. □

3.1.3. Convergence of the DQL Method

The DQL method's approach, as previously stated, is a two-stage procedure. When $k \leq$ MAX_SEARCH, all the direct, quadratic and linear steps are enabled, and the method focuses on the efficiency of finding a better solution. When $k >$ MAX_SEARCH, the method disables the quadratic and linear steps and switches the solution acceptance rule to the sufficient decrease rule. This switch allows us to prove the convergence of the method. In particular, if the objective function f is a function that satisfies Assumptions 1 and 4, then the method fits under Assumptions 2 and 3. Thus, Theorem 2 applies to the DQL method.

The following Theorem shows that Assumption 2 holds for the DQL method.

Theorem 3. *Let Assumption 1 hold. If there exists an $\alpha > 0$ such that $\delta^k > \alpha$, for all k, then the DQL method visits only a finite number of points.*

Proof. Since the number of points evaluated in an iteration is finite and the number of iterations in the exploration stage is finite, the evaluated points in the exploration stage of the DQL method is finite.

In the convergence stage, the DQL method accepts an improvement x if $f(x) < f(x^k) - (\delta^k)^2$. Therefore, Theorem 1 can be applied to the convergence stage of the DQL method. Therefore, the DQL method visits only a finite number of points. □

Let D^k be the rotation matrix produced by the DQL method at the iteration k. We denote the set of the columns of $\begin{bmatrix} D^k & -D^k \end{bmatrix}$ as $\bar{D}^k$. We have the following proposition.

Proposition 1. *Let $\bar{D}^k$ be the set of search directions generated by the DQL method at the iteration k and n be the dimension of the search space. Then,*
(a) $\|\bar{d}\| = 1$ for any $\bar{d} \in \bar{D}^k$,
(b) $cm(\bar{D}^k) = \frac{1}{\sqrt{n}}$.

Proof. This is easy to confirm. □

Proposition 1 indicates that in the DQL method, the cosine measure of the set of search directions and the norm of the search directions are constant, so we can find a lower bound ϵ_1 for the cosine measure of the set of search directions and an upper bound ϵ_2 for the norm of the search directions. Therefore, Assumption 3 holds for the DQL method.

We present the following convergence theorem for the DQL method.

Theorem 4. *Let $\{x_k\}$ be the sequence of iterations produced by the DQL method to a function $f : \mathbb{R}^n \to \mathbb{R}^n$ with a compact level set $L(x_0)$. In addition, let ∇f be Lipschitz continuous in an open set containing $L(x_0)$. Then, the DQL method results in*

$$\liminf_{k\to+\infty}\|\nabla f(x_k)\| = 0, \qquad (26)$$

and the sequence of iterates $\{x_k\}$ has a limit point $x_\star$ for which

$$\nabla f(x_\star) = 0. \tag{27}$$

Proof. Theorem 2 applies, since Assumptions 1–4 hold for the DQL method. □

3.2. Benchmark for Step Strategies

We have two strategies for the quadratic step and four strategies for the linear step. We denote a combination of strategies using three indexes as strategy ###. The first index is the index of the strategy used in the direct step. (We currently have only one option for the direct step, but we introduce more in the next Section. Hence, we use three indices to identify each strategy.) The second index is used to indicate the quadratic step, and the last index is used for the linear step. For example, strategy 111 means the combination of strategies of the direct step strategy 1, quadratic step strategy 1, and linear step strategy 1. Moreover, we can disable the quadratic or linear steps, and we denote the disabled step with 0. This gives us $1 \times 3 \times 5 = 15$ combinations in total. Notice that the direct step cannot be disabled because it is crucial to the convergence of the method. We would like to select the best strategy combination among them.

3.2.1. Stopping Conditions

In order to benchmark these strategy combinations, we need to define the stopping conditions. For our application, we hope to find an approximate solution that is close to an actual solution and stable enough for us to conclude that it is close to a critical point. We therefore stop when both the search step length and infinity norm of the centred simplex gradient are small enough. Three tolerance parameters ϵ_∇, $\epsilon_{\text{MAX\_STEP}}$, and $\epsilon_{\text{MIN\_STEP}}$ are used to define the stopping conditions.

The first parameter ϵ_∇ defines the tolerance for the infinity norm of the centred simplex gradient. If

$$\left\|\nabla_c f(x_{\text{best}}^k; \delta^k D^k)\right\|_\infty = \max_i\left\{\left\|\nabla_c f(x_{\text{best}}^k; \delta^k D^k)_i\right\|\right\} < \epsilon_\nabla, \tag{28}$$

then the current solution meets our stability requirement. However, if the current search step length is too large, then the gradient approximation is not accurate enough to stop. Thus, we use $\epsilon_{\text{MAX\_STEP}}$ to restrict the search step length. When

$$\delta^k < \epsilon_{\text{MAX\_STEP}}, \tag{29}$$

the search step length meets our accuracy requirement. When both stability and accuracy requirements (Equations (28) and (29)) are met, the method stops. The last parameter $\epsilon_{\text{MIN\_STEP}}$ is a safeguard parameter to stop the method whenever the search step length is so small that it could lead to floating-point errors. When

$$\delta_k < \epsilon_{\text{MIN\_STEP}}, \tag{30}$$

the method terminates immediately. In addition, the methods stop when the number of function calls reaches MAX_CALL. This safeguard prevents the method from exceeding the evaluation budget.

In our benchmark, the parameter settings are shown in Table 2. Since the accuracy of the centred simplex gradient is in $O((\delta^k)^2)$ [17], we take ϵ_∇ to be $\epsilon_{\text{MAX\_STEP}}^2$.

Table 2. Parameters for the Performance Benchmark

Parameter	Value
ϵ_∇	10^{-6}
$\epsilon_{\text{MAX\_STEP}}$	10^{-3}
$\epsilon_{\text{MIN\_STEP}}$	10^{-12}
MAX_SEARCH	10,000
δ_0	10
γ	0.3
β	3

3.2.2. Performance Benchmark

We used the 59 test functions from Section 2 of [22] and [23]. These problems were transformed to the sum of square problems to fit into our code environment. The dimensions of these problems range from 2 to 20. A large portion (26%) of the problems are in $\mathbb{R}^5$, which is identical to the first solid-tank design problem discussed in Section 5. We note that Problem 2.13 and 2.17 from [22] were omitted due to scaling problems.

The benchmarking and analysis followed the processes recommend in [24].

We first solved all the problems using the same accuracy and stability requirement by the FMINCON function from MATLAB. We used these solutions as a reference to the quality of our solutions. Then, we solved the problems by each strategy combination and recorded their number of function calls and the STOP_FLAG.

Since the direct step strategy uses a random rotation, we performed each method multiple times to obtain its average performance. We denoted the function calls used by strategy combination s for problem p at trial r as $t_{s,p,r}$ and the average performance of strategy combination s for problem p as $t_{s,p}$. If a method failed at some trial, we proceeded with the next trial until a successful trial or until the evaluation budget was exhausted. If the method found a solution, then we considered the function calls it used as the summation among all the previously failed trials plus this successful trial. Therefore, the average performance of strategy combination s for problem p was defined as

$$t_{s,p} = \frac{\sum_r t_{s,p,r}}{r_{\text{total}} - r_{\text{fail}}}, \tag{31}$$

where r_{total} is the number of total trials and r_{fail} is the number of failed trials.

If $t_{s,p}$ was larger than MAX_SEARCH, then we said that the strategy combination could not find the target solution within the evaluation budget and reset $t_{s,p} = \infty$.

We used the performance profile described in [25] to compare the performance among the strategy combinations. The performance profile first evaluated the performance ratio,

$$r_{s,p} = \frac{t_{s,p}}{\min\{t_{s,p} : s \in S\}}, \tag{32}$$

where S is the set of all strategy combinations. This ratio told us how the performance of strategy s at problem p compared to the best performance of the strategy at the problem. Then, we plotted the performance profile of strategy s as

$$\rho_s(\tau) = \frac{1}{|P|}|\{p \in P : r_{s,p} \leq \tau\}|, \tag{33}$$

where P is the set of all problems and $|\cdot|$ denotes the number of elements in a set. The performance profile told us the portion of the problems solved by strategy s when the performance ratio was not greater than a factor $\tau \in \mathbb{R}$. In all results, we validated the performance profile by also creating profiles with fewer strategies to check if the switching effect occurred [26]. The switching effect never occurred.

3.2.3. Discussion on the Experiment Results

The performance profile for all the DQL strategies is shown in Figure 2. From Figure 2, we can see that the performance profile formed three clusters. The best performing strategy combinations were strategies 123, 122, 121, 120, and 124. The underperforming strategy combinations were strategies 102, 103, 101, 100, and 104. In addition, this ranking held for any τ. We therefore drew the following conclusions.

- Quadratic step strategy 2 outperformed quadratic step strategy 1, which outperformed disabling the quadratic step. This showed that the quadratic step led to a performance improvement.
- Linear step strategy 4 was the worst strategy in every cluster. This strategy slowed down the performance. In addition, linear step strategies 1, 2, and 3 and disabling the linear step showed a mixed performance. Their performance differences were too small to find a clear winner.

These conclusions above gave us the insight to develop the SMART DQL method. In the SMART DQL method, we allow the method to choose the appropriate strategy dynamically and adaptively. First, since both quadratic step strategies were better than disabling the quadratic step, we decided to include both quadratic step strategies in the SMART DQL method. For the linear step strategies, we decided to remove linear step strategy 4 and we allowed the method to choose appropriate linear step strategies. In addition, we developed a better rotation strategy that selected the rotation direction using the results of previous iterations. The SMART DQL method is discussed in the next section.

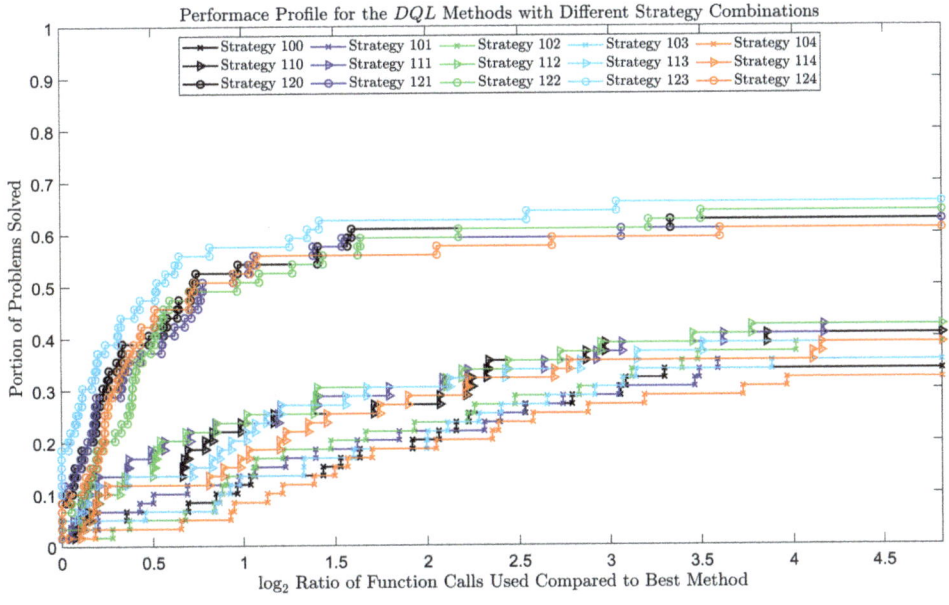

Figure 2. The performance profile for the DQL method with different strategy combinations.

4. SMART DQL METHOD

In this section we introduce the SMART DQL method. The SMART DQL method fits under the same framework as the DQL method. However, while the DQL method applies a static strategy, the SMART DQL method chooses the search strategies dynamically and adaptively.

4.1. Frameworks of Smart Steps

4.1.1. Smart Quadratic Step

In the smart quadratic step, we aim to combine both quadratic step strategy 1 and quadratic step strategy 2. We know that quadratic step strategy 2 performs best compared to other options, so the method should choose to perform quadratic step strategy 2 whenever the conditions are met. To perform quadratic step strategy 2, we require that both gradient and Hessian approximation at x_0^k are well-defined. This can be checked by examining whether $\nabla_s^2 f(x_0^k; S, \{\delta_h^j D_h^j\}) \in \mathbb{R}^{n \times n}$. If this does not hold, then the method should perform quadratic step strategy 1. To do so, we require that the $2n + 1$ evaluated points from the previous direct step are well-defined. This can be checked by examining whether $\nabla_c f(x_0^k; \delta^k D^k) \in \mathbb{R}^n$. The pseudocode for the smart quadratic step is shown in Algorithm 7.

Algorithm 7 SMART_QUADRATIC_STEP($\nabla_c f(x_0^k; \delta^k D^k)$, $\nabla_s^2 f(x_0^k; S, \{\delta_h^j D_h^j\})$)

1: **if** $\nabla_s^2 f(x_0^k; S, \{\delta_h^j D_h^j\}) \in \mathbb{R}^{n \times n}$ **then**
2:     Find $\mathbb{Q}^k$ using quadratic step strategy 2
3: **else**
4:     **if** $\nabla_c f(x_0^k; \delta^k D^k) \in \mathbb{R}^n$ **then**
5:        Find $\mathbb{Q}^k$ using quadratic step strategy 1
6:     **else**
7:        $\mathbb{Q}^k \leftarrow \phi$
8:     **end if**
9: **end if**
10: Return $\mathbb{Q}^k$

4.1.2. Smart Linear Step

In the smart linear step, the method should choose among the linear step strategies. Linear step strategy 4 ranked worse than disabling the linear step. Therefore, we removed linear step strategy 4 from our strategy pool. Our goal was to design an algorithm that chose among linear step strategies 1, 2, and 3 to give the method a higher chance to find an improvement at the current iterate.

We propose that when the last descent distance $\left\| x_0^k - x_0^s \right\|$ is larger than the current search step length, it is likely that the solution is even further, so the method should initiate an exploration move. Since linear step strategy 3 had better exploration ability, this strategy should be initiated under this condition. Notice that linear step strategy 2 had better exploitation ability, however, it was more computationally expensive than linear step strategy 1. Thus, linear step strategy 2 should perform better when x_0^k is close to an approximate solution and linear step strategy 1 should perform better when x_0^k is still far away from an approximate solution. The comparison between $\epsilon_{\text{MAX\_STEP}}$ and the search step length is a good indicator for this situation. When the search step length was smaller than $\epsilon_{\text{MAX\_STEP}}$, we found that x_0^k was close to an approximate solution, so spending more effort on local exploitation, i.e., using linear step strategy 2, might give the better result. In the case when the search step length is larger than $\epsilon_{\text{MAX\_STEP}}$, the method should spend less computational power on local exploitation. In some case, such as the first iteration, the conditions for any of above the linear step strategies do not hold. In this case, the linear step is disabled. The pseudocode for the smart linear step is shown in Algorithm 8.

Algorithm 8 SMART_LINEAR_STEP(x_0^k, x_0^s, $\nabla_c f(x_0^k; \delta^k D^k)$)

1: **if** $k \geq 2$ **and** $\left\| x_0^k - x_0^s \right\| \geq \delta^k$ **then**
2:     Find $\mathbb{L}^k$ using linear step strategy 3
3: **else**
4:     **if** $\nabla_c f(x_0^k; \delta^k D^k) \in \mathbb{R}^n$ **then**
5:         **if** $\delta^k \leq \epsilon_{\text{MAX\_STEP}}$ **then**
6:             Find $\mathbb{L}^k$ using linear step strategy 2
7:         **else**
8:             Find $\mathbb{L}^k$ using linear step strategy 1
9:         **end if**
10:     **else**
11:         $\mathbb{L}^k \leftarrow \phi$
12:     **end if**
13: **end if**
14: Return $\mathbb{L}^k$

4.1.3. Smart Direct Step

In the smart direct step, we aimed to design a rotation strategy that outperformed random rotation. Particularly, this smart direct step should be a deterministic strategy such that the method returns the same result for the same problem setup. To design such an algorithm, we first studied the results from a successful or failed direct, quadratic, or linear step.

A successful direct step skips both quadratic and linear step and proceeds with the direct step in the next iteration. In this case, the same search directions should be used because these directions have proven to be successful.

If the direct step fails, then the method proceeds with the quadratic step. For both quadratic step strategies, the method builds a quadratic model. If the quadratic step succeeds, then it is likely that this quadratic model is accurate. Therefore, the method uses the gradient of this model as desired rotation direction for the direct step.

If the gradient of the quadratic model was 0, then the quadratic step would fail. If the quadratic step fails, then the method proceeds with the linear step. For any linear step strategy, if the linear step succeeds, then the direction used in the linear step is likely to be a good descent direction. Therefore, the direct step uses the same direction as the previous linear step as the desired direction. Otherwise, if the linear step fails, then we know that the linear step direction at x_0^k is a nondecreasing direction. Therefore, at iteration $k+1$, the linear step direction at x_0^{k+1} is set as an undesired direction.

Algorithm 9 provides the pseudocode of the process to determine r^k in the direct step. Note that since the linear step decision process requires information from the previous iteration, at the first iteration, the method uses the coordinate direction as the desired direction.

4.2. Benchmark for SMART DQL Method

4.2.1. Experiment Result

We marked the smart strategy as strategy S, so the strategy SSS of the DQL method is the SMART DQL method. We performed the numerical experiment with the same setup as the benchmark for the step strategies from the previous section. Then, we constructed the performance profile as shown in Figure 3.

4.2.2. Discussion

As we can see from Figure 3, the SMART DQL method preformed best at any given τ. The SMART DQL method solved more than 45% of the problems as the fastest method. In addition, it solved more than 75% of the problems, which was more than any DQL method. Therefore, we attained a considerable improvement over the original DQL method. In the next section, we apply the SMART DQL method in a real-world application.

Algorithm 9 DETERMINE_ROTATION_DIRECTION(D^{k-1}, $m^{k-1}(x)$, d^{k-1})

1: **if** $k = 1$ **then**
2:     $r^k = e_1$ is a desired direction
3: **else**
4:     **if** the direct step at iteration $k - 1$ succeeds **then**
5:         $r^k = r^{k-1}$
6:     **else**
7:         **if** the quadratic step at iteration $k - 1$ succeeds **then**
8:             **if** $\nabla m^{k-1}(x_0^k) = 0$ **then**
9:                 $r^k = e_1$ is a desired direction
10:             **else**
11:                 $r^k = \nabla m^{k-1}(x_0^k)$ is a desired direction
12:             **end if**
13:         **else**
14:             **if** the linear step at iteration $k - 1$ succeeds **then**
15:                 $r^k = d^{k-1}$ is a desired direction
16:             **else**
17:                 $r^k = d^{k-1}$ is an undesired direction
18:             **end if**
19:         **end if**
20:     **end if**
21: **end if**
22: Return r^k

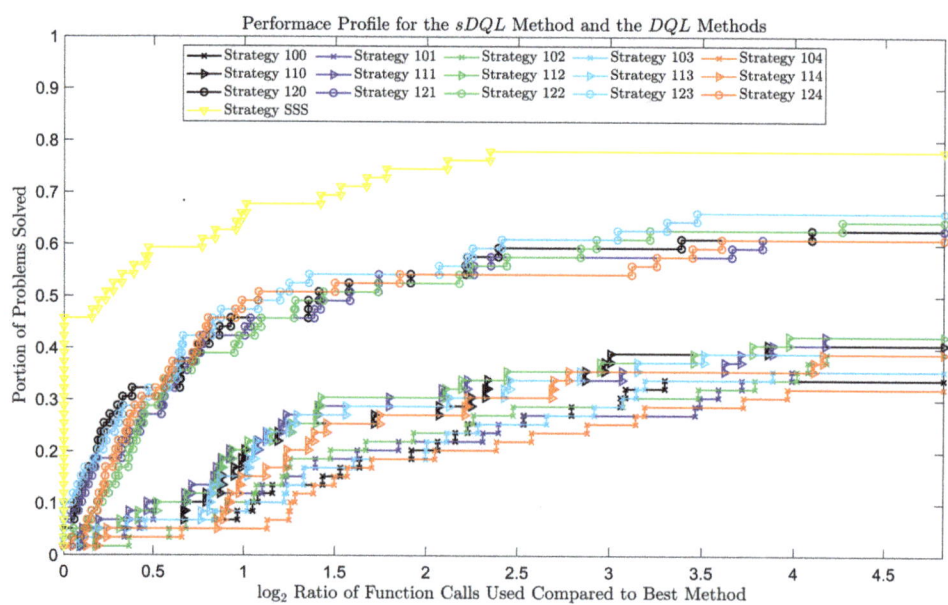

Figure 3. The performance profile for the SMART DQL method and all the DQL methods.

5. Solid-Tank Design Problem

5.1. Background

The solid-tank design problem [16] aims to create a design for a solid-tank fan-beam optical CT scanner with minimal matching fluid, while maximizing light collection, minimizing image artifacts, and achieving a uniform beam profile, thereby maximizing the usable dynamic range of the system. For a given geometry, a ray-path simulator designed by the UBCO gel dosimetry group is available in MATLAB and outputs tank design quality scores. The simulator is computationally expensive, so the efficiency of the method is crucial for solving this problem.

In the original problem, there are five parameters that control the geometry design. As shown in Figure 4, these are block length x_{bl}, bore position x_{bc}, fan-laser position x_{lp}, lens block face's semi-major axis length x_{ma}, and the lens block face's eccentricity x_{be}.

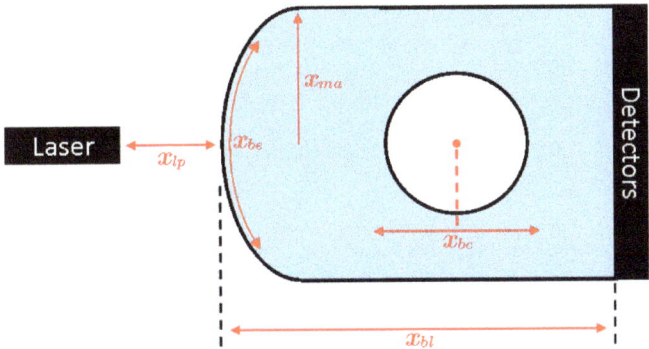

Figure 4. The geometry of the solid-tank fan-beam optical CT scanner.

These parameters give us an input $x \in \mathbb{R}^5$. The following bounds are the constraints for the problem.

$$x = \begin{bmatrix} x_{bl} & x_{bc} & x_{lp} & x_{ma} & x_{be} \end{bmatrix}^\top \in \mathbb{R}^5 \tag{34}$$

$$x_{bl} \leq 400 \tag{35}$$

$$x_{bl} \geq 2l + 2|x_{bc}| \tag{36}$$

$$x_{bc} \in [-30, 30] \tag{37}$$

$$x_{lp} \in [40, 100] \tag{38}$$

$$x_{ma} \in [40, 80] \tag{39}$$

$$x_{be} \in [0, 1], \tag{40}$$

where $l = 52$ mm (bore radius) + 5 mm (safeguard distance). The parameters x_{bl}, x_{bc}, x_{lp}, and x_{ma} are in mm and x_{be} is dimensionless.

An advanced version of the simulation software tool is currently being developed. This version introduces three new variables (x_{be2}, x_{ecc2} and x_{d3}), resulting in an eight-variable problem with the following constraints.

$$x = \begin{bmatrix} x_{bl} & x_{bc} & x_{lp} & x_{ma} & x_{be} & x_{be2} & x_{ecc2} & x_{d3} \end{bmatrix}^\top \in \mathbb{R}^8 \tag{41}$$

$$x_{bl} \in [2l + 2|x_{bc}|, 400] \tag{42}$$

$$x_{bc} \in [-40, 40] \tag{43}$$

$$x_{lp} \in [40, 100] \tag{44}$$

$$x_{ma} \in [40, 160] \tag{45}$$

$$x_{be} \in [0, 1] \tag{46}$$

$$x_{be2} \in [70, 120] \tag{47}$$

$$x_{ecc2} \in [0, 2.5] \tag{48}$$

$$x_{d3} \in [0, 400 - x_{bl}], \tag{49}$$

where $l = 52$ mm (bore radius) + 5 mm (safeguard distance). The parameters $x_{bl}, x_{bc}, x_{lp}, x_{ma}, x_{be2}$, and x_{d3} are in mm and x_{be} and x_{ecc2} are dimensionless.

At this time, the five-variable model is ready for public use. The eight-variable model is still undergoing detailed physics validation, but will be released along with the solid-tank simulation software tool. (See Data and Software Availability Statement for release details.)

In this section, we optimize the solid-tank design problems using the DQL and SMART DQL methods.

5.2. Transforming the Optimization Problem

We defined $f_{simu} : \mathbb{R}^n \to \mathbb{R}$ as the simulating scores at a given geometry, where $n = 5$ for the original problem and $n = 8$ for the redesigned problem. The output was normalized to give a final value between zero and one. Since the DQL and SMART DQL methods were designed for minimizing unconstrained problems, we transformed the problems as follows,

$$-\min\{-f_{simu}(\text{Proj}_C(x)) : x \in \mathbb{R}^n\} \tag{50}$$

where $\text{Proj}_C(x)$ is the projection of the input x onto the constraints C. For ease of interpretation, we shall report the optimized results as a value between zero and one with the goal of maximizing this value.

5.3. Experiment Result and Discussion

The stopping parameters for the solid-tank design problems are shown in Table 3; all other parameters remained the same as in Table 2. The maximum accepted step length $\epsilon_{\text{MAX\_STEP}}$ was designed to be the target manufacturing accuracy of the design. The minimum accepted step length $\epsilon_{\text{MIN\_STEP}}$ was designed to be the manufacturing error of the design. ϵ_∇ ensured the accuracy of the stability of the solution to be within 10^{-3}.

Table 3. The Stopping Parameters for the Solid-Tank Design Problems

Parameter	Value
ϵ_∇	2×10^{-3}
$\epsilon_{\text{MAX\_STEP}}$	0.5
$\epsilon_{\text{MIN\_STEP}}$	0.001
MAX_SEARCH ($n = 5$)	5000
MAX_SEARCH ($n = 8$)	8000

For each experiment, the method was assigned a random initial point within the constraints. Then, if the method was able to find a solution with unused function calls, it was assigned with a new initial point and began a new search. This process was repeated until the evaluation budget was exhausted.

Each experiment was performed with three different profile settings: water, FlexyDos3D, and ClearView™. These represented three standard dosimeters used in gel dosimetry and each had unique optical parameters (index of refraction and linear attenuation coefficient). As such, we had six related but distinct case problems.

To compare the performance of the DQL and SMART DQL methods, we ran the experiment with both methods. For each individual case, both methods were assigned the same list of initial points and evaluation budget. The optimum scores found by different methods for distinct profiles are shown in Table 4. Recall that values were between zero and one with the goal of maximizing these values.

Among the six individual tests, the SMART DQL method found a solution with a higher score for five of them under the same evaluation budget and initial points. In two cases ($n = 8$ water and $n = 8$ ClearView™), the SMART DQL method found a significant improvement. For the only case where DQL returned a higher score ($n = 8$ FlexyDos3D), the improvement was only 0.003. This showed that the SMART DQL method was more reliable in this application than the DQL method. The experiment results agreed with our conclusion from the performance benchmark.

Table 4. Optimum Scores for Solid-Tank Design Problem

Dimension	Method	Water $r^1 = 1.3316$	FlexyDos3D $r = 1.4225$	ClearView™ $r = 1.3447$
$n = 5$	DQL	0.801	0.979	0.952
$n = 5$	SMART DQL	0.829	0.981	0.956
$n = 8$	DQL	0.767	0.977	0.686
$n = 8$	SMART DQL	0.857	0.974	0.831

[1] The index of refraction of the corresponding dosimeter.

We show the optima from the SMART DQL method in Tables 5 and 6 for the five- and eight-variable models, respectively.

Table 5. Optima for Solid-Tank Design Problem ($n = 5$).

Profile	x_{bl} (mm)	x_{bc} (mm)	x_{lp} (mm)	x_{ma} (mm)	x_{be}
Water	252.4	19.2	71.8	70.1	0
FlexyDos3D	282.0	5.8	51.8	67.0	0
ClearView™	225.1	21.2	63.1	69.0	0

Table 6. Optima for Solid-Tank Design Problem ($n = 8$).

Profile	x_{bl} (mm)	x_{bc} (mm)	x_{lp} (mm)	x_{ma} (mm)	x_{be}	x_{be2} (mm)	x_{ecc2}	x_{d3} (mm)
Water	122.6	−4.3	94.0	79.8	0.8	70.0	0	23.4
FlexyDos3D	114.0	0	100.0	68.3	0.1	70.0	0	0.5
ClearView™	114.0	0	100.0	93.3	1.0	70.8	0.3	46.1

We were not able to identify a uniform design that was competitive for all profiles. The optimal design of the solid tank varied for different models and among different profiles. We noticed that in the eight-variable design, the method tried to minimize the block length x_{bl} and maximize the laser position x_{lp} for both FlexyDos3D and ClearView™; this suggested that further improvement may be gained by extending the range for these parameters.

6. Conclusions

In this research, we presented a DFO framework that allowed for direct search methods and model-based methods to be united into a single algorithm.

The DQL framework showed advantages over other methods in the literature. First, unlike heuristic based methods, convergence was mathematically proven under reasonable assumptions. Second, unlike more rigid DFO methods, the DQL framework was flexible, allowing the combination of direct search, quadratic step, and linear step methods into a single algorithm. This balance of mathematical rigour and algorithmic flexibility created a framework with a high potential for future use.

The algorithm was further examined numerically. In particular, we benchmarked the developed DQL method's strategy combinations to determine the optimal combination. The benchmark implied that there was no obvious winner. This motivated the development of the SMART DQL method. We presented the pseudocode for the SMART DQL method and conducted an additional benchmark. The SMART DQL method outperformed all other DQL methods in the benchmark. Last, the SMART DQL method was used to solve the solid-tank design problem. The SMART DQL method was able to produce higher-quality solutions for this real-world application compared to the DQL method, which verified the high performance of the decision-making mechanism.

While the DQL and SMART DQL methods both balanced mathematical rigour and algorithmic flexibility, it is worth noting their drawbacks. The most notable one is that the implementations of DQL and SMART DQL are both at the prototype stage. In comparison to more mature implementations (such as that of SID-PSM [13]), DQL and SMART DQL are unlikely to compete at this time. Another drawback is the need to asymptotically focus on direct search to ensure convergence. Further study will work to advance the SMART DQL method both in the quality of its implementation and the requirements for convergence.

Author Contributions: Conceptualization, method, validation, and writing and editing: Z.H. and W.H.; first draft: Z.H.; revisions: W.H. and Z.H.; DQL and SMART DQL software: Z.H.; solid-tank software: A.O.; discussion and insight: Z.H., W.H., A.J., A.O., S.C., and M.H.; supervision and funding: W.H. and A.J. All authors have read and agreed to the published version of the manuscript.

Funding: This research was funded by NSERC, Discovery Grant #2018-03865, and the University of British Columbia.

Institutional Review Board Statement: Not applicable.

Informed Consent Statement: Not applicable.

Data Availability Statement: Publicly available datasets and software were analyzed in this study. These data can be found here: https://github.com/ViggleH/STD-DQL-Data (accessed on 5 Feburary 2023); DQL and SMART DQL software: https://github.com/ViggleH/DQL (accessed on 5 Feburary 2023); DQL and SMART DQL benchmarking scripts: https://github.com/ViggleH/Performance-Benchmark-for-the-DQL-and-Smart-DQL-method (accessed on 5 Feburary 2023); solid-tank simulation: https://github.com/ViggleH/Solid-Tank-Simulation (accessed on 5 Feburary 2023).

Conflicts of Interest: The authors declare no conflict of interest. The funders had no role in the design of the study; in the collection, analyses, or interpretation of data; in the writing of the manuscript; or in the decision to publish the results.

Abbreviations and Nomenclature

The following abbreviations and nomenclature are used in this manuscript:

DFO	Derivative-free optimization	
BBO	Black-box optimization	
MBTR	Model-based trust region	
MBD	Model-based descent	
$A^\dagger$	Moore–Penrose pseudoinverse	Definition 1
$\nabla_c f$	Generalized centred simplex gradient	Definition 2
$\nabla_s^2 f$	Generalized simplex Hessian	Definition 3
$cm(D)$	Cosine measure	Definition 4
δ^k	Search step length	Section 2
x_0^k	Initial search point	Section 2
x_{best}^k	Current best solution	Section 2
$\bar{D}^k$	Direct step search directions	Section 2.2
$\mathbb{Q}^k$	Quadratic step search candidates	Section 2.3
$\mathbb{L}^k$	Linear step search candidates	Section 2.4

References

1. Ali, E.; Abd Elazim, S.; Balobaid, A. Implementation of coyote optimization algorithm for solving unit commitment problem in power systems. *Energy* **2023**, *263*, 125697. [CrossRef]
2. Abd Elazim, S.; Ali, E. Optimal network restructure via improved whale optimization approach. *Int. J. Commun. Syst.* **2021**, *34*, e4617.
3. Ali, E.; Abd Elazim, S. Mine blast algorithm for environmental economic load dispatch with valve loading effect. *Neural Comput. Appl.* **2018**, *30*, 261–270. [CrossRef]
4. Alarie, S.; Audet, C.; Garnier, V.; Le Digabel, S.; Leclaire, L.A. Snow water equivalent estimation using blackbox optimization. *Pac. J. Optim.* **2013**, *9*, 1–21.
5. Gheribi, A.; Audet, C.; Le Digabel, S.; Bélisle, E.; Bale, C.; Pelton, A. Calculating optimal conditions for alloy and process design using thermodynamic and property databases, the FactSage software and the Mesh Adaptive Direct Search algorithm. *Calphad* **2012**, *36*, 135–143. [CrossRef]

6. Gheribi, A.; Pelton, A.; Bélisle, E.; Le Digabel, S.; Harvey, J.P. On the prediction of low-cost high entropy alloys using new thermodynamic multi-objective criteria. *Acta Mater.* **2018**, *161*, 73–82. [CrossRef]
7. Marwaha, G.; Kokkolaras, M. System-of-systems approach to air transportation design using nested optimization and direct search. *Struct. Multidiscip. Optim.* **2015**, *51*, 885–901. [CrossRef]
8. Chamseddine, I.M.; Frieboes, H.B.; Kokkolaras, M. Multi-objective optimization of tumor response to drug release from vasculature-bound nanoparticles. *Sci. Rep.* **2020**, *10*, 1–11. [CrossRef] [PubMed]
9. Conn, A.; Scheinberg, K.; Vicente, L. *Introduction to Derivative-Free Optimization*; SIAM: Philadelphia, PA, USA, 2009.
10. Audet, C.; Hare, W. *Derivative-Free and Blackbox Optimization*; Springer: Cham, Switzerland, 2017.
11. Audet, C. A survey on direct search methods for blackbox optimization and their applications. In *Mathematics without Boundaries*; Springer: Berlin/Heidelberg, Germany, 2014; pp. 31–56.
12. Hare, W.; Nutini, J.; Tesfamariam, S. A survey of non-gradient optimization methods in structural engineering. *Adv. Eng. Softw.* **2013**, *59*, 19–28. . [CrossRef]
13. Custodio, A.L.; Vicente, L.N. *SID-PSM: A Pattern Search Method Guided by Simplex Derivatives for Use in Derivative-Free Optimization*; Departamento de Matemática, Universidade de Coimbra: Coimbra, Portugal, 2008.
14. Custódio, A.L.; Rocha, H.; Vicente, L.N. Incorporating minimum Frobenius norm models in direct search. *Comput. Optim. Appl.* **2010**, *46*, 265–278. [CrossRef]
15. Manno, A.; Amaldi, E.; Casella, F.; Martelli, E. A local search method for costly black-box problems and its application to CSP plant start-up optimization refinement. *Optim. Eng.* **2020**, *21*, 1563–1598. [CrossRef]
16. Ogilvy, A.; Collins, S.; Tuokko, T.; Hilts, M.; Deardon, R.; Hare, W.; Jirasek, A. Optimization of solid tank design for fan-beam optical CT based 3D radiation dosimetry. *Phys. Med. Biol.* **2020**, *65*, 245012. [CrossRef] [PubMed]
17. Hare, W.; Jarry–Bolduc, G.; Planiden, C. Error bounds for overdetermined and underdetermined generalized centred simplex gradients. *arXiv* **2020**, arXiv:2006.00742.
18. Hare, W.; Jarry-Bolduc, G.; Planiden, C. A matrix algebra approach to approximate Hessians. *Preprint* 2022. Available online: https://www.researchgate.net/publication/365367734_A_matrix_algebra_approach_to_approximate_Hessians (accessed on 7 November 2021).
19. Masson, P. Rotations in Higher Dimensions. 2017. Available online: https://analyticphysics.com/Higher%20Dimensions/Rotations%20in%20Higher%20Dimensions.htm (accessed on 7 November 2021).
20. MathWorks. MATLAB Version 2020a. Available online: https://www.mathworks.com/products/matlab.html (accessed on 15 November 2021).
21. Mifflin, R.; Strodiot, J.J. A bracketing technique to ensure desirable convergence in univariate minimization. *Math. Program.* **1989**, *43*, 117–130. [CrossRef]
22. Lukšan, L.; Vlcek, J. Test problems for nonsmooth unconstrained and linearly constrained optimization. *Tech. Zpráva* **2000**, *798*, 5–23 .
23. Moré, J.; Garbow, B.; Hillstrom, K. Testing unconstrained optimization software. *ACM Trans. Math. Softw. (TOMS)* **1981**, *7*, 17–41. [CrossRef]
24. Beiranvand, V.; Hare, W.; Lucet, Y. Best practices for comparing optimization algorithms. *Optim. Eng.* **2017**, *18*, 815–848. [CrossRef]
25. Dolan, E.; Moré, J. Benchmarking optimization software with performance profiles. *Math. Program.* **2002**, *91*, 201–213. [CrossRef]
26. Gould, N.; Scott, J. A note on performance profiles for benchmarking software. *ACM Trans. Math. Softw. (TOMS)* **2016**, *43*, 1–5. [CrossRef]

Disclaimer/Publisher's Note: The statements, opinions and data contained in all publications are solely those of the individual author(s) and contributor(s) and not of MDPI and/or the editor(s). MDPI and/or the editor(s) disclaim responsibility for any injury to people or property resulting from any ideas, methods, instructions or products referred to in the content.

Article

Clinical Validation of a New Enhanced Stent Imaging Method

Chadi Ghafari [1], Khalil Houissa [2], Jo Dens [3], Claudiu Ungureanu [1,4], Peter Kayaert [5], Cyril Constant [6] and Stéphane Carlier [1,7,*]

[1] Department of Cardiology, University of Mons (UMONS), 7000 Mons, Belgium; chadi.ghafari@umons.ac.be (C.G.); claudiu-mih.ungureanu@jolimont.be (C.U.)
[2] Department of Cardiology, Military Hospital of Tunis, Tunis 1000, Tunisia; khalilhouissa@gmail.com
[3] Cardiology Department, Ziekenhuis Oost-Limburg, 3600 Genk, Belgium; jo.dens@zol.be
[4] Cardiology Department, Hopital Jolimont, 7100 La Louvière, Belgium
[5] Cardiology Department, Jessa Ziekenhuis, 3500 Hasselt, Belgium; peter.kayaert@jessazh.be
[6] Faculty of Medicine, Free University of Brussels (ULB), 1050 Bruxelles, Belgium; cyril.constant@ulb.ac.be
[7] Cardiology Department, CHU Ambroise Paré, 7000 Mons, Belgium
* Correspondence: stephane.carlier@umons.ac.be

Abstract: (1) Background: Stent underexpansion is the main cause of stent thrombosis and restenosis. Coronary angiography has limitations in the assessment of stent expansion. Enhanced stent imaging (ESI) methods allow a detailed visualization of stent deployment. We qualitatively compare image results from two ESI system vendors (StentBoost™ (SB) and CAAS StentEnhancer™ (SE)) and report quantitative results of deployed stents diameters by quantitative coronary angiography (QCA) and by SE. (2) Methods: The ESI systems from SB and SE were compared and graded by two blinded observers for different characteristics: 1 visualization of the proximal and distal edges of the stents; 2 visualization of the stent struts; 3 presence of underexpansion and 4 calcifications. Stent diameters were quantitatively measured using dedicated QCA and SE software and compared to chart diameters according to the pressure of implantation. (3) Results: A total of 249 ESI sequences were qualitatively compared. Inter-observer variability was noted for strut visibility and total scores. Inter-observer agreement was found for the assessment of proximal stent edge and stent underexpansion. The predicted chart diameters were 0.31 ± 0.30 mm larger than SE diameters ($p < 0.05$). Stent diameters by SE after post-dilatation were 0.47 ± 0.31 mm smaller than the post-dilation balloon diameter ($p < 0.05$). SE-derived diameters significantly differed from QCA; by Bland–Altman analysis the bias was -0.37 ± 0.42 mm ($p < 0.001$). (4) Conclusions: SE provides an enhanced visualization and allows precise quantitative assessment of stent expansion without the limitations of QCA when overlapping coronary side branches are present.

Keywords: stent; percutaneous coronary intervention; quantitative coronary angiography

1. Introduction

Coronary angiography is the primary diagnostic imaging modality for the evaluation and classification of coronary artery lesions as well as for guiding percutaneous coronary interventions (PCIs). Percutaneous interventions are the most performed coronary revascularization procedure, improving the quality of life of patients along with their clinical outcomes [1]. Despite major advances in coronary stent technology, acute and late PCI-related complications still occur [2–4]. Successful PCI results relate directly to proper stent placement and deployment. Stent underexpansion was shown to be a major predictor of stent restenosis and thrombosis by quantitative coronary angiography (QCA) [5]. Moreover, insufficient stent expansion and malapposition found by intracoronary imaging were shown as major predictors of stent thrombosis in several studies [6–10].

Although optimizing stent implantation under intravascular imaging guidance is widely supported by the current literature [11–17], its routine clinical use remains limited due to the added time and cost to the procedure along with the image interpretation difficulties. Despite conventional angiography often falling behind in the detection of stent underexpansion and presenting a suboptimal accuracy assessing stent position, it is still carried out during routine clinical practice especially with newer generation scaffolds that are implanted at a higher pressure followed by a post-dilatation step and rely on the radiopaque nature of the material used for visualization.

Thicker stent struts were associated with higher in-stent restenosis rates in the ISAR STEREO trials [18,19]. On the other hand, thinner strut scaffolds used in new generation stents have been advocated to significantly reduce the risk of myocardial infarction at the expense of being more radiolucent on fluoroscopy [3,20–23]. Moreover, the trend towards the use of lower X-ray power during angiographic procedures presents another challenge for stent visualization which is further altered due to motion during the angiography sequence secondary to X-ray scattering.

More recently, several enhanced stent imaging (ESI) methods have been developed. These angiography-based software improve stent visualization and provide quantitative as well as qualitative data post-stent deployment but remain dependent on the X-ray angiographic system of each vendor [24,25]. The StentBoost® system (SB) (Philips Healthcare, Andover, MA, USA) is a motion-corrected X-ray stent visualization software that allows better assessment of stent expansion without using contrast [25]. It was designed as an add-on to conventional X-ray angiographic system and was found to be superior to conventional angiography in detecting stent underexpansion. The algorithm relies on the motion-compensated noise reduction by using landmarks (balloon markers) on 45 registered frames acquired over 3–4 s [26]. These images are transferred automatically to a workstation and corrected by averaging the images from each cine frame in relation to the two balloon markers. The software enhances stent visibility, fading out anatomical structures and background noise [25]. SB was found to have good correlation with IVUS regarding stent diameter and was found to be superior to quantitative coronary angiography (QCA) [14,17,24,27–31].

Pie Medical Imaging (Maastricht, The Netherlands) introduced the CAAS StentEnhancer® (SE), a method similar to SB with the main advantage of being completely independent of the X-ray angiographic system of the vendor and hence, runs on a side station. SE uses a maximum of 40 frames from a Digital Imaging and Communications in Medicine (DICOM) file. Its algorithm automatically detects the markers of the stent balloon or of the balloon used for post-dilation in order to compute a single image in which the visibility of a deployed stent is improved. Following background subtraction, all frames are transformed into a common reference frame. The resulting images are combined into a single image after weighted averaging. A sharpening filter is then applied. This filter works by first extracting the high-frequency components from the image. These high-frequency components are then added, using a predefined amount, to the original image. High-frequency components are extracted by first creating a blurred version of the image through performing a convolution of a Gaussian filter at a predefined scale with the original image. Subtracting the blurred version from the original yields the high-frequency components. An optimally contrasted enhanced stent image is then generated to improve the visibility using a linear scaling within a predefined width around the peak pixel value which is established from a histogram analysis. Furthermore, the SE system allows for a manual contrast adjustment of the generated images as well as a quantitative assessment of the deployed stent through manual measurements of different diameters along the stent length.

Quantitative coronary angiography (QCA) is a tool to measure coronary arteries filled with contrast based on the use of a dedicated software allowing automated measurements (that can be manually corrected) of vessel diameter, percent stenosis, and minimal lumen of stent diameters [32]. After image acquisition, a digital quantification on a selected frame can be easily performed with or without magnification.

The aims of this study was to (1) qualitatively compare image results from the SE system to the currently available SB system and (2) report the comparisons between measured diameters of deployed stents by the SE system and the expected chart diameters upon deployment and after post-dilation as well as final QCA measurements.

2. Materials and Methods

2.1. Study Design

Between January 2016 and January 2018, patients in whom an ESI acquisition was performed after the implantation of a stent at the Centre Hospitalier Universitaire et Psychiatrique de Mons-Borinage (CHUPMB), Belgium, were retrospectively reviewed. The acquired ESI images were transferred to the SB and SE workstations (CAAS workstation software v.8.4) and reconstructed. The patients' baseline demographic and procedural characteristics were collected. The study was conducted according to the guidelines of the Declaration of Helsinki and approved by the Ethics Committee of CHUPMB and Erasme-ULB (Université Libre de Bruxelles) (protocol code P2017/462 on 16 October 2017) who waived the requirement for written consent. Two independent blinded and experienced interventional cardiologists compared and graded the stent images obtained by each technique. The images from the same sequence (SB and SE) were blindly compared side to side (on the left side, it was either a SB or SE image and on the right side the other one). The images were graded on a scale from 0 to 2 (0 = undetectable; 1 = seen unclearly; and 2 = clearly seen) for different characteristics: (1) visualization of the proximal edge of the stent; (2) visualization of the distal edge of the stent; (3) clear visualization of the struts of the stent; and (4) the presence of underexpansion and (5) calcifications. One month later, 50 sequences were randomly selected and re-analyzed a second time by one of the two observers for the intra-observer variation analysis.

A subset of images was processed using a custom-designed Matlab software (version R2017a, The MathWorks, Natick, MA, USA) that computed the signal-to-noise ratio (SNR) of SB and SE images defined as the ratio of the average signal value μ_{sig} to the standard deviation σ_{bg} of the background. As shown in Figure 1, a reference noise square of 100 by 100 pixels was manually placed in a region without interventional material (wire, previous stent, etc.) and without a bone structure such as a rib. Another rectangle was then traced around the stent, as close as possible to the struts. The same two regions were used in the SB and SE images for comparison. The standard deviation σ_{bg} of the background pixel values was calculated in the square region of interest (ROI) of noise whereas the average signal value μ_{sig} was calculated as the average of the values of the pixels in the ROI traced around the enhanced stent.

Furthermore, between January 2021 and July 2022, patients with mildly to moderately calcified de novo coronary lesions in 4 Belgian centers who were treated by stent implantation and ESI acquisition in 2 orthogonal views were prospectively included. This protocol with EudraCT code B7072020000065 was approved by the Ethics Committee Hospitalo-Facultaire Universitaire de Liège under reference 2020/87 on 13/11/2020, as well as by each local institution review board. The study was also conducted according to the guidelines of the Declaration of Helsinki and informed written consent were obtained. The patients' baseline demographic and procedural characteristics were collected. The ESI images were transferred to the SE and QCA workstations (CAAS software v.8.4) and reconstructed. Of note, one center used a Siemens X-ray system with the Clearstent ESI system, the others used a Philips system with StentBoost. SE and QCA could be measured on the DICOM files from these two manufacturers. The final QCA analysis was conducted and included maximal and minimal stent diameters as well as percent stenosis. A quantitative SE analysis of the 2 orthogonal views acquired including proximal and distal stent edge diameters as well as minimal stent diameter was conducted. Mean stent diameter as well as percent stenosis were calculated in both views and compared to the expected stent chart diameter according to the pressure of deployment of the stent and after post-dilatation when available as well as to the QCA measurements. A Bland–Altman analysis was performed to compare the SE and QCA diameters.

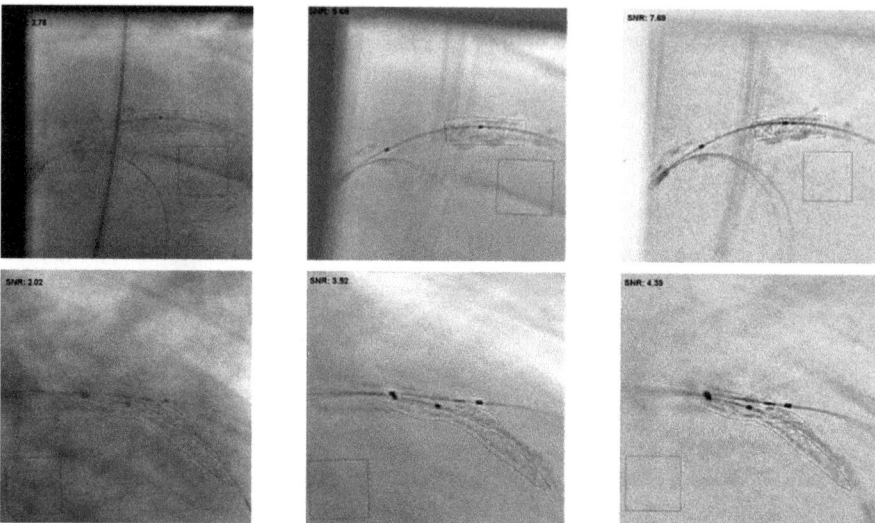

Figure 1. On the top, comparison between the original angiographic image (**left**), StentBoost (**middle**) and StentEnhancer (**right**) and the region where the noise was computed (red square) and the signal (blue region of interest around the stent). Bottom, original frame (**left**) and StentBoost (**middle**) and StentEnhancer (**right**) results where an underexpansion can be detected from the important calcifications outside of the stent. SNR in original image is 2.8, and, respectively, 5.7 and 7.7 for the SB and SE images (in area around stent).

2.2. Statistical Analysis

Categorical variables are reported as absolute values and percentages. Continuous variables are presented as means and standard deviations.

The Wilcoxon test was used to compare the two software and the two observers. After comparisons of the two methods, Kappa coefficients were calculated for repeatability and agreement between the reviewers.

The Kendall test was used to compare the two software for the presence of calcifications and stent underexpansion. Two McNemar tests were used for the evaluation of calcifications on underexpansion and post-dilatation efficacy. The SNRs of the SB and SE images were compared using a paired t-test. A p value < 0.05 was considered statistically significant. All statistical analyses was performed using SPSS software v.23 (IBM, New York, NY, USA).

3. Results

3.1. Patient and Lesion Characteristics

3.1.1. Qualitative Analysis

The qualitative analysis included 157 lesions with a total of 249 ESI sequences from 140 patients. The mean patient age was 64.7 ± 10.8 years, and 72.1% ($n = 101$) were men. Calcifications were reported on angiography in 72% ($n = 113$) of the cases. A total of 170 stents were placed, of which 140 (82.5%) were drug-eluting stents. Post-dilatation was performed in 68% of the cases; of these, 92% used a non-compliant balloon. The lesions were deemed highly calcified for 13 lesions (8%), moderately calcified for 40 (25%), slightly calcified for 60 (38%), and free of calcifications for 44 (28%). The baseline clinical, lesion, and stent characteristics of the study population are outlined in Table 1. Out of the 157 treated lesions, 26 (17%) were ST elevation myocardial infarctions (STEMI) and 46 (29%) non-ST elevation myocardial infarctions (NSTEMI). The indication to perform PCIs for the other patients was angina pectoris or arrhythmia, with ischemia proven non-invasively or after measurement of a fractional flow reserve. There were 18 total occlusions (11%). The lesions were localized in 34% of the cases in the right coronary artery (RCA), in 24% in the left circumflex artery (LCx), in 39% in the left anterior descending artery (LAD), and in 5% in the left main coronary artery.

Table 1. Qualitative cohort baseline clinical, lesion, and stent characteristics.

			N
Number of patients			140
Mean age (years)			64.7 ± 10.7
Male gender			101 (72.1%)
Mean body mass index (kg/m^2)			29.1 ± 5.9
Risk factors			
Hypertension			91 (65%)
Dyslipidemia			119 (85%)
Diabetes mellitus			54 (38.6%)
Current smoker			37 (26.4%)
Indication for PCI procedure			
Stable angina			45 (26.5%)
Unstable angina			
Non-ST elevation myocardial infarction			46 (27.1%)
ST elevation myocardial infarction			26 (15.3%)
Other			
Medical history			
Peripheral artery disease			38 (27.1%)
Treated coronary artery			
Number of lesions treated			157
Calcifications			113 (72%)
Left anterior descending artery			62 (39.5%)
Left circumflex artery			24 (15.3%)
Right coronary artery			53 (33.8%)
Left main coronary artery			8 (5.1%)
Other			10 (6.4%)
Stents			
Number of stents implanted			170
Coating	Scaffold	Struts Thickness (μm)	
Everolimus			
	PtCr	81	1 (0.6%)
	PtCr	74	67 (39.4%)
Sirolimus			
	CoCr	60	38 (22.4%)
	CoCr	80	29 (17.1%)
	316L	100	3 (1.8%)
	Mg	150	1 (0.6%)
Paclitaxel	PtCr	81	1 (0.6%)
TiNO	CoCr	75	5 (2.9%)
BMS			
	CoCr	80	25 (14.7%)

BMS = bare metal stent; **CoCr** = cobalt chromium; **PtCr** = platinum chromium; **TiNO** = titanium nitric oxide; **316L** = 316L stainless steel.

3.1.2. Quantitative Analysis

The quantitative analysis included 93 lesions treated in a total of 76 patients with a mean age of 69.2 ± 9.1 years, of which, 71.1% (n = 54) were men. The left anterior descending artery was treated in 63.4% (n = 59) and calcifications burden was moderate in 46.1% (n = 35) of cases. The baseline clinical, lesion, and stent characteristics of the study population are outlined in Table 2. A total of 98 stents were implanted with a mean diameter of 3.16 ± 0.46 mm at a mean inflation pressure of 11 ± 2 atm for which a mean chart diameter of 3.25 ± 0.47 mm was expected. Post-dilation was performed in 82.7% (n = 81) of cases using a non-compliant balloon in 85.5% (n = 71).

Table 2. Quantitative cohort baseline clinical, lesion, and stent characteristics.

	N
Number of patients	76
Mean age (years)	69.2 ± 9.1
Male gender	54 (71.1%)
Mean body mass index (kg/m^2)	28.1 ± 4.6
Risk factors	
Hypertension	56 (73.7%)
Dyslipidemia	57 (75.0%)
Diabetes mellitus	28 (36.8%)
Current smoker	12 (15.8%)
Family history of heart disease	24 (31.6%)
Peripheral vascular disease	8 (10.5%)
Previous myocardial infarction	14 (18.4%)
Previous PTCA	26 (34.2%)
Renal impairment	2 (2.6%)
Indication for PCI procedure	
Chronic coronary syndrome	28 (36.8%)
Unstable angina	6 (7.9%)
Non-ST elevation myocardial infarction	5 (6.6%)
Silent ischemia	37 (48.7%)
Treated coronary artery	
Number of lesions treated	93
Calcifications burden	
Mild	29 (38.2%)
Moderate	35 (46.1%)
Severe	12 (15.8%)
Lesion classification (AHA/ACC)	
A	6 (6.5%)
B1	62 (66.7%)
B2	22 (23.7%)
C	3 (3.3%)
Left anterior descending artery	59 (63.4%)
Left circumflex artery	8 (8.6%)
Right coronary artery	25 (26.9%)
Left main coronary artery	1 (1.1%)
Stents	
Number of stents implanted	98
Mean stent diameter (mm)	3.16 ± 0.46
Mean stent length (mm)	25 ± 9
Mean deployment pressure (atm)	11 ± 2
Expected chart diameter (mm)	3.25 ± 0.47
Post-dilation performed	81 (82.7%)
Non-compliant balloon	71 (85.5%)
Mean maximal post-dilatation balloon diameter (mm)	3.57 ± 0.54
Mean maximal balloon inflation pressure (atm)	18 ± 3

ACC/AHA = American College of Cardiology and the American Heart Association.

3.2. ESI Image Quality Evaluation

Table 3 shows the evaluation results of the two observers. The proximal and distal edge visualization grades did not differ between the two observers (1.42 ± 0.77 vs. 1.38 ± 0.62 and 1.46 ± 0.76 vs. 1.44 ± 0.61 for observer 1 and 2, respectively); however, a statistically significant difference ($p < 0.05$) was found between the mean total grade from observer 1 vs. observer 2 (4.12 ± 1.73 vs. 3.67 ± 1.49, respectively) for the evaluation of SB images

(Figure 1). A statistically significant difference ($p < 0.05$) was also found between the mean total grade from observer 1 vs. observer 2 (4.10 ± 1.86 vs. 3.76 ± 1.58, respectively) for the evaluation of SE images with no statistically significant difference noted for the proximal and distal edge visualization grades (1.46 ± 0.79 vs. 1.42 ± 0.64 and 1.43 ± 0.77 vs. 1.46 ± 0.59 for observer 1 and 2, respectively).

Table 3. Qualitative analysis of SB and SE.

	Observer 1		Observer 2		p-Value
	SE	SB	SE	SB	
Stent strut visibility	1.28 ± 0.73	1.35 ± 0.68	0.98 ± 0.69	0.96 ± 0.61	<0.001
Proximal stent edge visibility	1.46 ± 0.79	1.42 ± 0.77	1.42 ± 0.64	1.38 ± 0.62	NS
Distal stent edge visibility	1.43 ± 0.77	1.46 ± 0.76	1.46 ± 0.59	1.44 ± 0.61	NS
Total score	4.10 ± 1.86	4.12 ± 1.73	3.76 ± 1.58	3.67 ± 1.49	<0.001
Inter-observer Kappa coefficients (n = 249)					
	SE		SB		
Stent strut visibility	0.456		0.344		
Proximal edge visibility	0.434		0.498		
Distal edge visibility	0.416		0.386		
Stent underexpansion	0.394		0.480		
Calcifications	0.352		0.447		
Intra-observer Kappa coefficients (n = 50)					
Stent strut visibility	0.760		0.557		
Proximal edge visibility	0.629		0.710		
Distal edge visibility	0.647		0.783		
Stent underexpansion	0.584		0.473		
Calcifications	0.674		0.477		

NS = non-significant; **SB** = StentBoost; **SE** = StentEnhancer. Mean values of parameters graded out of 2 points and total score graded out of 6 points.

A Wilcoxon test demonstrated a statistically significant difference between the two observers ($p < 0.001$) indicating that they assessed the visualization of struts differently. This demonstrates the variability in such a qualitative assessment of any angiographic parameter.

The Kappa coefficients were calculated between the two observers (inter-observer Kappa) and between two different evaluations by the same observer (intra-observer Kappa). The evaluation system was simplified to a binary one. Inter-observer agreement between the two reviewers was observed (coefficient < 50% for the proximal stent edge with SB). The stent underexpansion and calcification coefficients showed similar results (coefficient < 48%). The intra-observer Kappa coefficients showed low reproducibility with perhaps a better reproducibility for the SB.

There was no significant difference between the two methods, SB or SE, according to the Wilcoxon test for each observer (Table 4). A final Kendall test demonstrated a significant difference between the two observers for the assessment of underexpansion and calcifications (Figure 2). While the first reviewer found a correlation of ±60%, the second one found ±90% (Table 5). This called for a more quantitative assessment of underexpansion which we validated prospectively in the second part of this research project.

Table 4. Different mean values of parameters by observer.

		SE	SB	*p*-Value
Observer 1	Stent strut visibility	1.28 ± 0.73	1.35 ± 0.68	NS
	Proximal edge visibility	1.46 ± 0.79	1.42 ± 0.77	NS
	Distal edge visibility	1.43 ± 0.77	1.35 ± 0.68	NS
	Total score	4.10 ± 01.86	4.12 ± 1.73	NS
Observer 2	Stent strut visibility	0.98 ± 0.69	0.96 ± 0.61	NS
	Proximal edge visibility	1.42 ± 0.64	1.38 ± 0.62	NS
	Distal edge visibility	1.46 ± 0.59	1.44 ± 0.61	NS
	Total score	3.76 ± 1.58	3.67 ± 1.49	NS

NS = non-significant; **SB** = StentBoost; **SE** = StentEnhancer. Mean values of parameters graded out of 2 points and total score graded out of 6 points.

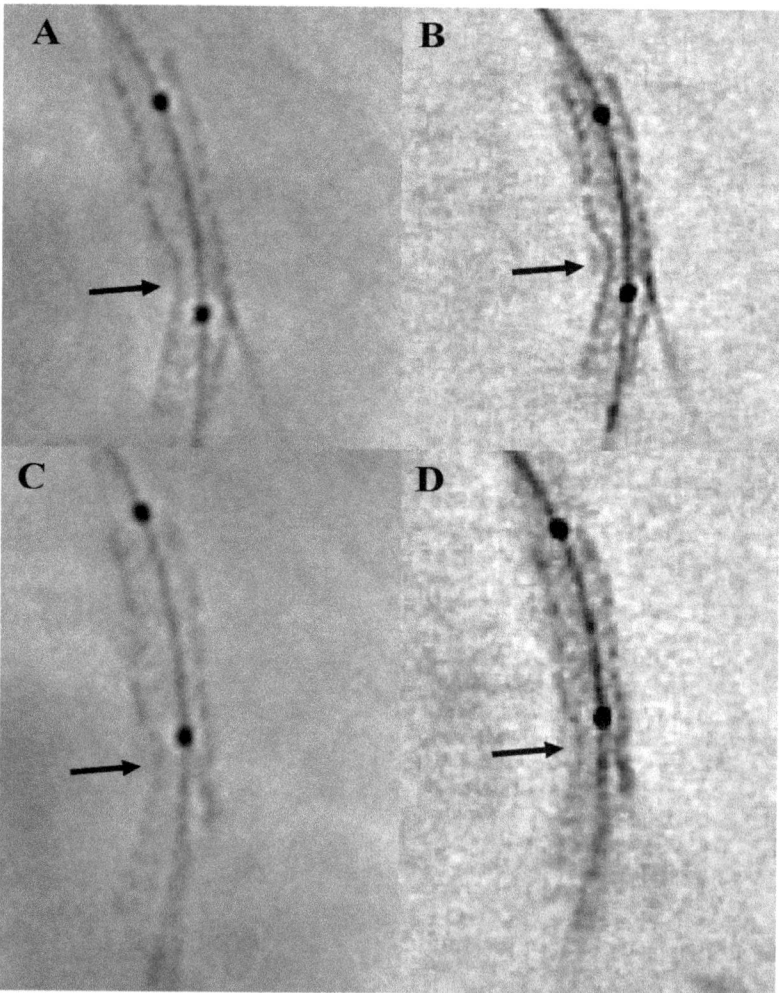

Figure 2. Underexpansion images before and after post-dilation (arrows). (**A**) StentBoost image before post-dilation; (**B**) StentEnhancer image before post-dilation; (**C**) StentBoost image after post-dilation; (**D**) StentEnhancer image after post-dilation.

Table 5. Comparison of rates of calcifications and underexpansion by SE and SB.

		SE	SB	Kendall Coefficient
Observer 1	Stent underexpansion (%)	71.5	73.9	61
	Calcifications (%)	64.0	43.8	58
Observer 2	Stent underexpansion (%)	47.0	47.0	92
	Calcifications (%)	63.9	62.7	91

3.3. Signal-to-Noise Ratio

The calculated SNR on a random part of the image and around the stent struts for a selection of 53 original frames was higher for SB and SE compared to the original frames (3.2 ± 1.0; 4.3 ± 1.5 and 2.2 ± 0.3, respectively). The SNR was statistically significantly higher for SE compared to SB ($p < 0.01$), as shown in Figure 3.

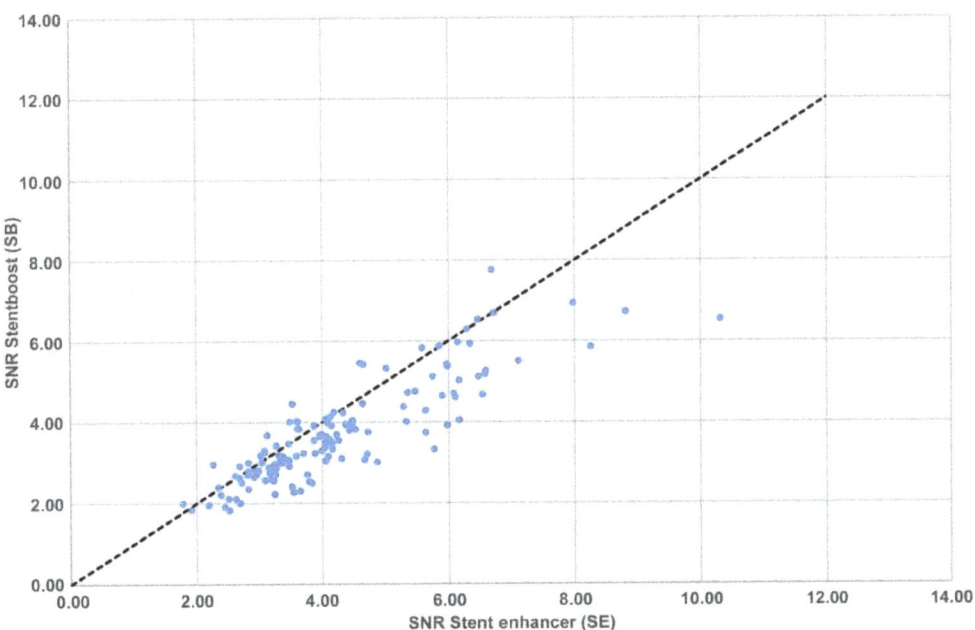

Figure 3. Linear regression between SNRs of StentBoost and StentEnhancer on 53 different frames.

3.4. Quantitative Analysis

Out of 93 lesions, reliable QCA analysis could be performed on the final PCI result in 90 lesions. Foreshortening or the overlap of branches precluded the analysis in five lesions. The mean stent diameter on QCA after stent implantation was 2.74 ± 0.53 mm and differed significantly from the predicted chart diameter ($p < 0.05$). On average, the predicted chart diameter upon stent implantation was 0.44 ± 0.44 mm larger than the mean stent diameter on QCA (95% CI; 0.34 to 0.53). This was also found upon comparison of mean stent diameter by QCA and maximal achieved post-dilation balloon diameter ($p < 0.001$). The stents diameters found by QCA tended to be 0.74 ± 0.48 mm smaller than the maximal achieved balloon diameter upon post-dilation (95% CI; 0.62 to 0.84). The remaining stents could not be quantified due to vessel overlapping.

A quantitative SE analysis could be performed in more stents (n = 91) using both orthogonal views after deployment of the stent and following post-dilation (Figure 4). The mean stent diameter post-implantation was 2.96 ± 0.45 mm (90% of predicted chart diameter) which was statistically different from the expected chart diameter ($p < 0.001$). The expected chart diameter was on average 0.31 ± 0.30 mm larger than the SE diameter (95% CI; 0.25 to 0.38). There was no statistically significant difference between the measured mean stent diameters and the measured diameters at the maximal stent underexpansion point between the two orthogonal views upon implantation (2.95 ± 0.46 mm vs. 2.95 ± 0.49 mm and 2.39 ± 0.46 mm vs. 2.44 ± 0.47 mm, respectively; $p > 0.05$). The mean stent diameter after post-dilatation by SE was 3.13 ± 0.49 mm (84% of predicted balloon diameter) and was, on average, 0.47 ± 0.31 mm smaller than the balloon diameter (95% CI; 0.39 to 0.56). The mean maximal stent underexpansion upon deployment was 19 ± 9% and 16 ± 7% after post-dilation. There was no statistically significant difference in the measured mean stent diameters between the two orthogonal views after post-dilation (3.11 ± 0.48 mm vs. 3.18 ± 0.55 mm; $p > 0.05$); however, a statistically significant difference was noted for the measured diameter at the site of maximal stent underexpansion point between the two views after post-dilation (2.58 ± 0.52 mm vs. 2.69 ± 0.52; $p = 0.004$). The achieved mean diameter by SE after post-dilation was more in line with the expected chart diameter upon implantation with a mean difference of 0.13 ± 0.32 mm (95% CI; 0.04 to 0.21). A statistically significant diameter gain of 0.23 ± 0.23 mm was noted at the site of maximal stent underexpansion after balloon post-dilation was noted upon comparison of mean minimal stent diameters upon implantation and after post-dilation (2.41 ± 0.44 mm vs. 2.63 ± 0.49 mm, respectively; $p < 0.001$). The detailed quantitative analysis results can be found in Table 6. The mean stent diameters after stent deployment by SE were, on average, 0.41 ± 0.44 mm [95% CI; 0.06 to 0.23] larger than the mean stent diameters by QCA ($p < 0.05$) and were 0.32 ± 0.38 mm [95% CI; 0.05 to 0.22] larger after post-dilation ($p < 0.05$).

Table 6. QCA and SE measurements.

QCA Analysis	
Post-Stent Implantation	n = 14
Mean stent diameter (mm)	2.74 ± 0.53
Minimal in-stent diameter (mm)	2.26 ± 0.48
Percentage stenosis (%)	13.86 ± 9.54
Post-balloon post-dilation	n = 75
Mean stent diameter (mm)	2.84 ± 0.53
Minimal in-stent diameter (mm)	2.23 ± 0.46
Percentage stenosis (%)	14.7 ± 11.9
SE analysis	
Mean stent diameter at deployment (mm)	2.96 ± 0.47
Minimal in-stent diameter at deployment (mm)	2.41 ± 0.44
Deployment diameter to chart (%)	90 ± 9
Mean stent underexpansion at deployment (%)	19 ± 9
Mean stent diameter after post-dilation (mm)	3.13 ± 0.49
Minimal in-stent diameter after post-dilation (mm)	2.63 ± 0.49
Post-dilation diameter to balloon (%)	13 ± 2
Mean stent underexpansion after post-dilation (%)	16 ± 7

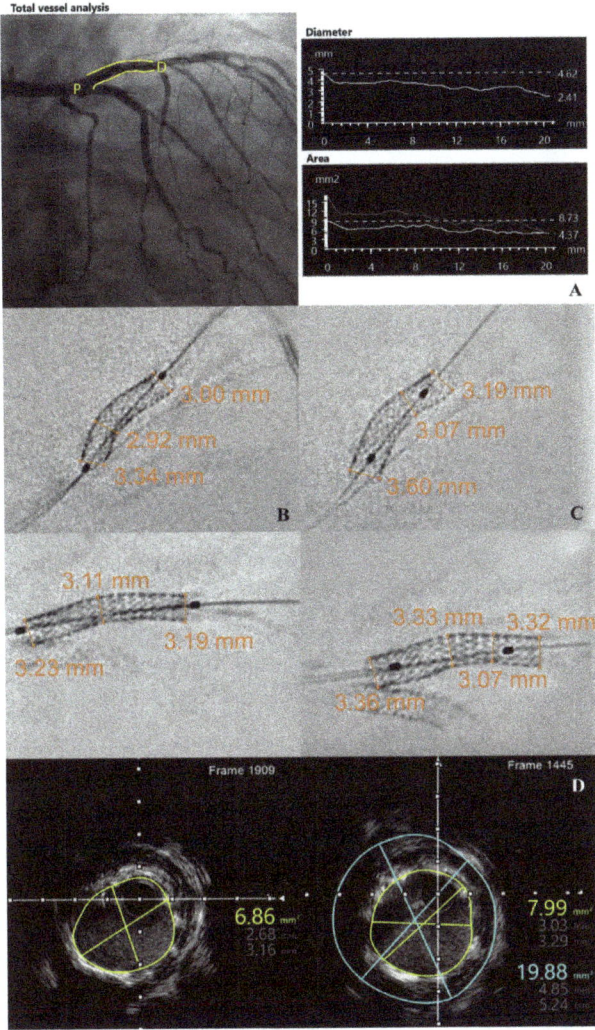

Figure 4. Quantitative analysis of an implanted proximal left anterior descending stent. Panel (**A**): quantitative coronary angiography analysis; Panel (**B**): StentEnhancer quantitative analysis post-implantation in two orthogonal views; Panel (**C**): StentEnhancer quantitative analysis after post-dilation. Stent expansion could be evaluated visually with clear stent struts and minimal calcifications. The pixels were transformed into millimeters using the calibration of the image. Note the presence of a second stent implanted in the ramus intermedius. Panel (**D**): Intravascular images at the minimal cross-sectional area in the stent after implantation (**left**) and after post-dilatation (**right**).

4. Discussion

The current study qualitatively compared the inter- and intra-observer results of different image criteria of a novel ESI software (SE) to the market-available one (SB) as well as a quantitative analysis of SE.

The results of the two ESI algorithms were compared as per each observer and finally SNRs for the two methods were calculated and compared to the SNR calculated from the angiographic image. ESI methods have been demonstrated to enhance contrast on fluoroscopic images, allowing better visualization of stent struts. This study demonstrated that SE is not inferior to SB for the criteria evaluated but a clear inter-observer variability calls for more quantitative methods. Despite this difference, both observers had a preference towards SE images to study parameters. SE can be easily integrated into procedures, independent of the X-ray angiography machine vendor, and was found in our study to provide good stent expansion assessment as well as a better stent strut visualization. The SNR of SE images was found to be superior compared to SB. We cannot provide a definite answer why this was the case, since we are unaware of the exact methods of StentBoost. However, based on the available papers, there are methodological differences. For instance, SB does not seem to perform background subtraction as can be seen in Figure 1.

Since newer generation scaffolds tend to use thinner struts or bioresobable materials in order to reduce the risk of stent thrombosis in addition to a trend towards the use of lower X-ray power during angiographic procedures, proper stent visualization is becoming challenging [3,20–23]. The use of ESI becomes pivotal for the assessment of proper stent expansion, a major risk factor for stent thrombosis [6–10].

QCA remains an important, readily available, and easy-to-use tool during PCIs allowing for a more practical and standardized angiography-based approach. QCA is particularly useful for the evaluation of the minimal lumen diameter, the reference vessel diameter, the diameter stenosis percentage, the lesion length, the acute gain, and late loss [14]. Our data failed to show any correlation between the expected stent diameter and the QCA-derived one. This could be explained by the foreshortening drawback of QCA as well as the two-dimensional evaluation by QCA of a three-dimensional vessel.

Our data demonstrated the feasibility of an accurate, quantitative, contrast-free assessment of stent expansion by SE. Post-dilatation remains an important step towards stent optimization. Our results are in-line with the current published literature in regard to the achieved stent diameter at a given implantation pressure being at least 10% lower than the given expected chart diameter [33,34]. These results could be attributed to the fact that the figures provided on the compliance charts are derived from bench tests performed in water at 37 °C while QCA and SE are measured on stents deployed in fibrotic and calcified lesions. The diameters measured by SE remain 2-dimensional measurements of a 3-dimensional structure. A second measurement using an orthogonal view would therefore overcome this limitation. The measured mean stent diameters by SE did not differ when using the two orthogonal views indicating precise measurements between the two views. However, a difference was noted for the measurements at the site of maximal stent underexpansion after post-dilation. This could be attributed to the eccentricity of lesions as well as to the visual assessment of the minimal diameter compared to adjacent ones.

Despite an era where modern flat-detector technology allows excellent angiographic images, coronary stent visualization has become a challenge especially with the on-going reduction in stent strut thickness. Stents are often suboptimally visualized on plain angiography hence limiting optimal PCI outcomes. High temporal resolution is needed to qualify a moving structure.

Adequate stent expansion has important short- and long-term effects after PCIs in clinical practice. It is crucial, yet challenging, to detect suboptimal stent deployment on qualitative and quantitative angiography since it is associated with an increased rate of in-stent restenosis and stent thrombosis [3,20]. Current stent delivery systems are still suboptimal for stent expansion, requiring, in most cases, a post-dilation using a larger, higher pressure, non-compliant balloon to improve the in-lumen area. This is particularly true when increased calcifications are found [24,35] as we demonstrated in our 157 lesions.

Intracoronary imaging, including intravascular ultrasound and optical coherence tomography, remains more sensitive than angiography and QCA in determining stent under expansion as illustrated in Figure 4; their use was found to improve stent expansion results and long term outcome [6,20,36]. However, these techniques are limited by cost, time, and technical expertise, calling for a simpler, ready-to-use visualization method. ESI was found very useful in identifying stents under expansion, thereby improving PCI outcomes [37]. Image processing algorithm softwares based on X-ray angiography images offer better stent visualization compared to angiography alone as validated by several previous studies [24,38]. ESI also shows no risk of complications and adds little additional time or radiation to the procedure [25,37]. Furthermore, ESI allows accurate measurements of the dimension of stents [29]. It was found useful in obese patients, long lesions, in-stent restenosis, and bifurcating lesions. Moreover, ESI was found to be superior to QCA and angiography and was highly correlated with IVUS [17,28,28,30,38].

We performed a comparison between the final diameters measured by QCA and by SE. We had 14 paired data available with no post-dilatation and 75 after final post-dilatation in the other patients. As shown in Figure 5, on average, the mean difference was -0.37 ± 0.42 mm and this bias for smaller QCA diameters was significant, with the 95% confidence interval not encompassing the 0. Using IVUS as the reference, Goto et al. also demonstrated that QCA underestimates MLDs in small vessels (<3.8 mm) and overestimates MLDs in vessels larger than 3.8 mm [39]. A direct head-to-head comparison of IVUS and SE might confirm a better agreement between IVUS and SE than with QCA. The wide agreement window between QCA and SE of ± 0.84 mm reflects the differences in the two methodologies, with only manual measurements being currently possible with the SE images, while automated contour calculation and minimal and reference diameters are available with QCA. However, when there were overlap of side branches or other vessels, no QCA could be reliably measured in 3 out of the 93 cases. Without contrast, hence without any overlap, SE could always be measured. Of note, no reliable reconstruction can be calculated on very long stents and/or with long balloons when the markers are more than 30 mm apart. Several ESI softwares are currently available on the market but each one can only be used on the specific vendor's angiographic system. The StentEnhancer software computes enhanced fluoroscopy images using the balloon markers as references, delivering an easily integrated, high-quality image independent of the angiography instrument vendor. Although an increase in radiation was reported during ESI acquisition, no significant impact on the patient radiation dose was found [40].

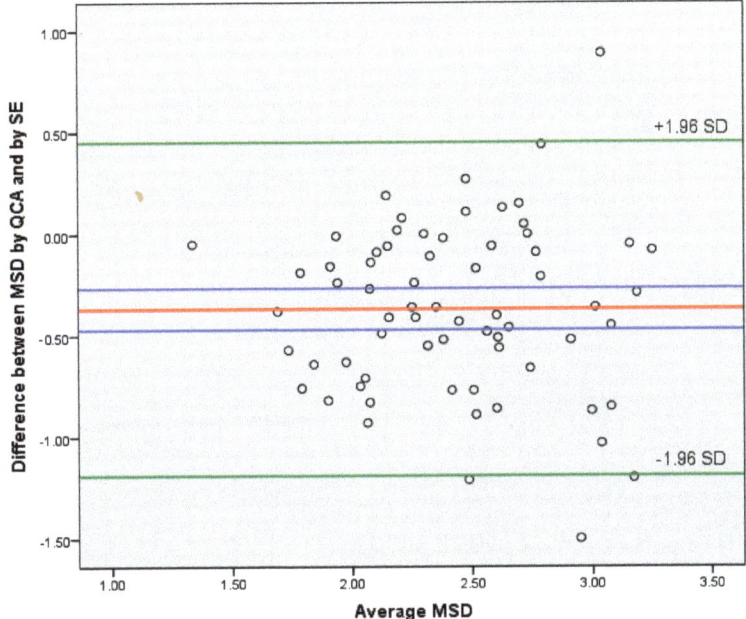

Figure 5. Bland-Altman analysis comparing QCA and SE. Red line: mean; green lines: $1.96 \times SD$; blue lines: 95%CI; circles: individual measurements. MSD: minimal stent diameter; SE: StentEnhancer; SD: standard deviation; QCA: quantitative coronary angiography.

5. Conclusions

StentEnhancer is a novel ESI modality that provides enhanced stent visualization and allows quantitative assessment of stent underexpansion. It is a simple, cost-effective, and minimally invasive method. We demonstrate that it is not inferior qualitatively to the validated StentBoost software on the market providing good stent visualization. The StentEnhancer workstation also allowed for a quantitative analysis of images to obtain stent expansion measurement as well as stent underexpansion quantitative assessment. A comparative study between StentEnhancer images and IVUS is needed in order to further validate the StentEnhancer measurements.

Author Contributions: Conceptualization, C.G., C.C., K.H. and S.C.; methodology, C.G.; software, C.G. and C.C.; validation, S.C., J.D., P.K. and C.U.; formal analysis, C.G. and C.C.; writing—original draft preparation, C.G.; writing—review and editing, S.C.; supervision, S.C. All authors have read and agreed to the published version of the manuscript.

Funding: This research received no external funding.

Data Availability Statement: Research data are available upon request.

Conflicts of Interest: The authors declare no conflict of interest.

References

1. Neumann, F.J.; Sechtem, U.; Banning, A.P.; Bonaros, N.; Bueno, H.; Bugiardini, R.; Chieffo, A.; Crea, F.; Czerny, M.; Delgado, V.; et al. 2019 ESC Guidelines for the Diagnosis and Management of Chronic Coronary Syndromes. *Eur. Heart J.* **2020**, *41*, 407–477. [CrossRef]
2. Kawaguchi, R.; Angiolillo, D.J.; Futamatsu, H.; Suzuki, N.; Bass, T.A.; Costa, M.A. Stent Thrombosis in the Era of Drug Eluting Stents. *Minerva Cardioangiol.* **2007**, *55*, 199–211. [PubMed]
3. Gopalakrishnan, M.; Lotfi, A. Stent Thrombosis. *Semin. Thromb. Hemost.* **2018**, *44*, 046–051. [CrossRef] [PubMed]
4. Choi, S.Y.; Maehara, A.; Cristea, E.; Witzenbichler, B.; Guagliumi, G.; Brodie, B.; Kellett, M.A.; Dressler, O.; Lansky, A.J.; Parise, H.; et al. Usefulness of Minimum Stent Cross Sectional Area as a Predictor of Angiographic Restenosis after Primary Percutaneous Coronary Intervention in Acute Myocardial Infarction (from the HORIZONS-AMI Trial IVUS Substudy). *Am. J. Cardiol.* **2012**, *109*, 455–460. [CrossRef]
5. Serruys, P.W.; Kay, I.P.; Disco, C.; Deshpande, N.V.; De Feyter, P.J. Periprocedural Quantitative Coronary Angiography after Palmaz-Schatz Stent Implantation Predicts the Restenosis Rate at Six Months: Results of a Meta-Analysis of the Belgian Netherlands Stent Study (BENESTENT) I, BENESTENT II Pilot, BENESTENT II and MUSIC. *J. Am. Coll. Cardiol.* **1999**, *34*, 1067–1074. [CrossRef]
6. Fujii, K.; Carlier, S.G.; Mintz, G.S.; Yang, Y.M.; Moussa, I.; Weisz, G.; Dangas, G.; Mehran, R.; Lansky, A.J.; Kreps, E.M.; et al. Stent Underexpansion and Residual Reference Segment Stenosis Are Related to Stent Thrombosis after Sirolimus-Eluting Stent Implantation: An Intravascular Ultrasound Study. *J. Am. Coll. Cardiol.* **2005**, *45*, 995–998. [CrossRef] [PubMed]
7. Okabe, T.; Mintz, G.S.; Buch, A.N.; Roy, P.; Hong, Y.J.; Smith, K.A.; Torguson, R.; Gevorkian, N.; Xue, Z.; Satler, L.F.; et al. Intravascular Ultrasound Parameters Associated with Stent Thrombosis After Drug-Eluting Stent Deployment. *Am. J. Cardiol.* **2007**, *100*, 615–620. [CrossRef] [PubMed]
8. Moussa, I.; Di Mario, C.; Reimers, B.; Akiyama, T.; Tobis, J.; Colombo, A. Subacute Stent Thrombosis in the Era of Intravascular Ultrasound-Guided Coronary Stenting without Anticoagulant: Frequency, Predictors and Clinical Outcome. *J. Am. Coll. Cardiol.* **1997**, *29*, 6–12. [CrossRef] [PubMed]
9. Choi, S.Y.; Witzenbichler, B.; Maehara, A.; Lansky, A.J.; Guagliumi, G.; Brodie, B.; Kellett, M.A.; Dressler, O.; Parise, H.; Mehran, R.; et al. Intravascular Ultrasound Findings of Early Stent Thrombosis after Primary Percutaneous Intervention in Acute Myocardial Infarction: A Harmonizing Outcomes with Revascularization and Stents in Acute Myocardial Infarction (HORIZONS-AMI) Substudy. *Circ. Cardiovasc. Interv.* **2011**, *4*, 239–247. [CrossRef]
10. Cheneau, E.; Leborgne, L.; Mintz, G.S.; Kotani, J.; Pichard, A.D.; Satler, L.F.; Canos, D.; Castagna, M.; Weissman, N.J.; Waksman, R. Predictors of Subacute Stent Thrombosis: Results of a Systematic Intravascular Ultrasound Study. *Circulation* **2003**, *108*, 43–47. [CrossRef]
11. Nerlekar, N.; Cheshire, C.J.; Verma, K.P.; Ihdayhid, A.R.; McCormick, L.M.; Cameron, J.D.; Bennett, M.R.; Malaiapan, Y.; Meredith, I.T.; Brown, A.J. Intravascular Ultrasound Guidance Improves Clinical Outcomes during Implantation of Both First- and Second generation Drug-Eluting Stents: A Meta-Analysis. *EuroIntervention* **2017**, *12*, 1632–1642. [CrossRef]
12. Buccheri, S.; Franchina, G.; Romano, S.; Puglisi, S.; Venuti, G.; D'Arrigo, P.; Francaviglia, B.; Scalia, M.; Condorelli, A.; Barbanti, M.; et al. Clinical Outcomes Following Intravascular Imaging-Guided Versus Coronary Angiography–Guided Percutaneous Coronary Intervention with Stent Implantation: A Systematic Review and Bayesian Network Meta-Analysis of 31 Studies and 17,882 Patients. *JACC Cardiovasc. Interv.* **2017**, *10*, 2488–2498. [CrossRef]

13. Maehara, A.; Matsumura, M.; Ali, Z.A.; Mintz, G.S.; Stone, G.W. IVUS-Guided Versus OCT-Guided Coronary Stent Implantation: A Critical Appraisal. *JACC Cardiovasc. Imaging* **2017**, *10*, 1487–1503. [CrossRef] [PubMed]
14. Ghafari, C.; Carlier, S. Stent Visualization Methods to Guide Percutaneous Coronary Interventions and Assess Long-Term Patency. *World J. Cardiol.* **2021**, *13*, 416–437. [CrossRef] [PubMed]
15. Truesdell, A.G.; Alasnag, M.A.; Kaul, P.; Rab, S.T.; Riley, R.F.; Young, M.N.; Batchelor, W.B.; Maehara, A.; Welt, F.G.; Kirtane, A.J. Intravascular Imaging During Percutaneous Coronary Intervention: JACC State-of-the-Art Review. *J. Am. Coll. Cardiol.* **2023**, *81*, 590–605. [CrossRef] [PubMed]
16. Lee, J.M.; Choi, K.H.; Song, Y.B.; Lee, J.-Y.; Lee, S.-J.; Lee, S.Y.; Kim, S.M.; Yun, K.H.; Cho, J.Y.; Kim, C.J.; et al. Intravascular Imaging–Guided or Angiography-Guided Complex PCI. *N. Engl. J. Med.* **2023**, *388*, 1668–1679. [CrossRef]
17. Tanaka, N.; Pijls, N.H.J.; Koolen, J.J.; Botman, K.J.; Michels, H.R.; Brueren, B.R.G.; Peels, K.; Shindo, N.; Yamashita, J.; Yamashina, A. Assessment of Optimum Stent Deployment by Stent Boost Imaging: Comparison with Intravascular Ultrasound. *Heart Vessels* **2013**, *28*, 1–6. [CrossRef]
18. Kastrati, A.; Mehilli, J.; Dirschinger, J.; Dotzer, F.; Schühlen, H.; Neumann, F.J.; Fleckenstein, M.; Pfafferott, C.; Seyfarth, M.; Schömig, A.; et al. Intracoronary Stenting and Angiographic Results: Strut Thickness Effect on Restenosis (Isar Stereo) Trial. *Circulation* **2001**, *103*, 2816–2821. [CrossRef]
19. Pache, J.; Kastrati, A.; Mehilli, J.; Schühlen, H.; Dotzer, F.; Hausleiter, J.; Fleckenstein, M.; Neuman, F.J.; Sattelberger, U.; Schmitt, C.; et al. Intracoronary Stenting and Angiographic Results: Strut Thickness Effect on Restenosis Outcome (ISAR-STEREO-2) Trial. *J. Am. Coll. Cardiol.* **2003**, *41*, 1283–1288. [CrossRef]
20. Mutha, V.; Asrar Ul Haq, M.; Sharma, N.; Den Hartog, W.F.; Van Gaal, W.J. Usefulness of Enhanced Stent Visualization Imaging Technique in Simple and Complex PCI Cases. *J. Invasive Cardiol.* **2014**, *26*, 552–557.
21. Doi, H.; Maehara, A.; Mintz, G.S.; Weissman, N.J.; Yu, A.; Wang, H.; Mandinov, L.; Popma, J.J.; Ellis, S.G.; Grube, E.; et al. Impact of In-Stent Minimal Lumen Area at 9 Months Poststent Implantation on 3-Year Target Lesion Revascularization–Free Survival. *Circ. Cardiovasc. Interv.* **2008**, *1*, 111–118. [CrossRef]
22. Ohlmann, P.; Mintz, G.S.; Kim, S.W.; Pichard, A.D.; Satler, L.F.; Kent, K.M.; Suddath, W.O.; Waksman, R.; Weissman, N.J. Intravascular Ultrasound Findings in Patients with Restenosis of Sirolimus- and Paclitaxel-Eluting Stents. *Int. J. Cardiol.* **2008**, *125*, 11–15. [CrossRef]
23. Iantorno, M.; Lipinski, M.J.; Garcia-Garcia, H.M.; Forrestal, B.J.; Rogers, T.; Gajanana, D.; Buchanan, K.D.; Torguson, R.; Weintraub, W.S.; Waksman, R. Meta-Analysis of the Impact of Strut Thickness on Outcomes in Patients with Drug-Eluting Stents in a Coronary Artery. *Am. J. Cardiol.* **2018**, *122*, 1652–1660. [CrossRef] [PubMed]
24. Sanidas, E.A.; Maehara, A.; Barkama, R.; Mintz, G.S.; Singh, V.; Hidalgo, A.; Hakim, D.; Leon, M.B.; Moses, J.W.; Weisz, G. Enhanced Stent Imaging Improves the Diagnosis of Stent Underexpansion and Optimizes Stent Deployment. *Catheter. Cardiovasc. Interv.* **2013**, *81*, 438–445. [CrossRef] [PubMed]
25. Rogers, R.K.; Michaels, A.D. Enhanced X-Ray Visualization of Coronary Stents: Clinical Aspects. *Cardiol. Clin.* **2009**, *27*, 467–475. [CrossRef]
26. Zaid, A.O.; Hadded, I.; Belhaj, W.; Bouallegue, A.; Abdessalem, S.; Mechmeche, R. Improved Localization of Coronary Stents Based on Image Enhancement. *Int. J. Biomed. Sci.* **2008**, *4*, 212–216. [PubMed]
27. Laimoud, M.; Nassar, Y.; Omar, W.; Abdelbarry, A.; Elghawaby, H. Stent Boost Enhancement Compared to Intravascular Ultrasound in the Evaluation of Stent Expansion in Elective Percutaneous Coronary Interventions. *Egypt. Heart J.* **2018**, *70*, 21–26. [CrossRef]
28. Zhang, J.; Duan, Y.Y.; Jin, Z.G.; Wei, Y.J.; Yang, S.L.; Luo, J.P.; Ma, D.X.; Jing, L.M.; Liu, H.L. Stent Boost Subtract Imaging for the Assessment of Optimal Stent Deployment in Coronary Ostial Lesion Intervention: Comparison with Intravascular Ultrasound. *Int. Heart J.* **2015**, *56*, 37–42. [CrossRef]
29. Davies, A.G.; Conway, D.; Reid, S.; Cowen, A.R.; Sivananthan, M. Assessment of Coronary Stent Deployment Using Computer Enhanced X-Ray Images-Validation against Intravascular Ultrasound and Best Practice Recommendations. *Catheter. Cardiovasc. Interv.* **2013**, *81*, 419–427. [CrossRef]
30. Blicq, E.; Georges, J.L.; Elbeainy, E.; Gibault-Genty, G.; Benjemaa, K.; Jerbi, B.; Livarek, B. Detection of Stent Underdeployment by Stentboost Imaging. *J. Interv. Cardiol.* **2013**, *26*, 444–453. [CrossRef]
31. Omran, O.M.; Sherif, M.H.; Saied, E.S.; El-Ashmawy, M.M.; El-guindy, A.D.; El-den, S.M.S. Evaluation of Coronary Stent Expansion during Percutaneous Coronary Interventions Using Stent Boost Visualization in Comparison with Intravascular Ultrasound. *J. Adv. Med. Med. Res.* **2022**, *34*, 205–215. [CrossRef]
32. Garrone, P.; Biondi-Zoccai, G.; Salvetti, I.; Sina, N.; Sheiban, I.; Stella, P.R.; Agostoni, P. Quantitative Coronary Angiography in the Current Era: Principles and Applications. *J. Interv. Cardiol.* **2009**, *22*, 527–536. [CrossRef] [PubMed]
33. Lozano, I.; López-Palop, R.; Pinar, E.; Pérez-Lorente, F.; Picó, F.; Valdés, M. Comparison between Theoretical and Actual Intracoronary Stent Dimensions in Non-Complex Lesions. *Rev. Española Cardiol.* **2006**, *59*, 624–627. [CrossRef]
34. De Ribamar Costa, J.; Mintz, G.S.; Carlier, S.G.; Costa, R.A.; Fujii, K.; Sano, K.; Kimura, M.; Lui, J.; Weisz, G.; Moussa, I.; et al. Intravascular Ultrasonic Assessment of Stent Diameters Derived from Manufacturer's Compliance Charts. *Am. J. Cardiol.* **2005**, *96*, 74–78. [CrossRef] [PubMed]

35. Blasini, R.; Neumann, F.J.; Schmitt, C.; Bökenkamp, J.; Schömig, A. Comparison of Angiography and Intravascular Ultrasound for the Assessment of Lumen Size after Coronary Stent Placement: Impact of Dilation Pressures. *Cathet. Cardiovasc. Diagn.* **1997**, *42*, 113–119. [CrossRef]
36. Hong, M.-K. Intravascular Ultrasound Predictors of Angiographic Restenosis after Sirolimus-Eluting Stent Implantation. *Eur. Heart J.* **2006**, *27*, 1305–1310. [CrossRef] [PubMed]
37. Silva, J.D.; Carrillo, X.; Salvatella, N.; Fernandez-Nofrerias, E.; Rodriguez-Leor, O.; Mauri, J.; Bayes-Genis, A. The Utility of Stent Enhancement to Guide Percutaneous Coronary Intervention for Bifurcation Lesions. *EuroIntervention* **2013**, *9*, 968–974. [CrossRef] [PubMed]
38. Cura, F.; Albertal, M.; Candiello, A.; Nau, G.; Bonvini, V.; Tricherri, H.; Padilla, L.T.; Belardi, J.A. StentBoost Visualization for the Evaluation of Coronary Stent Expansion during Percutaneous Coronary Interventions. *Cardiol. Ther.* **2013**, *2*, 171–180. [CrossRef]
39. Goto, K.; Mintz, G.S.; Litherland, C.; Lansky, A.J.; Weisz, G.; McPherson, J.A.; De Bruyne, B.; Serruys, P.W.; Stone, G.W.; Maehara, A. Lumen Measurements from Quantitative Coronary Angiography and IVUS: A PROSPECT Substudy. *JACC Cardiovasc. Imaging* **2016**, *9*, 1011–1013. [CrossRef] [PubMed]
40. Jin, Z.; Yang, S.; Jing, L.; Liu, H. Impact of StentBoost Subtract Imaging on Patient Radiation Exposure during Percutaneous Coronary Intervention. *Int. J. Cardiovasc. Imaging* **2013**, *29*, 1207–1213. [CrossRef]

Disclaimer/Publisher's Note: The statements, opinions and data contained in all publications are solely those of the individual author(s) and contributor(s) and not of MDPI and/or the editor(s). MDPI and/or the editor(s) disclaim responsibility for any injury to people or property resulting from any ideas, methods, instructions or products referred to in the content.

MDPI
St. Alban-Anlage 66
4052 Basel
Switzerland
www.mdpi.com

Algorithms Editorial Office
E-mail: algorithms@mdpi.com
www.mdpi.com/journal/algorithms

Disclaimer/Publisher's Note: The statements, opinions and data contained in all publications are solely those of the individual author(s) and contributor(s) and not of MDPI and/or the editor(s). MDPI and/or the editor(s) disclaim responsibility for any injury to people or property resulting from any ideas, methods, instructions or products referred to in the content.